John Dennis

Heroes of literature, English poets

A book for young readers

John Dennis

Heroes of literature, English poets
A book for young readers

ISBN/EAN: 9783337184865

Printed in Europe, USA, Canada, Australia, Japan

Cover: Foto ©Thomas Meinert / pixelio.de

More available books at **www.hansebooks.com**

HEROES OF LITERATURE.

ENGLISH POETS.

A BOOK FOR YOUNG READERS.

BY

JOHN DENNIS,

AUTHOR OF "STUDIES IN ENGLISH LITERATURE," AND EDITOR OF "ENGLISH
SONNETS; A SELECTION," ETC.

PUBLISHED UNDER THE DIRECTION OF THE COMMITTEE
OF GENERAL LITERATURE AND EDUCATION APPOINTED BY THE
SOCIETY FOR PROMOTING CHRISTIAN KNOWLEDGE.

LONDON:
SOCIETY FOR PROMOTING CHRISTIAN KNOWLEDGE,
NORTHUMBERLAND AVENUE, CHARING CROSS, W.C.;
43, QUEEN VICTORIA STREET, E.C.;
26, ST. GEORGE'S PLACE, HYDE PARK CORNER, S.W.
BRIGHTON: 135, NORTH STREET.
NEW YORK: E. & J. B. YOUNG AND CO.

1883.

PREFACE.

In asking the reader to travel with me for a season in the "realms of gold," or rather in that English realm, which is the richest, the widest, and the most fertile, I do not undertake fully to explore the country. So vast a journey is far beyond my power as a traveller. How, indeed, would it be possible to explore a territory so spacious, and to point out every lovely object in this enchanting region? The amplest leisure and the largest knowledge will scarcely suffice for such a task. My purpose is a more modest one—namely, to point out some of the impressive features of a road rich in all that is fitted to gladden the eye and soothe the heart. In other words, and dropping Keats's metaphor, the attempt is made in these pages to give brief biographies of illustrious English poets and such a sketch of their works as may attract young

readers to a study the delight in which must grow
in proportion to the knowledge.

Let it be understood, then, that this book is intended to excite interest, but not to satisfy it—to
show the reader where to look rather than to state
comprehensively what he is likely to find.   It may
be added that no attempt is made to estimate the
position of living poets, and that it has been found
necessary to omit many names which would hold
no mean place in a systematic history of English
verse.

CONTENTS.

CONTENTS.

CONTENTS. vii

CONTENTS. vii

CHAPTER XII.

THE GEORGIAN POETS (*Continued*).

PAGE

Robert Burns ... 257

CHAPTER XIII.

POETS OF THE NINETEENTH CENTURY.

William Wordsworth ... 278

CHAPTER XIV.

POETS OF THE NINETEENTH CENTURY (*Continued*).

Sir Walter Scott ... 300

CHAPTER XV.

POETS OF THE NINETEENTH CENTURY (*Continued*).

Samuel Taylor Coleridge—Robert Southey—Walter Savage Landor ... 322

CHAPTER XVI.

POETS OF THE NINETEENTH CENTURY (*Continued*).

Lord Byron ... 344

CHAPTER XVII.

POETS OF THE NINETEENTH CENTURY (*Continued*).

John Keats—Percy Bysshe Shelley ... 365

CHAPTER XVIII.

POETS OF THE NINETEENTH CENTURY (*Continued*).

Elizabeth Barrett Browning—John Keble ... 388

HEROES OF LITERATURE.

CHAPTER I.

INTRODUCTORY.

THERE is no study which should be more dear to an Englishman than the literature of his country, and there is no branch of that literature which has stronger claims on his attention than the works of our great poets. " Poetry," said Wordsworth, " is the first and last of all knowledge "—an assertion which will sound strange to readers who treat the poet's art as an agreeable accomplishment, instead of accepting it as the highest and noblest effort of which the intellect is capable. But poetry is not merely, nor chiefly, an intellectual achievement. It is the outcome of the singer's heart, and ex-presses in the choicest language the feelings of which all human hearts are conscious. It deals with universal truths, and there is nothing too great or too little for an instrument which is some-

B

times sublime as the organ, sometimes pathetic as the harp, and sometimes spirit-stirring like the trumpet. Language has a wider compass than music, painting, or sculpture ; and Poetry, being less restricted than either of these noble arts, to each of which she is closely linked, stands supreme among the works of man. This exaltation of poetry will not be accepted readily by all readers. There are men blind to beauty and deaf to song ; but he who loves the divine art, and knows how much it can yield of solace and delight, of wisdom and aspiration, of energy and calm, will find no exaggeration in my words. And if these words be true of poetry generally, they are certainly true of the poets who have given its greatest lustre to English literature. Noble indeed is the heritage they have handed down to us, and to appreciate by patient study the boon we have received forms no mean part of a liberal education.

I propose to assist my readers in this study, and to carry them, let me hope pleasantly and profitably, through three centuries of our poetical literature. In doing this it will be my effort so to associate the poets with their times and with their literary contemporaries, that the young student may gain much serviceable knowledge in what may be called the byways of literature and history. Dr. Johnson thought there was no reading more captivating than that of literary biography, and assuredly it will be the writer's fault if he cannot make the great subject he has selected alike instructive and entertaining.

Let me say at once that the criticism to be found in this book pretends to no special originality. I shall state frankly what I think upon matters poetical, and if the thought be not always new, it will not be less serviceable to the reader. In borrowing, knowingly, the authority will be acknowledged ; but the light I have myself gained from much reading will no doubt be often reflected unconsciously.

The earliest literature is poetical, and our first English poet was Cædmon the cowherd, who flourished about A.D. 670. The simple story of the way in which the gift of song came to him in his old age is related by the Venerable Bede, to whom we are indebted for an invaluable chronicle, mixed up with much that is beautiful and grotesque in legend, of the seventh century of Anglo-Saxon history. From this early date no poet of mark made his voice heard until the middle of the fourteenth century, when Langland gained a high reputation by his "Vision of Piers the Plowman," a religious poem, **William Langland, about 1332.** "which wrought so strongly in men's minds that its influence was almost as great as Wyclif's in the revolt which had now begun against Latin Christianity." * That poem, popular though it was at the time, had not vitality enough to give it a sustained life ; and the same **John Gower, 1330-1408.** may be said of the three poems of Gower, or rather of the one poem, the " Confessio

---

* Stopford Brooke.

Amantis," which the old poet wrote in English, his "Speculum Meditantis" having been written in French, and his "Vox Clamantis" in Latin. This English poem, in Mrs. Barrett Browning's judgment, "proves an abundant fancy, a full head, and a full heart, and neither ineloquent;" and she "considers that the poet has been much undervalued." Mr. Hallam's judgment of Gower is more in harmony with the general opinion. He observes that, though not, like Chaucer, a poet of nature's growth, Gower had some effect in rendering the language less rude, and adds, "If he never rises, he never sinks low ; he is always sensible, polished, perspicuous, and not prosaic in the worst sense of the word."

Gower calls Chaucer his "disciple," and it is possible, though not certain, that the author of the "Canterbury Tales" took some suggestions from his contemporary ; but Chaucer's superiority to the "moral Gower" is immeasurable. The one is a respectable versifier ; the other ranks with the noblest of English poets—with the greatest poets of the world. There is no gracious gift of song which Chaucer does not possess, unless it be that of lyrical utterance. Imagination, fancy, humour, pathos, dramatic skill, exquisite felicity of expression,—these are his gifts, and to him is assigned with justice the honourable title "Father of English Poetry." The attempt has been made unsuccessfully, by Dryden and others, to modernize Chaucer ; and even Wordsworth, with

Geoffrey Chaucer, 1340-1400.

his delicate sense of poetical simplicity and contempt for adventitious ornament, has not succeeded
in this dainty task. Chaucer must be admired in
his ancient dress or not at all, and there is nothing
in his archaic language that need daunt a studious
reader. Like all great poets, he had a fine ear
for rhythm, and when once the easy art of reading
Chaucer is acquired, the music of his verse will fall
as gratefully on the ear as the lovely melody of
Spenser or of Shelley. There never was a more
joyous poet or one more full of animal spirits.
These sometimes led him astray, to his deep after
regret ; but Chaucer's grossness is less hurtful than
the more refined immorality of later poets, and his
tender affection for the simplest objects in nature
marks a gentle, and in some respects a guileless,
spirit. The dew and freshness of morning rest
upon his song. He had faith in himself, faith in the
world, faith in God ; and, while knowing well the
secrets of sorrow, lived, as such a man well might,
in an atmosphere of mirth. This great artist and
poet, although he drew from the wells of French and
Italian romance, was English to the backbone. In
the earlier days of his poetical career the influence
of the Troubadours and of Boccaccio is evident in
his verse ; but just as Shakespeare, two hundred
years later, chose his plots from foreign sources,
and placed his scenes on foreign ground, without
lessening thereby the English character of his
poetry, so was it with Chaucer. His writings
served to fix the language, and his " Canterbury

Tales " is as genuine a product of England's soil as her oaks and elms.

The poetry of Chaucer does not fall within the plan of this volume ; but before opening our study with the age of Elizabeth, it is well to remember, not only that the well of English undefiled had sent forth its refreshing waters two centuries before, but that many lesser springs of poetry had from time to time given freshness to our literature. Chaucer died in 1400, and lies buried, as is meet, in the famous Abbey which has since received so many of his noble brotherhood. Between that period and the sixteenth century there is nothing in English verse likely to detain the young reader, unless he care more for what is quaint than for what is poetically good. The only name, perhaps, worthy of mention here is that of John Skelton—

John Skelton, 1460?-1529. who is, however, insufferably coarse, and deserving of more attention as a humorist than as a poet. Skelton's position and acquirements made him well known in his lifetime. From him the future king, Henry VIII., received his education, and that he was deeply learned is proved by the high praise bestowed on him by Erasmus. How far Skelton's buffoonery influenced the youthful prince can only be guessed at. His faults were common to the age, but the ability he possessed was as uncommon then as it is now, and it is impossible to believe it was wholly used for good. His writings, popular in his own day, are dead to the modern reader, and no republication can revive their fame.* He wrote one simple poem—"The Book of Philip Sparrow"—in which a girl is supposed to mourn the loss of her pet, that will surely please any reader. Mr. Minto observes that the "tender bits" in this poem remind one of Swift's "Journal to Stella," and "are written in exactly the same strain of fondling affection."† This is true; and there are other indications which will remind those familiar with the writings of Skelton and Swift that these clerical humorists and verse-makers had much in common.

With Sir Thomas Wyatt and his friend the Earl of Surrey a new era arose, which, though scarcely brilliant at the commencement, was destined to become one of unexampled literary splendour. Wyatt and Surrey, friends in life and in art, belong to the reign of Henry VIII., but their poems were published just before the accession of Elizabeth, and the influence of their poetry extended far into her reign. Like Chaucer, Wyatt had visited Italy, and, like him, both poets warmed themselves at the fire of Italian literature. The debt they owed to Petrarch they repaid in sonnets, and were the first to naturalize that difficult form of verse on English soil. This was no mean

Sir Thomas Wyatt, 1503-1542.

Earl of Surrey, 1517?-1547:

---

* An edition of Skelton's works, in two volumes, edited by Mr. Dyce, appeared in 1843.
† "Characteristics of English poets from Chaucer to Shirley," by William Minto, M.A., p. 114 (Blackwood).

achievement, but they have other claims to attention. Wyatt, who slightly preceded Surrey, imitated
Horace, and, according to Warton, may justly be
deemed the first polished English satirist.* Surrey
was the first poet who wrote heroic blank verse in
our language ; he did much to improve our versification, and the laws he established "have been
adopted by our standard writers with hardly any
variation ever since." And not only did he become
an authority on the construction of verse, but
proved that he possessed in some measure the
inspiration of the poet. Truly does Sir Philip
Sidney say that his lyrics contain "many things
tasting of a noble birth and worthy of a noble
mind." Both poets, we may add, attempted paraphrases of the Psalms, and both had poetical mistresses, upon whom they expended all the passion
and real or imaginary despondency they could
express in verse. Wyatt is conjectured to have
been in love with Anne Boleyn ; and Surrey's
Geraldine is also supposed by some of his critics
to have been a real woman.

"In Sir Thomas Wyatt and Henry Earl of
Surrey," writes Mr. Brewer, "we have poets of

---

* He has certainly a better claim to this position than Joseph
Hall (1574–1656), who, when he afterwards obtained a bishopric,
was the opponent of Milton. Hall's coarse but vigorous satires
were the work of his early life, and thus he writes concerning
them—

"I first adventure, with foolhardy might,
To tread the steps of perilous despight ;
I first adventure, follow me who list,
And be the second English satirist."

ripe age and growing families devoured by the
pangs of love, and devoting themselves to the
celebration of the charms of a youthful mistress—
their own woes, hopes, and despondency—with all
the imaginary ardour of youthful lovers not yet
arrived at the age of discretion. To this day it
is impossible to decide whether the fair Geraldine
in the case of the latter was the object of a real
or mythical attachment ; and in the former, whether
'his love called Anna,' a word 'that changeth not
though it be turned and made in twain,' was a
substantial incorporation of flesh and blood, or
only an incorporeal quibble." *

That some sort of flirtation existed between
the knight and the maid of honour prior to Anne
Boleyn's ill-fated marriage, seems probable enough,
not only from the circumstantial story told by
Wyatt's grandson, but also from what we know
of the lady's free manners and volatile disposition. On the other hand, if Surrey's Geraldine
was really the Lady Elizabeth Fitzgerald—a statement that has been recently disputed—the love
he lavished upon a child of twelve was an imaginary passion. The subject is of wider interest
than the mere settlement of the relations of
Wyatt and Surrey to their poetical mistresses.
It was as imperative in those days as in the
age of Petrarch that every verse-maker should have

---

* "Letters and Papers, Foreign and Domestic, of the Reign of
Henry VIII.," arranged and catalogued by J. S. Brewer, M.A.,
vol. iv. p. 240.

a mistress, no matter whether in the flesh or out of it. The amatory effusions of susceptible young poets were no doubt sometimes only too real, but for matters of poetic art it sufficed if they worshipped some imaginary goddess, a Dulcinea del Toboso of the fancy.

"There is not," says Cowley, "so great a lie to be found in any poet as the vulgar conceit of men that lying is essential to good poetry." Bacon, on the contrary, says, and he also is alluding to the divine art, "A mixture of a lie doth ever add pleasure." Is the poet right or the philosopher? It depends entirely upon what we understand by lying. All true poetry, and all genuine work whatsoever, must be based on truth, and the recognition of primal truths is to be found in every great work of imagination. It is the veracity of such writers as Shakespeare and Scott, of Wordsworth and Tennyson, of Jane Austen and George Eliot, that makes them so dear to us; and the form in which they utter what they know is a vivid creation, and not a deceptive shadow. All this is obvious enough, and the reader may be reminded that some of the most sacred truths uttered on our earth were conveyed through the medium of parable or allegory. The poet, then, does not lie when his imagination lifts him above the smoke and stir of earth, when he sees visions and dreams dreams. In his inspired moments he looks further than most of us may into the life of things, and the truest words man has ever spoken to his fellow-men have been generally said under the veil of fiction. How much of genuine feeling and of poetical enthusiasm is to be found in Wyatt and Surrey, and the sonneteers who followed them, cannot readily be estimated. Sometimes the true voice of song sounds forth without hindrance, as in the "My lute, awake!" of Wyatt, and in the brightly descriptive poems attributed to Surrey, in which "the lover describeth his whole state unto his love." Frequently, however, the notes we hear are discordant, and will perhaps appear false ; but what seems artificial to us may have been real to the singers, for poets, like other men, are creatures of circumstance and fashion. Goldsmith, in his bloom-coloured suit, would seem a strangely made-up creature, could we meet him to-day in the streets of London. Yet we know how true the man was to his nature, and what a generous heart beat under that tawdry costume. In reading the love-poetry of the Elizabethans it will be well, then, to bear in mind that if the diction of the age differs from our own, the expression of poetical feeling may be none the less genuine. To us the artifice is more evident than the sincerity, but it would be hard to call the most grotesque poet of that age a mere literary dandy, when we remember how great poets like Spenser and Shakespeare, and true poets like Surrey and Sidney, were affected by the habits of the time.

Queen Mary's reign, a period one would think unfriendly to all art, found a poet in Sackville, whose " Mirror of Magistrates " is as remarkable

Thomas Sack-
ville (Lord
Buckhurst),
1536-1608.
as it is poetical. "Sackville's genius,"
says Hallam, " stands absolutely alone
in the age to which, as a poet, he
belongs;" and in the following passage this
eminently sane critic gives a just estimate of the
one man who, in that dark period of our history,
"shone out for an instant in the higher walks of
poetry":—

" The 'Mirror of Magistrates,' " he writes, "published in 1559, is a collection of stories by different
authors, on the plan of Boccaccio's prose work, ' De
Casibus virorum illustrium,' recounting the misfortunes and reverses of men eminent in English
history. It was designed to form a series of
dramatic soliloquies united in one interlude. Sackville, who seems to have planned the scheme,
wrote an induction, or prologue, and also one of
the stories, that of the first Duke of Buckingham.
The induction displays best his poetical genius ; it
is, like much earlier poetry, a representation of
allegorical personages, but with a fertility of imagination, vividness of description, and strength of
language, which not only leave his predecessors far
behind, but may fairly be compared with some of
the most poetical passages in Spenser. . . . Sackville is far above the frigid elegance of Surrey, and
in the first days of Elizabeth's reign is the herald of
that splendour in which it was to close."

An elaborate account of the " Mirror of Magistrates " will be found in Warton's "History of

English Poetry," and other historians of English literature have given it considerable attention. Our words on the subject shall be extremely brief. The plan of the work was, perhaps, better fitted for prose than poetry. The "Mirror" is composed of a number of biographies in verse, and is a jeremiad on the melancholy fate of men who once occupied a high place in English history, and who, being visited in the land of shades, are supposed to relate the story of their woes. It was impossible that a work formed on a design like this, and destined to be carried out by various hands, should glow throughout with the white heat of poetry. It did, in fact, degenerate into a mere rhyming chronicle, and the imagination which gives vitality to Sackville's portion of the work is to be found nowhere else. As a poet, Sackville belongs to the reign of Mary ; as a statesman to the age of Elizabeth, by whom he was knighted, and ultimately promoted to the peerage, under the title of Lord Buckhurst. Like Chaucer, he was a man of affairs, and proved, as some later and greater poets have done, that it is possible to live two lives, and to live both well. Sackville's integrity was unimpeachable, and how highly the queen estimated his ability is proved by the fact that, on the death of Burleigh, he was appointed Lord High Treasurer. For us it is of greater interest to remember that he was the author of " Gorboduc," the first English tragedy.

Sackville's poetry is not what Spenser terms it,

"golden verse, worthy immortal fame;" but the feeling of the poet may be seen in his work, and there are indications in it which foretell the dawn of a new era. To that brighter period we will now direct our attention.

CHAPTER II.

THE ELIZABETHAN POETS.

EDMUND SPENSER.

THE reign of Queen Elizabeth is illustrious for great deeds and noble words, for the splendour of its achievements on sea and land, for sea-kings and statesmen like Drake and Burleigh, for profound thinkers like Hooker and Bacon, for knights versed in many accomplishments like Raleigh and Sidney. It was an age of enterprise and discovery, of freedom and speculation, and above all of an ardent desire for truth. " Then," in the fine language of Milton, "was the sacred Bible sought out of the dusty corners where profane falsehood and neglect had thrown it, the schools opened, divine and human learning raked out of the embers of forgotten tongues." That an age, full of eager life and rampant with its newly found strength, should have exhibited signs of literary eccentricity was inevitable. No doubt in such an age strength of thought and originality of conception would be more conspicuous than taste. English writers, like bold sportsmen, rode across country, heedless of all obstacles, and the signs of this rough-riding are evident in their works. Among the characteristics common to the Elizabethan poets we may note a comparative inattention to form and a prodigal expenditure of wealth. They are full of matter, but the manner frequently lacks shape and comeliness. They want the sense of proportion, they do not know where to stop, they are burdened with a weight of imagery and stifled by a plethora of wit. Defects like these, defects nearly allied to virtues, are chiefly evident in the lesser lights of that wonderful period—in Marlowe, Chapman, and Webster, in Sir Philip Sidney and John Lyly. The two great lights of the age, however—Edmund Spenser and William Shakespeare—while belonging to all time, are essentially Elizabethans in the royal extravagance with which they scatter broadcast their literary treasures. It is as though their store of fancy and imagination were unfailing; and perhaps it was. Assuredly, when one died at the comparatively early age of forty-six, and the other at fifty-three, there were no indications that the fountain of their genius was dried up.

Spenser was Shakespeare's senior by twelve years, and as a poet he has therefore

Edmund
Spenser,
1552-1598.

the first claim on our attention. What shall we say of the poets' poet—of him who, it might be supposed, did we not know

to the contrary, had lived his whole life in a dream
of glorious romance ; of him who is pre-eminently
the poet of the beautiful, and is yet at the same
time, to use Milton's words, " sage and serious," and,
in the highest sense of the term, a Christian poet ? *

The first thing that deserves notice is the paucity
of our information about him. He was accounted
a divine poet by his contemporaries ; he was the
friend of great men like Sidney and Raleigh ; the
queen made him her Laureate ; and when he died
he was buried in Westminster Abbey. Yet we
know not who were the parents of this splendid
poet, or whether he was an only child ; the date
even of his birth is not absolutely certain ; and the
writer who undertakes to tell the story of his life is
forced to feel his way by the help of probabilities
and conjectures, and by references to his poetry.
Mr. Hales, the editor of the Globe Spenser, states
that the poems are the one great authority for the
biography prefixed to that edition ; and if it be
true, as Dean Church observes, that we know more
about the circumstances of Spenser's life than about
the lives of many men of letters of that time, it is
also true that our knowledge is extremely limited.
Biography was not encouraged in the Elizabethan
age ; but considering what Spenser's fame was in

---

* The revered author of the " Christian Year " has paid the
noblest tribute to Spenser, in calling him " pre-eminently the sacred
poet of his country." That John Wesley so esteemed him is
evident, for he enjoined his divinity students to read the " Faerie
Queene."

his lifetime, and that his poetry raised him to a height which hitherto had been occupied by Chaucer alone, our ignorance about him may be accounted extraordinary.   There is probably no English poet save Shakespeare who has exercised so wide a sway in his own country.   Many a noble poet, and many a writer of high impulses, has acknowledged Spenser as his master.   "The 'Faerie Queene,'" says Mr. Stopford Brooke, "has never ceased to make poets," and the men who have borne witness to its power are among the most honoured names in our literature. It was by reading the "Faerie Queene" that Cowley became "irrecoverably a poet."   The author of this incomparable poem was the poetical guide of Milton, the admiration of Dryden, who styles him "inimitable," the delight of the youthful Pope, the inspirer of Gray, the constant companion of Scott and Southey, of Shelley and Keats, and the favourite poet of Charles Kingsley.   "Spenser," said Sir Walter, "I could have read for ever."   Southey read the great allegory through thirty times, and regarded Spenser as the greatest master of versification in our language.   "Do you love Spenser?" writes Landor.   "I have him in my heart of hearts." *
Keats, at seventeen, in the expressive words of Cowden Clarke, "ramped through the scenes of the romance like a young horse turned into a

---

* Elsewhere, however, he utters a different opinion.   Addressing ing Wordsworth, he says—

" Thee gentle Spenser fondly led,
But me he mostly sent to bed."

spring meadow ;" and Lord Houghton adds, "He could talk of nothing else ; his countenance would light up at each rich expression, and his strong frame would tremble with emotion as he read. The lines 'in imitation of Spenser' are the earliest known verses of his composition, and to the very last the traces of this main impulse of his life are visible." *

Spenser, then, lives for us in his works. Of the man himself, so little is known with certainty that it may be stated in two or three pages. He was born in London, in 1552, and was therefore about six years old when Elizabeth came to the throne. His school education was acquired at Merchant Taylors', and from thence he went as a sizar to Pembroke Hall, Cambridge. There seems to be evidence that his poetical genius blossomed early, and that he had written verses before entering the university, which he left in 1576, after taking his Master's degree. Meanwhile he had won two warm friends, Edward Kirke and Gabriel Harvey, the latter of whom was destined to influence, not always wisely, the genius of the poet. Some time was spent in the north of England,

---

* Spenser has not been the delight of poets alone. Lord Somers, one of the most accomplished men of his age, was passionately fond of the "Faerie Queene," and in the last picture which he sat for to Sir Godfrey Kneller, he desired to be painted with Spenser in his hand. Lord Chatham is said to have been always reading this poet, who also won the admiration of Fox and of Burke. "The nobility of the Spensers," said Gibbon, "has been illustrated and enriched by the trophies of Marlborough, but I exhort them to consider the 'Faerie Queene' as the most precious jewel of their coronet."

and there Spenser fell vainly in love with Rosalind, the "widow's daughter of the glen," who, according to Kirke, "was a gentlewoman of no mean house, nor endowed with any vulgar and common gifts both of nature and manners." The passion was not returned, and the poet found vent for his grief, and, no doubt, large compensation also, in the composition of eclogues. In 1579 Spenser was in London, and it seems to have been at the same time, or a little earlier, that he gained the acquaintance and friendship of Sir Philip Sidney, his junior by two years. It was in the closing month of that year that the poet published, anonymously, his "Shepherd's Calendar." The letters between Harvey and Spenser at this period upon literary matters contain also a fact for the biographers, since we read of a new sweetheart, another "little Rosalind," who appears for a moment, to pass away for ever. And now we hear for the first time of the "Faeric Queene," and that it did not suit the taste of Gabriel Harvey, a pedantic critic, who tried to form our English verse after classical models, and for a while infected Spenser with his folly. The intimacy with Sidney, and his acquaintance with Sidney's uncle, the Earl· of Leicester, failed to lead, as Spenser hoped it would have done, to promotion at court. It was probably well for the poet that it did not. He needed an "ampler ether" in which to breathe his poetic life, and found it in Ireland, whither he went as secretary to the Lord Deputy, Lord Grey of Wilton, in 1580. The country was at that time in a state of anarchy, which demanded vigorous action. Grey is said to have governed justly but severely, and the terrible scenes Spenser must have witnessed left, no doubt, their mark upon his character and genius. He found himself, in the words of Dean Church, "transplanted into a wild and turbulent savagery, where the elements of civil society hardly existed, and which had the fatal power of drawing into its own evil and lawless ways the English who came into contact with it." A poet's life is best nurtured by conflict, but the position in which the conquering race stood at that time to the conquered was not likely to encourage the noblest virtues of chivalry, courtesy, and forbearance. The Spartan rigour of Lord Grey's administration was afterwards praised in no niggard terms by his secretary, in his remarkable tractate, "A View of the Present State of Ireland," and we gather from it that the poet of the "Faerie Queene," gentle and lovable though his nature on its poetical side may seem, was not free from sternness or, from what on a modern estimate might be deemed, a strain of cruelty.

The posts accepted by Spenser in Ireland have been recorded. One was that of Clerk of Decrees and Recognizances in the Irish Court of Chancery, and another which he took up several years later was the appointment of Clerk to the Council of Munster. In a worldly point of view he seems to have prospered. We know that he had a lease of the Abbey and Manor of Inniscorthy, and that

Lord Grey presented him with some of the property forfeited by the rebels. Sir Walter Raleigh,
it may be remembered, had taken part in the
struggle in Ireland under Lord Grey, and it was
then in all probability that he and Spenser became
acquainted. A warm friendship followed, and when
Spenser settled with a large grant of land at Kilcolman, we know—for the visit has been recorded
in the poet's verse—that he welcomed Raleigh
under his castle roof. On this occasion it appears
that Spenser read to his friend some portion of his
unfinished poem, "The Faerie Queene."   Raleigh,
unlike Harvey, was quick to discern its merits,
and the sonnet in which he praised it—a sonnet
which, according to Archbishop Trench, is "about
the finest compliment which was ever paid by poet
to poet"—should be known to all readers ; * and it

---

* "Methought I saw the grave where Laura lay
   Within that temple where the vestal flame
   Was wont to burn ; and passing by that way
   To see that buried dust of living fame,
   Whose tomb fair Love and fairer Virtue kept,
   All suddenly I saw the Faerie Queen :
   At whose approach the soul of Petrarch wept ;
   And from thenceforth those Graces were not seen,
   For they this Queen attended ; in whose stead
   Oblivion laid him down on Laura's hearse.
   Hereat the hardest stones were seen to bleed,
   And groans of buried ghosts the heavens did pierce,
   Where Homer's spright did tremble all for grief
   And cursed the access of that celestial thief."

This sonnet, says Leigh Hunt, "flows with such nerve and will,
and is so dashing and sounding in the rest of its modulation, that no
impression remains upon the mind but that of triumphant force."
But Archbishop Trench concludes his generous estimate of the poem

is worth remembering that Raleigh, not contented with this splendid tribute to the genius of his friend, uttered his praise a second time, and in a form which, if less poetical, bears at least the mark of honesty. Here is the final couplet—

" Of me no lines are loved, nor letters are of price,
   Of all which speak our English tongue but those of thy device."

By Raleigh's invitation Spenser accompanied him to England, where he was presented to "the most High, Mighty, and Magnificent Empresse Elizabeth," to whom the first three books of the "Faerie Queene" are dedicated, "to live with the eternitie of her fame." His reception at court took place in 1589, and in the following year these books were published and received a hearty welcome. Unlike an illustrious poet of more recent times, Spenser's genius won instant recognition, and he sprung at once into the place he was entitled to hold as the successor of Chaucer, as the second English poet who had won a poetical immortality. Ten years earlier, it will be remembered, Spenser had published his "Shepherd's Calendar," so that at the age of thirty-eight he had risen to a height of fame which could scarcely be increased by any after-labour. He spent some time at court, and

---

with the just remark that it labours under a serious defect. "The great poets of the past," he writes, "lose no whit of their glory because later poets are found worthy to share it. Petrarch in his lesser and Homer in his greater sphere, are just as illustrious since Spenser appeared as before."

spent it in vain beyond gaining some experience
he would willingly have been spared.

> " Full little knowest thou, that hast not tried
> What hell it is in suing long to bide ;
> To lose good days that might be better spent ;
> To waste long nights in pensive discontent ;
> To speed to-day, to be put back to-morrow ;
> To feed on hope, to pine with fear and sorrow ;
>
> .   .   .   .   .
>
> To fawn, to crouch, to wait, to ride, to run,
> To speed, to give, to want, to be undone.
> Unhappy wight, born to disastrous end,
> That doth his life in so long tendence spend ! "

Spenser returned to Ireland, to find the richest
compensation for this neglect in a good wife, whose
praise he has sung magnificently in the " Faerie
Queene " (book vi. canto x.), and also in his immortal
nuptial song. If any one wishes to know how rich
this poet was in fancy, and what an ear for music
he possessed, let him read and read again the
" Epithalamion." What poet has ever so praised
his bride? And yet, strange to say, no one knows
to this day the family name of the lady who is thus
honoured. We know only that her Christian name
was Elizabeth, that the marriage took place in
1594, that she survived Spenser to marry a second
time, and had some litigation with one of her sons.
In the following year the poet again visited London,
and remained there many months. On returning
to Ireland he was appointed Sheriff of Cork. Two
sons were born to him, and baptized with the suggestive names of Sylvanus and Peregrine. There

seem also to have been other children, and of one at least we have sad mention. The great poet's days ended in gloom. In 1598 Kilcolman was attacked by the Irish rebels, sacked and burned. It is said that an infant child of Spenser's perished in the flames. The poet and his wife escaped to London, and there Spenser died shortly afterwards, in King Street, Westminster, apparently in great poverty. He was buried near Chaucer, in Westminster Abbey.

"His hearse," writes Dean Stanley, "was attended by poets, and mournful elegies and poems, with the pens that wrote them, were thrown into his tomb. What a funeral was that at which Beaumont, Fletcher, Jonson, and in all probability Shakespeare, attended!—what a grave, in which the pen of Shakespeare may be mouldering away!"

Spenser's "Faërie Queene," which is designed "to fashion a gentleman or noble person in virtuous and gentle discipline," is of so great a length that a youthful student, who takes up the poem for the first time, may be tempted either to leave it unread or to rest satisfied with the perusal of such passages as are generally given in selections. He will commit a blunder in either case. Spenser demands leisure and that absolute freedom from care which is the priceless possession of the young; but the reader who has these gifts, and a love, however untutored, for the divine felicities of verse, will gain a lasting delight from the perusal of this poet. Some of the critics of the last century, writing under the slavery of classic models, have found fault with Spenser for doing what he never in-

tended to do.   It may be readily admitted that the
"Faerie Queene" wants the unity of plan which
is regarded as essential to the epic.   It is broken
into many parts, and the design, as stated by the
poet in the preface, lacks fulfilment in the verse.
Prince Arthur is far too insubstantial and shadowy
a personage to form the hero of the poem, and
Spenser is assuredly not happy in representing his
"Faerie Queene" as "glory in general and Queen
Elizabeth in particular."

"There are a hundred faults in this thing, and
a hundred things might be said to prove them
beauties," writes Goldsmith of his immortal "Vicar
of Wakefield;" and a similar judgment may be
passed on the "Faerie Queene." Some of these
faults may be mentioned.   Spenser's plan was too
vast to be carried out satisfactorily, and it is probably a gain to the reader that some of the promised books were never written, or are lost.   As it
is, there are six books and a portion of a seventh,
instead of the twelve books designed by the poet,
and each book, it has been justly said, may be
considered as almost amounting in quantity to an
ordinary epic.   The vast length of the poem is
unfavourable to vigour of language and compression of thought, although sometimes the force
of the style is as conspicuous as its beauty, and
what the poet himself calls its "dark conceit" is
an obstacle to the reader's enjoyment.   On his
choice of allegory something more shall be said
presently, but it may be observed here that Spen-

ser's explanation of his purpose in the long letter
to Sir Walter Raleigh, prefixed to the work,
proves that he foresaw the necessity of furnishing
a key to his "dark sayings." A poem that does
not tell its own story is, in a measure, defective
as a work of art. Another fault due to the construction of the work is the abstract nature of the
characters. Unlike Shakespeare's men and women
of flesh and blood, who are as real to us as
the people with whom we have clasped hands,
Spenser's shadowy personages represent vices and
virtues, and finely drawn though they be, lack a
human interest. The adventures of his heroes, who
are pledged to relieve the distresses of forlorn
damsels, are the adventures of knights-errant; but
the moral purpose of the poem gives to every exploit
a sacred significance. Thus chivalry and religion are
linked together; and Spenser's warriors are bound
—as we also are bound by our baptismal vows—to
resist the world, the flesh and the devil, and to continue Christ's faithful soldiers and servants unto their
lives' end. But the scheme even as conceived by the
author is not clearly maintained, and while pouring
forth the wealth of his imagination, and revelling
in splendid imagery, Spenser frequently forgets his
purpose as an allegorist and moral teacher. On
this point Dean Church writes so clearly that I
am glad to substitute his words for my own. The
poem, says Spenser's latest critic and biographer—-

"is really a collection of separate tales and allegories as
much as the 'Arabian Nights,' or as its counterpart and

rival of our own century, the 'Idylls of the King.' As a whole it is confusing; but we need not treat it as a whole. Its continued interest soon breaks down. But it is probably best that Spenser gave his mind the vague freedom which suited it, and that he did not make efforts to tie himself down to his pre-arranged but too ambitious plan. We can hardly lose our way in it, for there is no way to lose. It is a wilderness in which we are left to wander. But there may be interest and pleasure in a wilderness if we are prepared for the wandering. Still the complexity, or rather the uncared-for and clumsy arrangement of the poem, is matter which disturbs a reader's satisfaction till he gets accustomed to the poet's way and resigns himself to it. It is a heroic poem in which the heroine who gives her name to it never appears; a story of which the basis and starting-point is whimsically withheld for disclosure in the last book, which was never written."

Another objection often made to the "Faerie Queene" is the archaic character of the language. Spenser is in the habit of using words that had ceased to be used in his own day. He goes to Chaucer for old forms, wishing probably to fix them permanently in our English tongue. Poets are makers in two senses. They give a shape to imaginative conceptions, and they form the language in which they write. It was therefore by no means unreasonable of Spenser, the first poet worthy to be named as the successor of Chaucer, to endeavour as far as he might, to recall words and expressions that had fallen out of use. But he was too daring in this exploit; for not only did he employ obsolete words, he also invented words with a contemptuous disregard of precedent or grammar, in order to suit the exigencies of rhyme. These eccentricities, although hurtful to the poet's fame, interfere but little with the pleasure of his readers, who, if they cannot sometimes explain a word, can always guess at a meaning. Dean Church has pointed out another fault in Spenser's poetry, which unhappily he shares in common with the poets of his own and of the next two centuries. The adulation of monarchs has been until of late years the glaring vice of poets. The disease was at its height in the reign of Queen Elizabeth, and Spenser, a great poet, offended greatly. This at least may be said, that there was more reasonableness in his flattery, absurd though it sometimes appears, than in the stupendous adulation lavished by smaller poets upon the Stuarts and Georges. Another count brought against the "Faerie Queene" is the offensiveness of the imagery sometimes employed by the poet. Spenser can excite the strongest feelings of disgust, and does this in such forcible language that the reader is compelled to remember what he would fain forget. All great poets, how-ever, know how much in their art, as in the art of the painter, may be effected by contrast. The pre-sentation of a disagreeable scene makes the reader all the more ready to welcome a scene of beauty; and Spenser, who is pre-eminently the poet of the beautiful, no doubt used repulsive imagery as a foil to the incomparable loveliness of the passages in which his genius expands most freely. In vivid power of representation and a belief in

what he sees, Spenser has been compared to
Homer. He is like him in the directness and force
of his imagery, in his simplicity and homeliness,
in the faith with which he narrates impossible
adventures. To an artificial, world-ridden nature,
Spenser may seem childish; he is really childlike,
and to him may be applied with more exquisite
pertinence, the fine lines which Collins dedicated to
Tasso—

" Prevailing poet ! whose undoubting mind
　　Believed the magic wonders which he sung !
　　Hence at each sound, imagination glows !
　　Hence at each picture, vivid life starts here !
　　Hence his warm lay with softest sweetness flows !
　　Melting it flows, pure, murmuring, strong and clear,
　　And fills the impassion'd heart and wins the harmonious
　　　　ear ! "

To many readers the principal stumbling-block
in the " Faerie Queene " is the allegory. The
modern mind is not attracted by the figurative
representation of ideas; and if the " Pilgrim's
Progress " continues to be the most popular of
books, it is because Bunyan's pictures are regarded
as real, because the personations of spiritual
agencies speak and move in his pages as if endowed with bodily life. We forget the allegory
while reading about Christian and Christiana,
Great-heart and Giant Despair, and we may, without
much loss, forget the allegory (which, by the way,
Spenser himself often forgets) while reading the
" Faerie Queene." The student will do well to

master the purport of the poem, as explained by
its author in his letter to Raleigh; but, having done
this, it is not necessary that he should perplex
himself with the attempt, often a vain one, to interpret the allegorical meaning which is supposed
to pervade the work. Moreover, although a fault
in the construction of the "Faerie Queene," it is to
the reader's advantage that each book can be regarded as a separate poem. The first book, which
is, as Hallam observes, the finest of the six, is indeed
a complete poem in itself, and it is one with which
the student will do well to gain a thorough familiarity. He should learn by heart all its finest
stanzas ; he should master all the difficult passages,
the allusions with which it abounds, the purpose
with which it is written ; and in doing this he cannot
have a better guide than the edition published by
Mr. Kitchin in the Clarendon Press Series. But
I hope the student will discover for himself, without the aid of a teacher, the noble lessons to be
gathered from this divine poem—lessons which,
like flowers by the wayside, instruct unconsciously
and through the potent influence of beauty. The
reader who, like Keats, "ramps" through this
splendid work, will overlook or forget its faults, in
his admiration of its gorgeous imagery, the enchanting melodiousness of the verse, the wealth of
fancy and imagination, which the poet lavishes so
freely. Spenser is diffuse ; he takes his own way,
and, like a river, winds "at his own sweet will."
Do you find fault with this method of a poet's

workmanship, which enables him to reveal at every
turn some fresh vision of beauty? or do you prefer
to the secret movements of the stream that "winds
about and in and out," and "murmurs under moon
and stars in brambly wildernesses," the open and
orderly but sluggish course of the canal?

The metre used by Spenser is a striking feature
of the poem. He was the inventor of it, and it is
therefore termed Spenserian. The stanza, consisting of nine lines, and ending with an Alex-
andrine—a measure termed by Shelley "inexpres-
sibly beautiful," and by Professor Wilson the finest
ever conceived by the soul of man—is not well
fitted for rapid narrative; but for meditative verse,
and for the dreamy pictures of beauty in which
Spenser delighted, it is an incomparable instrument.
And this has been felt so strongly by later poets, that
several of the most familiar poems in the language—
Thomson's "Castle of Indolence," Burns's "Cotter's
Saturday Night," Keats's "Eve of St. Agnes," and
Byron's "Childe Harold," for example—are written
in the Spenserian stanza. But not one of these
poets can be said to have treated it with the mastery
displayed by Spenser.*

---

* The following passage from the first canto of the poem, in
which the Red Cross Knight and "heavenly Una" seek shelter
from a storm, will suffice to illustrate Spenser's metre and spelling:—

"Enforst to seeke some covert nigh at hand,
A shadie grove not farr away they spide
That promist ayde the tempest to withstand;
Whose loftie trees, yclad with sommers pride
Did spred so broad, that heavens light did hide,

Perhaps, considering the purpose of this volume, enough has been said of this glorious poem. It will surely be enough if it lead the reader to give to Spenser the reverent study which such a high-souled poet claims ; and it may be observed that, while reading his poetry, the student will not only be led to love and honour what is pure and honest and of good report, but will gain also some know-

---

Not perceable with power of any starr ;
And all within were pathes and alleies wide,
With footing worne, and leading inward farr.
Faire harbour that them seems so in they entred ar.

"And foorth they passe with pleasure forward led,
Joying to heare the birdes sweete harmony,
Which, therein shrouded from the tempest dred
Seemd in their song to scorne the cruell sky.
Much can they praise the trees so straight and hy,
The sayling Pine ; the Cedar proud and tall ;
The vine-propp Elme ; the Poplar never dry ;
The builder Oake, sole king of forrests all ;
The Aspine good for staves ; the Cypresse funerall ;

"The Laurell, meed of mightie Conquerours
And Poets sage ; the Firre that weepeth still ;
The Willow worne of forlorne Paramours ;
The Eugh, obedient to the benders will ;
The Birch for shaftes ; the Sallow for the mill ;
The Mirrhe sweete-bleeding in the bitter wound ;
The Warlike Beech ; the Ash for nothing ill ;
The fruitfull Olive ; and the Platane round ;
The carver Holme ; the Maple seeldom inward sound.

"Led with delight, they thus beguile the way,
Untill the blustring storme is overblowne ;
When, weening to returne whence they did stray,
They cannot finde that path which first was showne,
But wander too and fro in waies unknowne,
Furthest from end then, when they neerest weene,
That makes them doubt their wits be not their owne :
So many pathes, so many turnings seene,
That which of them to take in diverse doubt they been."

D

ledge of an age which still dazzles us with its glory. Writing of the " Faërie Queene," Mr. Stopford Brooke observes—

"As the nobler Puritanism of the time is found in it, so also are the other influences of the time. . . . It represents the new love of chivalry, the new love of classical learning, the new delight in mystic theories of love and religion. It is full of those allegorical schemes in which doctrines and heresies, virtues and vices, were contrasted and personified. It takes up and uses the popular legends of fairies, dwarfs, and giants, and mingles them with the savages and the wonders of the New World of which the voyagers told in every company. Nearly the whole spirit of the English Renaissance under Elizabeth, except its coarser and baser elements, is in its pages. Of anything impure, or ugly, or violent, there is not a trace."

I do not know that it is necessary to dwell at any length upon Spenser's minor poems. A good deal might be said about the " Shepherd's Calendar " (published in 1579), for it is a poem characteristic alike of the period and of the author. The form in which the work is moulded belongs to an age which delighted in the discussion of political and religious themes by poetical shepherds, but the verse itself is such as none but Spenser could have written ; and remembering that "the 'Calendar' is not only our first English pastoral, but our earliest poetical work of any description written since the language has been substantially the same that it now is which can be called a classical work," * it will be seen that it possesses a literary interest

_____

* George L. Craik.

apart from its value as a poem. Among the
shorter poems of Spenser, his "Muiopotmos," or
the "Fate of the Butterfly," should not be overlooked. In Mr. Lowell's judgment the poem is
a marvel for delicate conception and treatment,
and he adds that " in Clarion, the butterfly, he
has symbolized himself. And surely never was the
poetic temperament so picturesquely exemplified.
We see 'young Clarion' soaring over the wide
country, over rivers and fens, over woods and
meadows. But his chief delight is in gardens, and
as he flits from bed to bed and from border to
border, he pastures on the pleasures of each place."

> " And evermore with most variety
> And change of sweetness (for all change is sweet)
> He casts his glutton sense to satisfy,
> Now sucking of the sap of herbs most meet,
> Or of the dew which yet on them doth lie,
> Now in the same bathing his tender feet ;
> And then he percheth on some branch thereby
> To weather him and his moist wings to dry.

> " And then again he turneth to his play,
> To spoil the pleasures of that paradise ;
> The wholesome sage, the lavender still gray,
> Rank-smelling rue and cummin good for eyes,
> The roses reigning in the pride of May,
> Sharp hyssop good for green wounds' remedies,
> Fair marigolds, and bees-alluring thyme,
> Sweet marjoram, and daisies decking prime.

> " And whatso else of virtue good or ill,
> Grew in this garden, fetched from far away,

Of every one he takes and tastes at will,
And on their pleasures greedily doth prey ;
Then, when he hath both played and fed his fill,
In the warm sun he doth himself embay,
And there him rests in riotous suffisance
Of all his gladfulness and kingly joyance.

" What more felicity can fall to creature
Than to enjoy delight with liberty,
And to be lord of all the works of nature ?
To reign in the air from earth to highest sky,
To feed on flowers and weeds of glorious feature,
To take whatever thing doth please the eye ?
Who rests not pleasèd with such happiness
Well worthy he to taste of wretchedness."

"To reign in the air," writes Mr. Lowell, in commenting
on these stanzas, "was certainly Spenser's function. And
yet the commentators, who seem never willing to let their
poet be a poet pure and simple—though had he not been so
they would have lost their only hold on life—try to make out
from his ' Mother Hubberd's Tale' that he might have been
a very sensible matter-of-fact man if he would. For my own
part, I am quite willing to confess that I like him none the
worse for being *un*practical, and that my reading has con-
vinced me that being too poetical is the rarest fault of poets.
Practical men are not so scarce, one would think ; and I am
not sure that the tree was a gainer when the hamadryad
flitted and left it nothing but ship-timber. Such men as
Spenser are not sent into the world to be part of its motive
power. The blind old engine would not know the difference
though we get up its steam with ottar of roses, nor make one
revolution more to the minute for it. What practical man ever
left such an heirloom to his country as the 'Faery Queen'?"

This unworldly and pre-eminently un-American
statement will recall to the reader of Carlyle's
" Hero-Worship" the question he asks with regard

to Shakespeare and our Indian empire. If we English were compelled to give up India or the poet, which should it be? Despite Mr. Lowell, there can be no question that the greatest poets, unlike many smaller singers, have been men eminent for worldly sagacity and business tact.* Grant that the poetical nature is of rarer value, and therefore more precious than the practical wisdom so needful in this working-day world, the poet is surely better as a poet in proportion to the free play and full development of his nature as a man.

Spenser has one more claim upon our admiration which can never be overlooked. He is a great lyric poet, and the " Epithalamion," or " Wedding Hymn," written on his own marriage, to which I have already alluded, is perhaps the most triumphant love-poem in the language ; it is beyond question one of our most splendid lyrics. No extract can convey a notion of its peerless beauty. Enough to say that it is worthy of the purity, the rich fancy, and the mastery of language which distinguish this noble poet, whose place is with Chaucer and Shakespeare, with Milton and with Wordsworth.

[The literature associated with Spenser is extensive. It may suffice to call the student's attention to the Globe edition of Spenser, edited by Mr. R. Morris, with a memoir by J. W. Hales (Macmillan and Co.) ; to the finely printed edition, in five vols., brought out about ten years ago by that literary veteran Mr. J. P.

---

* Chaucer and Shakespeare, for example, were both men of affairs, and Mr. Lowell allows that Dante was supremely practical.

Collier; to Dean Church's "Spenser," in "English Men of Letters;"
and to "Spenser and his Poetry," by the late Professor Craik. A
series of papers on Spenser, written by "Christopher North," in
Blackwood's Magazine, in the years 1833–1835, are worthy of the
subject and of the eloquent—sometimes perhaps too eloquent—
writer. Professor Wilson's admiration of Spenser is unbounded.
There is no affectation in his praise ; and it is better sometimes
for a young student to read such generous, if occasionally un-
guarded, criticism, catching as he reads the glow of the writer's
enthusiasm, than to follow the tamer comments of more cautious
critics. Every word about Spenser in Leigh Hunt's delightful
volume " Imagination and Fancy " should be read, and cannot fail
to be read with pleasure.]

CHAPTER III.

THE ELIZABETHAN POETS (*Continued*).

SIR PHILIP SIDNEY—SAMUEL DANIEL—MICHAEL DRAY-
TON—CHRISTOPHER MARLOWE—GEORGE CHAPMAN.

THERE are several poets of this period who, although never likely to be much read, will always keep an honoured place in the history of English verse. Prominent among the number stand the names of Sir Philip Sidney, Samuel Daniel, Michael Drayton, Christopher Marlowe, and George Chapman; and I will try to tell the young reader as much about these poets as it is perhaps necessary that he should know.

The name of Sir Philip Sidney stands pre-eminent in the Elizabethan age, not so much for his poetry as for his many virtues as a gentleman, a soldier, and a scholar. A recent editor of Sidney's works has

Sir Philip
Sidney,
1554-1586.

advised students to give days and nights to the study of his poetry. Such advice addressed to a youthful and enthusiastic reader can only breed vexation and disappointment. Sidney's verse, although not without distinct poetical worth, has many crudities and conceits. There is little in it comparatively of high value, and assuredly nothing that calls for a large sacrifice of time and labour. In his fine treatise, the "Apologie for Poetrie," Sidney objects to far-fetched words and impertinent conceits. In his day, as in our own, verse-makers were apt to mistake extravagant allusions and a fantastic use of words for the inspiration of the poet. Sidney himself was not free from the fault he had the critical sagacity to discover. He often plays upon words; his imagery is sometimes strained and affected, his fancy "high fantastical;" and as conceits in poetry retain no life beyond the age that produced them, there is much in his verse that is without significance for the modern reader. Charles Lamb has said that some of Sidney's sonnets are among the very best of their sort. It would be more correct to say that Sidney's best work is to be found in them. Several of the sonnets, indeed, read like the painful efforts of a scholar's wit rather than of a poet's fancy; but there are others which possess sweetness and strength, and much of that subtle charm of rhythm which belongs to the Elizabethan lyrists. The following sonnet, for instance, has a quaint melodiousness characteristic of the time :—

"O kiss, which dost those ruddy gems impart,
  Or gems or fruits of new-found paradise ;
  Breathing all bliss and sweet'ning to the heart ;
  Teaching dumb lips a nobler exercise !
  O kiss, which souls, even souls together, ties
  By links of love and only nature's art,
  How fain would I paint thee to all men's eyes !
  Or of thy gifts, at least shade out some part.
  But she forbids ; with blushing words she says
  She builds her fame on higher-seated praise.
  But my heart burns ; I cannot silent be.
  Then, since, dear life, you fain would have me peace,
  And I, mad with delight, want wit to cease,
  Stop you my mouth with still, still kissing me."

Sidney's love-poetry was inspired by Lady Rich,
who, when a young girl—her maiden name was
Lady Penelope Devereux—seems to have been
affianced to the poet. Sidney's life and her life
might have been different had this early attachment been brought to a happy ending. Worldly
guardians, however, thought they were doing the
girl profitable service by marrying her to Lord
Rich, a nobleman whom she regarded with indifference. Lady Rich's career was brilliant and
sad. In the court of England, says Mr. Minto,
she was "the most conspicuous and fascinating
woman of her generation." Her wit and beauty
were praised in no measured language by the Elizabethan poets, and that she should form the theme
of Sidney's verse is not surprising in that age of
courtly gallantry. As a lyric poet, Sidney, like so
many of his contemporaries, was occasionally very
happy, and Mr. Palgrave, in his invaluable " Golden

Treasury," has inserted a favourable specimen of the
poet's craft as a lyrist.   By repeating the burden of
the first line at the end of the stanzas, and omitting
four or five lines, Mr. Palgrave has added to the
music of the verse.   The poem shall be transcribed
from his version, although it may be questioned
whether such a treatment of the piece is wholly
justifiable on the part of an editor.

> " My true love hath my heart and I have his ;
> By just exchange one for the other given.
> I hold his dear, and mine he cannot miss.
> There never was a better bargain driven ;
> My true love hath my heart and I have his.

> " His heart in me keeps him and me in one ;
> My heart in him his thoughts and senses guides.
> He loves my heart, for once it was his own ;
> I cherish his because in me it bides ;
> My true love hath my heart and I have his."

The weakest portion of Sidney's poetry is his version of the Psalms, or, rather, of about forty psalms,
his sister, the Countess of Pembroke, having done
the largest and by far the best portion of the work.

[Sir Philip Sidney's best sonnets are to be found in selections.
His " Apologie for Poetrie " should be read.   It forms one of Mr.
Arber's cheap and valuable " English Reprints."]

Samuel Daniel, it will be seen, was born two years
before Shakespeare, and died three
Samuel Daniel, 1562-1619. years later than that poet.   He has
been styled by Southey " the tenderest
of all tender poets "—a judgment which has in it
more of affection than of criticism ; but the opinions

expressed by Daniel's contemporaries are still more eulogistic, and the chief authors of the day treated him as a friend and brother.* At seventeen he was admitted a commoner of Magdalen College, Oxford, and, after staying there three years, left without taking a degree. Then we read that Daniel was patronized by Sir Philip Sidney's sister, the Countess of Pembroke, by Lord Mountjoy, by Shakespeare's friend the Earl of Southampton, and by the Countess of Bedford, who befriended several poets and was repaid by verses. Men of letters, it should be remembered, looked to patronage in those days as naturally as in our own they anticipate the support of the public. This dependence upon the great strikes us as ignoble now, but it was not so regarded then, and it was, moreover, inevitable. Sometimes it led to splendid friendships, and in most cases the patron received back more than he gave ; but the system grew to be in time a canker at the heart of literature.

To return to Daniel. The facts of his life are the records of his works. He wrote tragedies and masques, gained high applause, and on the death of Spenser, in 1598, was appointed Poet-Laureate. His great work—great assuredly in length, if not in quality—is a poem in eight books, which was dedicated to Prince Charles, entitled " The History of the Civil Wars between the Houses of York and Lancaster." It is written in octave stanzas, a

---

* Ben Jonson did not join in this chorus of praise, but called Daniel " a good honest man, but no poet."

favourite metre with some of the Italian poets, and
one well fitted for narrative.   The genius of a poet
is seen in his choice of a subject as well as in his
treatment of it, and it seems strange Daniel did not
see that to write a history in verse must inevitably
prove a failure.   If good as a history, it must be bad
as a poem ; if fine poetically, its historical value will
be slight.   The Wars of the Roses lasted sixteen
years, and that there are episodes in that period of
civil strife which can be nobly treated has been
proved by Shakespeare ; but it is one thing to select
actions for poetical uses, and quite another thing
to chronicle in due order, as Daniel undertakes to
do, a long series of historical events.   Truly does
Drayton say of his contemporary—

> " His rhymes were smooth, his metres well did close,
>   But yet his manner better fitted prose."

The poem, however, is not without significance.
Daniel was born ten years after Spenser, whose old-
world style, quaint in his own age, will not allow
us to forget that three centuries have gone by since
he lived and wrote ; but Daniel, on the contrary,
writes in the purest, and I had almost said the
most modern, English.   His " History " from beginning to end may be understood by the youngest
reader.   He is never obscure in language or in
thought, and of the few obsolete words used in this
long poem we doubt if there is one which will perplex
the student. The same remark holds good for all the
poems of Daniel. Among his epistles, the most
notable, addressed to the Countess of Cumberland,

has been warmly praised by Wordsworth. It has many weighty lines, and among them will be found the couplet so often quoted by Coleridge—

> "Unless above himself he can
> Erect himself, how poor a thing is man!"

Daniel's "Musophilus," called by Mr. Lowell "the best poem of its kind in the language," is intended for a defence of learning. The ambition that prompts a man to "scorn delights and live laborious days," that he may leave behind him something the world will not let die was felt by Daniel as by all poets. To him also poetry held out an earthly immortality, and he anticipates by the power of song—

> "That when our days do end they are not done,
> And though we die we shall not perish quite,
> But live two lives where others have but one."

And then he bursts forth into this noble praise of knowledge and of literature—

> "O blessed letters! that combine in one
> All ages past and make one live with all.
> By you we do confer with who are gone
> And the dead-living unto council call;
> By you the unborn shall have communion
> Of what we feel and what doth us befall.
> Soul of the world, knowledge without thee
> What hath the earth that truly glorious is?
> Why should our pride make such a stir to be,
> To be forgot? What good is like to this,
> To do worthy the writing, and to write
> Worthy the reading, and the world's delight?"

These words are supposed to be uttered by Musophilus, but this love of fame is, as Milton says, an "infirmity;" and Philocosmus, who deems it such, replies in a strain of argument which will be rejected by all ardent spirits if it cannot well be contradicted. How poor a thing, he says in effect, is fame at the best! how uncertain! how much in danger of being thrust aside by the attempts of fresh adventurers! and how limited in extent!

> "Is this the walk of all your wide renown,
>   This little point, this scarce-discernèd isle?"

And even within these poor narrow limits how many thousands never heard the name of Sidney or of Spenser, or their books?* Present action he avers is more important than future fame, and this search after "sweet, enchanting knowledge" takes a man "out from the fields of natural delight." After Philocosmus has pleaded for action instead of words, for the grace to do rather than to say, Musophilus replies at some length and not always with much point, but towards the close he rises into eloquence, foretells the time when the "treasure of our tongue" shall be carried to the far West, and ends with a fine tribute to the power of verse. The poem should be read by the more advanced students of our poetry, but the few words we have said about it will probably suffice for young readers. Indeed, "well-languaged Daniel," though he wrote much and gained high repute for it, has left few poems

---

* "The life of literary men," says Mr. Bagehot, "is often a kind of sermon in itself; for the pursuit of fame, when it is contrasted with the grave realities of life, seems more absurd and trifling than most pursuits, and to leave less behind it."

which command attention now. His "Complaint
of Rosamond" does not, and his fifty-seven sonnets
addressed to Delia possess a literary but not a
poetical interest. It has been suggested, and it is
possible, that they formed the model upon which
Shakespeare worked. The most poetical of Daniel's
sonnets, and the one best known, is addressed to
Sleep—a favourite subject with the sonnet-writers—

"Care-charmer Sleep, son of the sable night ;"

but in most of the sonnets there is a sweetness and
gentleness of expression which make it just to link
the epithet "tender" to Daniel's name.

Drayton had a greater reputation than Daniel in
his lifetime, and deserved it. He is
one of the most copious writers of verse
in the language—an evil sign for his
fame—but much that he has written is of solid
worth. He was born at Hartshill, near Atherstone,
in Warwickshire, in 1563, and is said, like Pope, to
have "lisped in numbers." In one of his poetical
epistles he refers to this precocity, and says—

Michael
Drayton,
1563-1632.

"For from my cradle you must know that I
Was still inclined to noble poesy ;"

and he tells how he went to his tutor when a
pigmy boy, and, clasping his slender arms round
his leg, exclaimed—

"'O my dear master, cannot you,' quoth I,
'Make me a poet? Do it if you can,
And you shall see I'll quickly be a man.'"

Like other poets of the age, Drayton depended

upon patrons, and to one of them he appears to
have owed his education. Of his life we know
little beyond the catalogue of his numerous poems.
He seems to have been a man of high character,
amiable in disposition, honest in conversation, and
of a "well-governed carriage," and when he died,
in the sixty-eighth year of his age, he obtained
a resting-place among the poets in Westminster
Abbey. The Countess of Dorset raised the monument to this "memorable poet," and the quaint
Francis Quarles (1592–1644) is said to have written
his epitaph. His works show that Drayton deserved the honours awarded to him by patrons and
contemporary poets. Jonson, who loved well to
praise his friends and poetical rivals in vigorous
lines, has reviewed in succession Drayton's most
notable poems in an epistle to the author. Drayton wrote upwards of sixty irregular sonnets under
the title of "Ideas," which Jonson found "pure
and perfect poesy." He praises, too, his "Heroical
Epistles," one of which, describing the miseries of
Queen Margaret, makes his eyes "overflow;" his
"Fairy Court," his "Owl," his "Barons' Wars," his
"Polyolbion," and above all his "Agincourt," of
which he writes—

> "Look how, we read, the Spartans were inflamed
> With bold Tyrtæus' verse. When thou art named
> So shall our English youth urge on, and cry,
> 'An Agincourt! an Agincourt!' or die!
> This book it is a catechism to fight,
> And will be bought of every lord and knight
> That can but read."

The poem thus praised by Jonson is of considerable length, and not without merit; but Drayton wrote also a ballad on the subject, which despite the brilliant achievements of Campbell, Mr. Tennyson, and other poets, is still one of the most spirited battle-songs in the language. Listen to some of the stanzas, and I shall be surprised if, while hearing them or reading them aloud, they do not keep a place in your memory.

> " Fair stood the wind for France,
>   When we our sails advance,
>   Nor now to prove our chance
>   Longer will tarry ;
>   But putting to the main,
>   At Caux, the mouth of Seine,
>   With all his martial train,
>   Landed King Harry.
>
> "And taking many a fort,
>   Furnished in warlike sort,
>   Marcheth tow'rds Agincourt,
>   In happy hour ;
>   Skirmishing day by day
>   With those that stopp'd his way,
>   Where the French gen'ral lay,
>   With all his power.
>
> "And turning to his men,
>   Quoth our brave Henry then,
>   'Though they be one to ten,
>   Be not amazed.
>   Yet have we well begun ;
>   Battles so bravely won,
>   Have ever to the sun
>   By fame been raised.

E

"'And for myself,' quoth he,
　'This my full rest shall be,
　England ne'er mourn for me,
　　　Nor more esteem me.
　Victor I will remain,
　Or on this earth lie slain ;
　Never shall she sustain
　　　Loss to redeem me.

"'Poitiers and Cressy tell,
　When most their pride did swell,
　Under our swords they fell ;
　　　No less our skill is,
　Than when our grandsire-great,
　Claiming the regal seat,
　By many a warlike feat,
　　　Lopp'd the French lilies.'

"They now to fight are gone,
　Armour on armour shone,
　Drum now to drum did groan,—
　　　To hear was wonder ;
　That with the cries they make,
　The very earth did shake,
　Trumpet to trumpet spake,
　　　Thunder to thunder.

"Well it thine age became,
　O noble Erpingham,
　Which didst the signal aim
　　　To our hid forces ;
　When from a meadow bý,
　Like a storm suddenly,
　The English archery
　　　Struck the French horses.

"With Spanish yew so strong,
  Arrows a cloth-yard long,
  That like to serpents stung,
    Piercing the weather ;
None from his fellow starts,
  But playing manly parts,
  And like true English hearts,
    Stuck close together.

"When down their bows they threw,
  And forth their bilboes drew,
  And on the French they flew,
    Not one was tardy ;
Arms were from shoulders sent,
  Scalps to the teeth were rent,
  Down the French peasants went,
    Our men were hardy.

" This while our noble king,
  His broad sword brandishing,
  Down the French host did ding,
    As to o'erwhelm it ;
And many a deep wound lent,
  His arms with blood besprent,
  And many a cruel dent
    Bruisèd his helmet.

" Gloucester, that duke so good,
  Next of the royal blood,
  For famous England stood,
    With his brave brother ;
Clarence in steel so bright,
  Though but a maiden knight,
  Yet in that furious fight
    Scarce such another.

"Warwick in blood did wade,
Oxford the foe invade,
And cruel slaughter made,
     Still as they ran up ;
Suffolk his axe did ply,
Beaumont and Willoughby,
Bare them right doughtily—
     Ferrers and Fanhope.

" Upon Saint Crispin's Day
Fought was this noble fray,
Which fame did not delay
     To England to carry ;
Oh when shall English men
With such acts fill a pen,
Or England breed again
     Such a King Harry ! "

The colossal amplitude of Drayton's works is
likely to daunt young readers, who, it is to be
feared, will sometimes yawn at what Ben Jonson
would have expected them to admire. But in spite
of his prolixity this poet has sterling merit. There
are moral qualities which make themselves felt in
literature as well as in life. Earnestness of purpose,
sincerity, a regard for truth,—these are virtues which,
when combined with the faculties especially characteristic of the poet, cannot fail to place a man
upon a high level ; and they are virtues prominent
in Drayton. He had some imagination and more
fancy, some ear too for melody, as beseems a poet ;
but one can scarcely doubt that the exhaustless
energy and patience which mark such poems as
" The Barons' Wars " and the " Polyolbion " would in

another age have been expended more wisely upon prose. Drayton says of Daniel that he was "too much historian in verse," a criticism which in some cases applies with equal truth to Drayton himself.

Mrs. Browning, who, with the instinct of a true poet, often hits in a word or two the faults or beauty of a poem, its fictitious value or lasting worth, has called "The Barons' Wars" "somewhat tame and level." The poem is written in the eight-line stanza employed by Daniel in his "History of the Civil Wars." Being scarcely more than half the length, Drayton's chronicle in rhyme is twice as readable, and it is, perhaps, purer in style, being free from the alliteration and play upon words, of which Daniel is too fond. "Polyolbion," a poem of enormous length—it contains, I believe, more than thirty thousand lines—is, in regard to quantity, Drayton's most remarkable work. In lines of twelve syllables which, "like a wounded snake, drag their slow length along," he travels through the length and breadth of England "with the fidelity of a herald and the painful love of a son who has not left a rivulet so narrow that it may be stepped over without honourable mention, and has animated hills and streams with life and passion above the dreams of old mythology." * It is a difficult poem to read, but one from which a great deal may be learnt; and so accurate are Drayton's statements, so close his observation, that

* Charles Lamb.

local historians are always glad to quote pertinent passages from his verse.

It would be treason to Drayton's fame to pass by unnoticed his " Nymphidia, or the Court of Fairy," a poem full of the brightest fancy, and written with a nimbleness of metre which forms a happy contrast to the weightier works of the poet. Two short extracts may be welcome. They will not show the beauty of the work, but they will illustrate its fantastic grace, and in their measure also the wealth of the poet's fancy. Shakespeare's Queen Mab is a tiny lady well known to poetry-lovers. In Drayton's hands she is equally small and equally contrary. So, without asking King Oberon's permission, she resolves to visit a knight called Pigwiggen, who is "at home" in a "fair cowslip flower."

> "Her chariot ready straight is made,
>   Each thing therein is fitting laid,
>   That she by nothing might be stayed,
>   For naught must her be letting ;
>   Four nimble gnats the horses were,
>   Their harnesses of gossamer,
>   Fly Cranion, her charioteer,
>   Upon the coach-box getting.

> " Her chariot of a snail's fine shell,
>   Which for the colours did excel
>   The fair Queen Mab becoming well,
>   So lively was the limning ;
>   The seat the soft wool of the bee,
>   The cover (gallantly to see)
>   The wing of a pied butterfly—
>   I trow 'twas simple trimming.

.   .   .   .   .

" She mounts her chariot with a trice,
   Nor would she stay for no advice
   Until her maids, that were so nice,
      To wait on her were fitted,
   But ran away herself alone ;
   Which when they heard, there was not one
   But hasted after to be gone,
      As she had been diswitted.

" Hop and Mop and Drop so clear,
   Pip and Trip and Skip that were
   To Mab their sovereign ever dear,
      Her special maids of honour ;
   Fib and Tib and Pinck and Pin,
   Tick and Quick and Jill and Jin,
   Tit and Nit and Wap and Win,
      The train that wait upon her.

" Upon a grasshopper they got,
   And what with amble and with trot,
   For hedge and ditch they spared not,
      But after her they hie them ;
   A cobweb over them they throw
   To shield the wind if it should blow ;
   Themselves they wisely could bestow
      Lest any should espy them."

Then there is rare sport, and some fear too ; for
the dancing and fun of the maidens in the presence
of the queen and Pigwiggen is interrupted by the
news that Puck has been sent by the king to fetch
them home again ; so they all creep into an empty
hazel-nut. Meanwhile Nymphidia plays Puck all
kinds of tricks, until at length—

> " When stumbling at a piece of wood,
> He fell into a ditch of mud,
> Where to the very chin he stood,
> In danger to be choked."

Whereupon poor Puck yells and roars at such a rate that the noise wakes Queen Mab in her nut-shell, who, upon hearing what had happened—

> "Well-near cracked her spleen
> With very extreme laughter."

Then Pigwiggen challenges King Oberon to fight; and, having taken a hornet's sting for his rapier, which "was a very dangerous thing," and a fish's scale for armour, the poet completes his description of the doughty knight by saying—

> " His helmet was a beetle's head,
> Most horrible and full of dread,
> That able was to strike one dead,
>   Yet did it well become him;
> And for a plume a horse's hair,
> Which, being tossèd with the air,
> Had force to strike his foe with fear
>   And turn his weapon from him.

> " Himself he on an earwig set,
> Yet scarce he on his back could get,
> So oft and high he did corvet
>   Ere he himself could settle;
> He made him turn and stop and bound,
> To gallop and to trot the round;
> He scarce could stand on any ground,
>   He was so full of mettle."

One lovely sonnet, marked by a glow of feeling

seldom to be met with in Drayton, deserves to be
quoted before parting from this worthy poet.

"Since there's no help, come, let us kiss and part.
Nay, I have done, you get no more of me.
And I am glad, yea, glad with all my heart,
That thus so cleanly I myself can free.
Shake hands for ever, cancel all our vows,
And when we meet at any time again,.
Be it not seen in either of our brows
That we one jot of former love retain.
Now at the last gasp of Love's latest breath,
When, his pulse failing, Passion speechless lies,
When Faith is kneeling by his bed of death,
And Innocence is closing up his eyes,—
Now if thou wouldst, when all have given him over,
From death to life thou mightst him yet recover ! "

[Daniel's poems are to be found in vol. iii. of Chalmers' "English
Poets," and Drayton's in vol. iv. About the middle of the last
century Drayton's works appeared in an edition of four volumes.
In his case, however, the half is better than the whole. A privately
printed volume, " Selections from the Poems of Michael Drayton,"
edited by A. H. Bullen, has recently appeared. Only 155 copies
have been printed of this beautiful work—beautiful in form as well
as in contents—but it is to be hoped that ere long the editor will be
able to reproduce it in a cheaper form.]

Marlowe's "mighty line" holds a place of no
slight significance in our early poetry. Christopher
There was in this poet an untutored Marlowe,
1564-1593.
greatness which influenced Shakespeare,
and, through Shakespeare, all the dramatists of the
age. Genius is more visible in Marlowe than art ;
his Titanic conceptions astound the reader, his
characters exercise a force that is not human. He
was the first to introduce blank verse into our

plays; he "created the English tragic drama;"*
and his verse, though full of bombast, sound, and
fury, is full also of energy and power. It has
been well said that "the strength of our old poets
lay in their unconscious independence." This is
true of Marlowe; yet, if independence gave him
robust strength, it was the source also of his weakness. The poet, like all artists, is bound by laws
which he cannot slight with impunity; but in his
writings, as in his life, Marlowe was a despiser of
restraint.

Christopher Marlowe, like so many of our poets,
belonged to the common people. His father was a
shoemaker at Canterbury, and there the future poet
was born in 1564, the year that gave birth to
Shakespeare. By good fortune, which means probably the kindness of some wealthy friend, the
young man was sent in due time to Cambridge, and
took the usual degrees. How he first became connected with the stage we do not know, but he began
his dramatical career at a very early period, and
was the predecessor, not the follower, of Shakespeare.† Marlowe's short life appears to have been
spent in dissipation. We know little about him,
but that little, unfortunately, is wholly bad, and he
died at last in a tavern brawl, at the early age of
thirty.

---

* Stopford Brooke.
† "King Richard II." is the earliest play by Shakespeare entered on
the Stationers' register (August 1597), but Marlowe's "Tamburlaine"
was entered and published in 1590. Whatever virtues Marlowe
possesses as a dramatist are due to himself alone.

Of Marlowe's plays, "Tamburlaine," 'Dr. Faustus," "The Rich Jew of Malta," "Edward I.," and the "Massacre of Paris," I need say nothing, for the plan of this volume excludes the literature of the drama. Yet I may linger a moment to observe that in these plays many a gem of poetic beauty is hidden away. The couplet in "Dr. Faustus"—

> "Oh, thou art fairer than the evening air,
> Clad in the beauty of a thousand stars"—

is, indeed, worthy of Shakespeare. Of Marlowe's poems one is familiar, having been for many years stereotyped in selections. I allude to "The Passionate Shepherd to his Love," which opens with the following lines :—

> "Come, live with me and be my Love,
> And we will all the pleasures prove
> That hills and valleys, dale and field,
> And all the craggy mountains yield.

> "There will we sit upon the rocks
> And see the shepherds feed their flocks,
> By shallow rivers, to whose falls
> Melodious birds sing madrigals." *

To this poetical invitation, it may be remembered, Sir Walter Raleigh replied in verses similar in metre but inferior in beauty. The only poem of any length written by Marlowe is a piece left

---

* Izaak Walton, whose lovely prose pastoral, "The Complete Angler," is as refreshing as the breath of summer and as fragrant as her flowers, calls this poem "that smooth song made by Kit Marlowe." "The milkmaid's mother," he adds, "sang an answer to it which was made by Sir Walter Raleigh in his younger days. They were old-fashioned poetry, but choicely good."

imperfect and continued by Chapman, the famous
translator of Homer, entitled, " Hero and Leander."
Beauty of language and wealth of colour are to be
found in it, but the absence of purity leaves the
poem at a low level, and justifies the severe criticism
of Hallam.

Of Chapman, who took up the thread of Marlowe's story, little need be said here ;
but it is worth observing that he numbered amongst his friends the choicest
wits of the age ; that his picturesque, swiftly flow-
ing but often crude version of Homer called forth
the immortal sonnet of John Keats; and that his
plays, sixteen in number, while coarse and ignoble
in conception, contain many lines and pithy
aphorisms which impress us with the imaginative
fire and weighty sense of the writer.   At the same
time, there was much in him hollow and pretentious,
and his lofty estimate of his own writings is not
the estimate of posterity.   Chapman, who was
born in 1557, studied, it is said, for two years at
Trinity College, Oxford, and left the university
without a degree.   In 1611 his translation of the
"Iliad" appeared, written in fourteen-syllabled verse
—" an unmeasurable length of verse," Pope calls it
—and four years later this was followed by the
" Odyssey."   The young student should not fail to
read at least some books of this translation, not
for its accuracy as a rendering of Homer, but for
the robust strength of the language, and for the
poetic glow which gives it life and warmth.   Chap-

George
Chapman,
1557?-1634.

man declared that he translated the last twelve books of the "Iliad" in fifteen weeks—a feat that . seems well-nigh incredible ; but there is every sign that the work was done with great rapidity.

"The great obstacle," writes Charles Lamb, "to Chapman's translations being read is their unconquerable quaintness. He pours out in the same breath the most just and natural and the most violent and fierce expressions. He seems to grasp whatever words come first to hand during the impetus of inspiration, as if all other must be inadequate to the divine meaning. But passion, the all in all in poetry, is everywhere present, raising the low, dignifying the mean, and putting sense into the absurd."

The story of George Chapman's life is untold. We know scarcely anything about him beyond the dates of his publications and the fact that his patron was Sir Thomas Walsingham, through whom he is supposed to have gained some position at court. He died in 1634.

[Two editions of Chapman's Homer have appeared within the last half-century ; one of the "Iliad," in two vols., with introduction and notes by Dr. Cooke Taylor, and another containing the whole works of Homer, in four vols., edited by Richard Hooper. "Conversations on Some of the Old Poets," by James Russell Lowell, a little volume published in 1845, contains the author's youthful thoughts on several of our early poets. Considerable attention is paid to Chapman, and probably more praise awarded than the author of the "Biglow Papers" would give now ; but the book is delightful for its freshness and enthusiasm.]

CHAPTER IV.

THE ELIZABETHAN POETS (*Continued*).

WILLIAM SHAKESPEARE.

THE Elizabethan poets mentioned in the last chapter still stand like landmarks in the literature of their country. The place they hold is not exalted, but it is secure, and to each of them a measure of respect is due. But we come now to a name that towers far above them all.

William Shakespeare is the greatest of our poets —the greatest of all poets—and his gifts are so infinitely varied that it is almost impossible to criticize him justly. One reader will be enthralled by one phase of his genius, a second reader by another, and no one has enough of imagination and intellectual capacity to grasp the whole. Shakespeare was great all round ; his best critics, including even men of consummate power, like Coleridge and Goethe, were great but in parts, and if they could not fully interpret this

William
Shakespeare,
1564-1616.

myriad-minded poet, an ordinary lover of poetry can but touch the theme with humility and reserve.

Feeling, then, how much there is to say about Shakespeare—whose works are in themselves a literature—and how impossible it is to say it adequately, I shall content myself with making a few concise remarks, and with referring the student to the best sources of information open to him for the study of this incomparable poet. Moreover, this reticence is in accordance with the purport of my volume. Shakespeare's genius is expressed almost entirely in the dramatic form, and in these pages the drama is "out of court." Neither Shakespeare's youthful poems, "Venus and Adonis" and "Lucrece," nor his beautiful but obscure sonnets, would claim much attention from us apart from the plays. In these may be found in richest abundance every element of poetry—imagination, fancy, wit, humour, pathos, dignity of thought, aptness of expression, the loveliest strains of melody, the largest sagacity, and a creative power, the highest possession of the poet—which has never been surpassed. No man can venture to say that he has mastered Shakespeare. As well might he imagine, after visiting a scene of great loveliness or sublimity, that he had learnt every lesson Nature can teach him. The works of all great poets, indeed, will yield much in beauty of blossom and wealth of fruit to the man who studies them most heartily ; but the time may perhaps come when he has gained all they have to give him. This can never be the case with Shake-

speare. Great though he be, it is sheer idolatry
and folly to write of him as a faultless poet. His
faults are on the surface, and are due for the most
part to his superabundant vitality, and in a measure
to the influences of his age. The reader is sometimes offended by grossness of language and of
plot, and sometimes irritated by the poet's love of
puns and quibbles. Happily for England and for
the honour of our literature, Shakespeare is, in the
main, a thoroughly moral writer. He paints vice
with the hand of a master, but he does not glorify
it ; he is coarse in expression, but the spirit that
pervades his poetry is pure and on the side of
virtue. His intellect is robust, and he has at the
same time the gentleness and tenderness we
admire so much in women. The highest minds,
it has been said, are never wholly masculine, and
Shakespeare's sweetness is as conspicuous as his
strength. We see this in the pure womanliness
of his feminine characters—in Rosalind and Juliet,
in Imogen and Perdita, in Beatrice and Desde-
mona, in Isabella and Portia. And it may be
seen, too, in his tender love of nature, a love which
lights up pages of tragic horror or of coarse world-
liness, so that the reader still feels the grateful
warmth of the sunshine, and sees the steadfast
beauty of the stars. The lavish prodigality of this
wonderful poet reminds us of Nature herself. He
scatters his gifts broadcast, as if he had no fear of
exhausting the matchless resources of his genius.
And yet it cannot be said that there is much in

his plays, certainly not in his later plays, which can be called waste, or which fails to contribute to the action of the drama. It is possible in certain cases to write of a man's poetry as something apart from his art as a dramatist. We can do so, for instance, in writing of Ben Jonson or of Dryden, but with regard to Shakespeare this is impossible. There are dramatists who are not poets, and poets who, when writing plays, have not given scope to their poetical genius. In Shakespeare, as I have said already, the poet predominates over the dramatist, or rather the poetry is so interfused with the action of the drama that the two are linked together inseparably. Of all his plays the most purely poetical are, perhaps, the "Midsummer Night's Dream," the "Tempest," and the "Winter's Tale;" and it is remarkable that the two last-mentioned plays belong to the latest season of his poetical activity. Lyric verse of the most enchanting beauty is scattered over his thirty-five dramas, and in this department of poetry, as in most others, Shakespeare stands without a rival. Yet he was not without great competitors in that wonderful age of song, and John Fletcher, the dramatic associate of Beaumont, had upon rare occasions a voice almost John Fletcher. 1579-1625. equal to that of Shakespeare himself. Poets could sing in Shakespeare's time, and several of his fellow-dramatists sang with a bird-like impulse that seemed like "unpremeditated art." By degrees this art was lost, and with rare exceptions the poets

F

of the eighteenth century were not singers. Indeed,
the voice of song was mute before that century
began.   There is, for example, no greater contrast
in our poetical literature than between the artificial songs of Dryden and the musical notes of
Shakespeare, Fletcher, and Ben Jonson.   Listen
to one of Dryden's songs and then to one of
Fletcher's.

> "Go, tell Amynta, gentle swain,
>   I would not die, nor dare complain ;
> Thy tuneful voice with numbers join,
> Thy words will more prevail than mine.
> To souls oppressed and dumb with grief,
> The gods ordain this kind relief—
> That music should in sounds convey
> What dying lovers dare not say.

> "A sigh or tear perhaps she'll give ;
>   But love on pity cannot live.
> Tell her that hearts for hearts were made,
> And love with love is only paid.
> Tell her my pains so fast increase,
> That soon they will be past redress.
> But ah ! the wretch that speechless lies,
> Attends but death to close his eyes."

In eight peerless lines Fletcher sings the death-
song of a maid dying for love.

> " Lay a garland on my hearse
>   Of the dismal yew,
> Maidens, willow branches bear ;
>   Say, I died true.

"My love was false, but I was firm
From my hour of birth.
Upon my buried body lie
Lightly, gentle earth!"

Another illustration of Fletcher's genius as a
lyrist shall be given here, because there is nothing
more interesting than to note how one poet is
indebted to another. The origin of Milton's "Il
Penseroso" is to be found in the following lovely
lines :—

"Hence all you vain delights,
As short as are the nights
  Wherein you spend your folly!
There's nought in this life sweet,
If men were wise to see't,
  But only melancholy,
  O sweetest melancholy!

"Welcome, folded arms and fixèd eyes,
A sigh that piercing mortifies,
A look that's fastened to the ground,
A tongue chained up without a sound,
Fountain-heads and pathless groves,
Places which pale passion loves,
Moonlight walks, when all the fowls
Are warmly housed save bats and owls;
A midnight bell, a parting groan,—
These are the sounds we feed upon.
Then stretch our bones in a still gloomy valley;
Nothing's so dainty sweet as lovely melancholy."

As a lyrist, Fletcher was a younger brother to
Shakespeare, and therefore, although he will not
claim separate attention, it is not irrelevant to have

halted at his name with a " Hail and Farewell ! "
Let us return to Shakespeare.

The facts of his life, apart from the traditionary
stories that have gathered round his name, can be
concisely stated, and are probably familiar to the
youngest reader.

Shakespeare belonged to the yeoman class. He
was born probably on the 23rd of April, 1564, at
Stratford-on-Avon, where his father, who was a
farmer, had a shop for the sale of gloves as well as
of farm produce. John Shakespeare, in his son's
early days, was a well-to-do citizen, and enjoyed
the honour of being elected chief alderman. There
was a free school in the town, to which in all likelihood William was sent. He left it, we may conclude, at an early age, for when the boy was four-
teen his father had fallen into pecuniary difficulties,
and what he did afterwards, as well indeed as the
amount of schooling he received, are mere matters
of conjecture. This we do know from the records
of the corporation, that Stratford was frequently
visited by companies of players, and it is a safe
conclusion that the wonderful boy's genius for the
drama was first awakened at these local entertainments. In 1582 the youth, for he was not yet
nineteen, married Anne Hathaway, a woman eight
years older than her husband. Their first child
was born in the following year. The story that
Shakespeare, in a youthful freak, stole Sir Thomas
Lucy's deer may or may not be true. It is certain
that a few years after his marriage he left his birth-

place for London. Of the way in which he lived
there and of the steps by which he rose to fame
we know nothing. Now and then we have slight
glimpses of him, and they testify to the sweet
nature and large-heartedness of this prince of poets.
He found a friend in the young Earl of Southampton, and seems to have early gained a professional
reputation, for he acted twice before Queen Elizabeth in 1593. His growth in worldly prosperity
was not slow, and at the age of thirty-three he was
able to purchase a residence in Stratford. Before
that time he lost his only son Hamnet, and learnt
thus early, what all of us learn before long, that
"the thread of our life is a mingled yarn, good
and ill together." It is evident that throughout his
active London life Shakespeare never forgot his
birthplace. It was there he would make his home
when fortune was propitious; it was there, in the
full maturity of his powers, that he was destined to
die. One purchase after another of land at Stratford is recorded by the biographers; and in that
town, according to a statement recorded in the
diary of a Stratford vicar forty years or more after
the poet's death, he lived "in his elder days, and
supplied the stage with two plays every year, and
for it had an allowance so large that he spent at
the rate of £1000 a year"—an incredible statement,
seeing that money in Shakespeare's time was about
ten times the value it is at present. The same
diary states: "Shakespeare, Drayton, and Ben
Jonson had a merry meeting, and, it seems, drank

too hard, for Shakespeare died of a fever there contracted." Let us hope the tradition is a false one.*
No English poet has expressed in such forcible language the evils of excess, and one does not like to believe that he was fatally overtaken in a fault of this kind. It is as though the spirit of Stephano had taken possession of Prospero.

There is a contrast worth noting between Ben Jonson and Shakespeare. The former is sometimes said to have had a crabbed nature, yet no poet has written more genially of his contemporaries; the disposition of Shakespeare was said to be eminently sweet, yet he has scarcely a line of praise to bestow on his brother poets. In his writings he seems to stand apart from them. That he had a profound consciousness of his own greatness cannot be questioned, for, though it was a habit of every poet who wrote love-sonnets to promise immortal fame to the lady he addressed, Shakespeare's expressions in his " sugared sonnets " are too frequent and too emphatic to be treated as mere poetical diction.

> " Not marble nor the gilded monuments
> Of princes shall outlive this powerful rhyme."

> " My love shall in my verse ever live young."

> " So long as men can breathe or eyes can see,
> So long lives this, and this gives life to thee."

Words such as these express—can we doubt it ?—

* Mr. Dyce observes that " we should hardly be justified in determining the cause of Shakespeare's death on the authority of a tradition which was not written down till nearly half a century after the event."

the inmost conviction of the poet's soul; and yet, strange to say—and it is one of the most insoluble problems in literary history—Shakespeare left his great dramas as the ostrich drops her eggs, with an indifference as to their ultimate fate that appears well-nigh incredible. But, indeed, every portion of Shakespeare's career is marvellous. Not that, as some French critics have said, he was a monster in literature, but because his mighty but well-ordered genius was large enough to embrace all human wisdom; because in tragedy and comedy he was alike supreme; because he resembles Nature in her largeness and minuteness, in her sublimity and beauty, in the delicacy and perfection of her colouring, in the grandeur and variety of her forms. The language of hyperbole is scarcely inappropriate when we write of Shakespeare, so impossible is it to do justice to his transcendent powers in the simple speech of common life.

Shakespeare has in recent years become a school classic, like Homer and Virgil. His plays are prepared for school use and for Oxford and Cambridge examinations, so that most young readers gain their earliest acquaintance with the poet through the grammatical study of his words. This is, no doubt, useful labour, and will enable students to read Shakespeare at a later period with intelligence and accuracy. What it cannot do is to impart that sense of poetic art and beauty without which we open in vain the pages of a great poet. Scholarly knowledge is invaluable and forms a solid basis

on which the student of poetry may build, but he
who would enter into the secrets of the art must
not rest content with acquisitions that satisfy the
examiner. It is something, no doubt, to understand the framework of a drama, but it is more
difficult and more essential to enter into the spirit
which may be said to make a Shakespearian
tragedy or comedy " a being full of life and
breath." All poetry worthy of the name is alive ;
it has in it no element of dissolution ; and he is
the best student and the wisest critic who can
realize most distinctly this poetical vitality. The
life of Shakespeare's poetry is, of course, principally exhibited in dramatic representation. There
are few characters in history that we know better
than his men and women, still fewer that we care
for so much; but this life also imparts its energy
to passages in which Shakespeare as a descriptive poet tells us what Nature has taught him,
or as a lyric poet lifts his song to heaven. But
even his descriptive passages and the enchanting
music of his songs have a dramatic consistency
which does not allow them to be rudely severed
from the context. To talk much of Shakespeare's
" beauties " is absurd. The real splendour and
glory of his work are to be seen in the genius which
enables him not merely to write beautiful passages
and sweet snatches of song, but to make these
passages and these songs subservient to his chief
purpose as an artist. They are to be found where
they are because they could not be anywhere else.

Truly does Coleridge say, that great as was the genius of Shakespeare, his judgment was at least equal to it.

[Every reader should possess a good edition of Shakespeare, an edition which, like the Cambridge Shakespeare, or the Shakespeare edited by the Rev. A. Dyce, has been made as perfect as love and scholarship can make it.

The Globe Shakespeare (Macmillan) may be recommended for cheapness of cost and accuracy of text, but the print is small, and . the book cannot be carried in the pocket. A charming edition in twelve little volumes has been published by Kent and Co., and Messrs. Bradbury and Evans and George Bell and Sons have also issued a Shakespeare in a similar form. I do not know which is to be preferred. Separate plays with elaborate notes have been printed by the Clarendon Press and by the Pitt Press, and to these the student who needs to be "coached up" in Shakespeare may refer with confidence. They will tell him all that he ought to know. He will also do well to gain a thorough acquaintance with Dr. Abbott's "Shakesperian Grammar," which is "an attempt to illustrate some of the differences between Elizabethan and modern English." The most concise and, considering its brevity, the most useful introduction to Shakespeare is Professor Dowden's tiny volume—one of the "Literature Primers," published by Macmillan and Co. Coleridge, one of the few great poets who is also a great critic, has written the best comments upon Shakespeare which we possess, and his "Notes and Lectures" should be read with care. Hazlitt's "Lectures," Mrs. Jameson's "Characteristics," Lamb's "Tales from Shakespeare," Landor's "Citation and Examination of Shakespeare," Guizot's "Shakespeare and his Times," and Gervinus's "Commentaries on Shakespeare," all deserve to be read or consulted. Gervinus stands, perhaps, at the head of the German critics, if we except the profound and subtle remarks of Goethe, the prince of German poets, on the greatest poet of England. The books that have been written on the sonnets of this great master are not generally to be commended. In endeavouring to unravel the purpose of the writer they make it more intricate.]

CHAPTER V.

THE ELIZABETHAN AND JACOBEAN POETS
(*Continued*).

BEN JONSON—WILLIAM DRUMMOND—GEORGE SANDYS
— GEORGE WITHER — GEORGE HERBERT — HENRY
VAUGHAN—WILLIAM BROWNE—ROBERT HERRICK.

BEN JONSON, Shakespeare's friend and rival, is
alike distinguished as a dramatist and
as a lyrist, and his commanding genius
was largely felt and amply acknow-
ledged by the younger poets of his age. His plays
were popular ; his masques won the applause of the
court ; his genius was appreciated and rewarded
by the king ; men of learning, like Camden and
Selden, did honour to the learning of the poet ; and
it was owing to the faults of the man rather than to
the forgetfulness of the age that he suffered in his
latter days from poverty and neglect. Ben Jonson,
like so many men of genius, neither knew how to
treat friends nor how to use money. His temper
was irritable, his pocket was a sieve, he loved wine

*Ben Jonson,
1573-1637.*

too well, and it was probably when under the influence of wine that he spoke unguardedly even of his friends. It has been said that he was envious ; it is certain that he was rash, and that his innermost feelings found vigorous expression ; but he had many sterling qualities, and in praising contemporary genius Jonson showed a generous nature. Donne, Constable, Francis Beaumont, Lord Bacon "England's High Chancellor," Selden, Chapman, Drayton, Browne, and Fletcher, are honoured in his verses ; and above all, the lines, "To the memory of my beloved master, William Shakespeare," bear the force and fervour of the most genuine enthusiasm and admiration.*

Ben Jonson was born in London in 1573, and his earliest education was received at a school in St. Martin's parish. From thence, thanks to the kindness of Camden, which Jonson always remembered with gratitude, he was sent to Westminster, where no doubt a solid foundation was laid for the learn-

---

* Ben Jonson received much honour in return from his contemporaries. Here is a tribute by John Cleveland, which deserves note for its own merits :—

"The Muses' fairest light in no dark time,
The wonder of a learnèd age ; the line
Which none can pass ; the most proportioned wit
To nature, the best judge of what was fit ;
The deepest, plainest, highest, clearest pen ;
The voice most echoed by consenting men ;
The soul which answered best to all well said
By others, and which most requital made ;
Tuned to the highest key of ancient Rome,
Returning all her music with his own ; .
In whom with nature study claimed a part,
And yet who to himself owed all his art."

ing which afterwards distinguished him. His step-
father was a master-bricklayer, and the boy was
taken from school to follow that occupation. Fuller
says that "he helped in the structure of Lincoln's
Inn, when, having a trowel in his hand, he had a
book in his pocket." The young man, full of ambition and of genius, was not likely long to follow
so uncongenial an employment. In those days
Englishmen of all ranks were in the habit of trying
their fortune in foreign wars, and Jonson went to
Flanders, where, as he afterwards boasted, he killed
an enemy in single combat. Probably he soon
tired of the life of a mercenary. At all events, we
next hear of him in London, following the profession of playwright, for which he was endowed by
nature. Like Shakespeare, and apparently with as
little success, he also acted his part upon the stage.
The first comedy written by Ben Jonson was "Every
Man in his Humour," and there is a tradition, not
perhaps of much account, that Shakespeare, then
a member of the Globe Company, read the piece,
recommended it to the theatre, and afterwards
played in it himself. Certain it is that between the
poets there was frequent intercourse, and this makes
it delightful to read Ben Jonson's after assertion,
"I loved the man, and do honour to his memory on
this side idolatry as much as any can."

A characteristic and tragic incident occurred at
the beginning of Jonson's London life. Having
fought a duel with a player of the name of Gabriel
Spencer and killed his man, he was thrown into

prison and narrowly escaped the gallows. The prospect of death made the impulsive poet serious, and, being visited by a Romish priest, he joined the Roman Catholic Church. Twelve years later he returned to the English communion. When Jonson was released from prison his means of living must have been extremely precarious, and so, to quote the words of Gifford, "with that happy mode of extricating himself from a part of his difficulties which men of genius sometimes adopt, he now appears to have taken a wife." Of her we know nothing beyond the statement made by Jonson twenty years later, that she was "shrewish but honest."

At a later period of life the poet was again imprisoned. A play called "Eastward Hoe!" written by Jonson in conjunction with Marston and Chapman, contained a passage reflecting upon the Scotch. His two associates were arrested, and Jonson, considering himself implicated, voluntarily accompanied them to prison. When they were first committed it was said the three dramatists would have their ears and noses slit, which was one of the barbarous punishments of the day. The news reached Ben Jonson's mother, and at an entertainment given by the poet on his release she drank to him, and showed him a paper containing poison, which, had the sentence taken effect, she intended to mix with his drink. "To show that she was no churl," her son adds, "she designed to have first drank of it herself."

Another notable incident of Jonson's life was his walk to Scotland and visit to Hawthornden, the seat of the poet Drummond. Drummond kept notes of "rare Ben's" conversations, and the greater part of what we know about him is derived from this source.

To Jonson's long life as a dramatist—his quarrels, his friendships, his prosperity at one period, when he seems to have been courted by the nobility and honoured by the king, his poverty and loneliness at another period, when, beggar-like, he sued for bread —it is unnecessary to do more than allude. Slight though the details be which have come down to us, we can form a fair estimate of what he was in person and in character. In several respects he reminds us of his great namesake, Samuel Johnson. Vigour of mind, indomitable persever-ance, and the most ardent love of knowledge, marked both the men. Both were humorists and shrewd observers of mankind ; both were omnivo-rous readers and remembered what they read ; both loved society and intellectual predominance ; both were dogmatic, hasty, and forgiving ; and to both honour and fealty were paid by reverent dis-ciples. At the Mermaid Tavern, in Bread Street, took place those wit combats, as Fuller calls them, between Shakespeare and Jonson ; the latter, to quote Fuller's happy illustration, a great Spanish galleon, "built far higher in learning than his opponent," and solid but slow in performance ; the former an English man-of-war, "lesser in bulk but lighter in sailing, turning with all tides, tacking about and taking advantage of all winds by the quickness of his wit and invention." Beaumont, twin dramatist with Fletcher, was one of the poets who listened to and joined in this talk at the Bread Street tavern, and in his lines to Jonson he writes—

> " What things have we seen
> Done at the Mermaid ! heard words that have been
> So nimble, and so full of subtile flame,
> As if that every one from whom they came
> Had meant to put his whole wit in a jest,
> And had resolved to live a fool the rest
> Of his dull life."

In personal appearance Ben Jonson and Samuel Johnson had much in common. Every young reader can picture the famous doctor, with his ungainly figure but powerful physique, his scars, his convulsive movements, his shabby wig and shabbier brown coat, and can realize, from the vivid descriptions of Boswell, how he was wont to enforce an argument and demolish an opponent while seated upon his tavern throne at the Mitre. So, too, in imagination can we see Ben Jonson, " a man of enormous girth and colossal height, weighing close upon twenty stone, his stormy head looking as solid and wild as a sea-rock, his rugged face knotted and seamed by jovial excesses acting on a scorbutic habit, and his brawny person enveloped in a great slovenly wrapper, like a coachman's greatcoat, with slits under the arm-pits, which

Lacy, the player, told Aubrey was his usual costume." *

If the points of resemblance between the two men are strong, it may be well to remember that in the noble moral qualities that give a purpose and dignity to life there is but little resemblance between them. Ben Jonson was a man of many failings, some of which have grievously infected his writings. Samuel Johnson had many a fault also, of which he was profoundly conscious ; but, like a good man, he fought vigorously against evil, and his one aim was to follow the leadings of a sensitive, although not always enlightened, conscience. To him, cast down in many a struggle, but finally a victor in the strife, may be applied the immortal lines of his friend Goldsmith—

> " As some tall cliff that rears its awful form,
>   Swells from the vale, and midway leaves the storm,
>   Though round its breast the rolling clouds are spread,
>   Eternal sunshine settles on its head."

With Ben Jonson's position as a dramatist the readers of this volume are not concerned, but I may observe in passing that what we miss in his comedies is human interest. He describes manners rather than men ; his characters, it has been justly said, are caricatures, and their interest consists chiefly in the exhibition of strange humours and conceits. His plots and dramatic dialogue appear to be designed for the purpose of displaying the

---

* Robert Bell.

poet's curious and ample learning, and the wild improbability of incident in his plays might seem better fitted for farce than comedy. But Jonson's dramas, whatever faults they may possess, are among the most remarkable works of a great literary age, and in all of them there are marks of a robust intellect, of satirical humour, of subtle observation, and extensive knowledge. As a writer of masques, Ben Jonson occupies a unique position. He was the court poet, and was the first to give what may be called literary form to these courtly entertainments. King James's queen and her ladies took part in these representations, which were "of the most costly and splendid kind," calling into exercise the arts of the musician and scene painter as well as the genius of the poet. Ben Jonson's masques were famous, and no doubt justly so, but they have no attraction now save for curious readers. There is, indeed, but one poem of this class which holds its place in literature—the immortal masque of "Comus." With the exception of his latest production, "The Sad Shepherd," a pastoral drama written on his death-bed, Ben Jonson's plays contain little of the pure poetry which imparts a freshness and fragrance to Shakespeare's least attractive scenes. But that Jonson had the poet's sense of natural beauty and the poet's love of a country life is evident from his poems. The little volume which contains his " Epigrams," " The Forest" and "Underwoods," presents the writer to us under a new aspect. There is in some of these

G

poems a manly wisdom pithily expressed, in some
a lyrical sweetness which attests his claims as a
singer, in others a lively and wholly unconventional
description of rural scenes, and in others, unfortunately, a fulsomeness of flattery and a coarseness
of expression which are only too characteristic of
the age and of the man.   The young reader who
wishes to see the poet at his best, and only at his
best, may be advised to read the poem " To Pens-
hurst ; " the epistle " To Sir Robert Wroth," a fine
specimen of Jonson's work ; the poem already mentioned written in memory of Shakespeare; and the
songs beginning with the lines, " Still to be neat,
still to be drest," " See the chariot at hand here of
Love," " Men, if you love me, play no more "—a
song absurdly styled by Gifford " the most beautiful
in the language; " and the well-known song, married
to lovely music, " Drink to me only with thine eyes."

[Many of the best of Jonson's poems are to be found in anthologies, but no editor has, I believe, made a selection from " The
Forest " and " Underwoods."]

William Drummond, the poet who was visited
by " rare Ben " at his lovely estate of
Hawthornden, does not occupy a striking place in literature, but he has
written several fine sonnets, and, as the reader will
discover who reads Mr. Masson's interesting biography, has many claims on the attention of the
student.   In early life he had a great love-sorrow,
which coloured his after-history and his poetry.

William
Drummond.
1585-1649.

As a man of letters, as a politician, and as a writer whose purpose was eminently serious, Drummond is entitled to respect. His verse is sometimes beautiful, it is always sincere, and rises occasionally to a strain which, as in the sonnet " Saint John Baptist," seems to anticipate the solemn aim of Milton. His record of "Conversations with Ben Jonson " has awakened much wrath in some virtuous critics, for the book contains passages which present the dramatist in a very unfavourable light. But this at least should be remembered to Drummond's credit. He did not rush into print with the work upon the death of Jonson, when its interest for scandal-lovers and Grub Street poets would have been great, but kept the record by him in manuscript ; and in that form it remained for two centuries.

[Drummond's poetical works, edited by William B. Turnbull, appeared in 1856, and they are also to be found in that vast repository of worth and weakness, of poets and poetasters, the collection made by Chalmers.]

When Sir Philip Sidney was about twenty-three years old, George Sandys was born; and about fifty years after Sidney's early death, Sandys' version of the Psalms was published. It is difficult to believe that so brief a period separated the versions of the two men. Sidney's rhymes are for the most part rough and halting, while Sandys' verse, masculine and careful in construction, glides smoothly along

George Sandys, 1577-1643.

and delights the ear with its music.   The "so much admired Sandys," as Dryden calls him, is now almost unknown; but in his own day, and long after his day, his fame as a versifier and translator was considerable.   Dryden said that if Sandys, who translated the first book of the "Æneid," had completed the work, he would not have attempted his version.   Joseph Warton declared that Sandys had done more by his paraphrases to polish the English language than either Denham or Waller; and Richard Baxter said, "Next the Scripture poems, there are none so savoury to me as Mr. George Herbert's and Mr. George Sandys';" and he adds, "It did me good when Mrs. Wyat invited me to see Boxley Abbey, in Kent, to see upon the old stone wall in the garden a summer-house with this inscription in great golden letters, that in that place Mr. G. Sandys, after his travels over the world, retired himself for his poetry and contemplations."   Pope, when a boy, is said to have liked Sandys' version of Ovid extremely; and when we come nearer to our own day, we find James Montgomery writing that Sandys' rendering of the Psalms is "incomparably the most poetic in the English language."   Sandys produced also several other paraphrases, and turned the Book of Job into heroic couplets.   Such attempts are not to be commended, and all we need say of Sandys' honest effort is that it is greatly to be preferred to the feeble, commonplace version of a part of the book written by Young, who confesses that he has omitted, added, and transposed and has "thrown the whole into a method more suited to our notions of regularity;" from which you may judge that the author of the " Night Thoughts " was not especially distinguished for taste or modesty. It is always · interesting to note the links which bind our poets together, and there is one, slight, indeed, but note-worthy, that joins Sandys to Milton—the ardent loyalist and Churchman to the great Puritan and iconoclast. Both of these poets tried their skill in metrical versions of the Psalms. Milton failed utterly in the attempt, while Sandys had a large measure of success.

[An admirable edition of Sandys' poetical works, "now first collected," appeared in 1872 (John Russell Smith). It is edited, with introduction and notes, by the Rev. Richard Hooper.]

George Wither, who was born eleven years later than Sandys, also published the "Psalms of David, translated into Lyric Verse," and not content with this, produced a volume called " Hymns and Songs of the Church." In the first part of the volume Bible songs, prayers, and prophecies, and even the Ten Commandments, are put into metre, and it need scarcely be said injured in the process ; but the smoothness of the versification is remarkable. The second part may have suggested the plan of the "Christian Year" to Keble. Wither's " Songs," however, celebrate only the principal festivals and saints' days of the Church, and in beauty and poetic art are infinitely

George Wither, 1588-1667.

inferior to the verses of the latest and greatest of
Church singers.   Wither does not, like Herbert,
Vaughan, and Keble, live on his reputation as a
sacred poet.   He tried his verse-making skill in
a variety of directions, and is sometimes eminently
successful, his verses being marked by tenderness,
pathos, and much sweetness of expression.   The
poem written " When upon the Seas " is worthy of
a place in any selection, and his charming lyric—

> " Shall I, wasting in despair,
>   Die because a woman's fair ? "—

is universally known, and uninjured by popularity.

Wither had a poet's eye for natural beauty.   His
chief fault is diffuseness, a habit which he defends.
If readers find his verses tedious, he says they can
let them alone, but he will not " change a syllable
or measure."

> " Pedants shall not tie my strains
>   To our antique poets' veins ;
>   As if we in latter days
>   Knew to love but not to praise.
>   Being born as free as these,
>   I will sing as I shall please ;
>   Who as well new paths may run
>   As the best before have done.
>   I disdain to make my song
>   For their pleasures short or long ;
>   If I please I'll end it here,
>   If I list I'll sing this year.
>   And though none regard of it,
>   By myself I pleased can sit,

And with that contentment cheer me,
As if half the world did hear me."

Much might be said of George Wither, did the plan of this volume allow of more than a brief reference to minor poets. On parting with him it will be interesting to recall a suggestive fact in his history—I mean the warm friendship that existed between him and William Browne. At one time, indeed, the two poets linked their fortunes together in the same volume.

[In the "Library of Old Authors" (John Russell Smith) George Wither's "Songs of the Church" appeared in 1856, and a very dainty edition of his "Fair Virtue" appeared in the early years of the century, edited by Sir Egerton Brydges ; but there has been no recent demand for his poems, which are only to be met with in large libraries. "The two critical essays on Sidney and Wither," says Mr. Ainger, "contain some of Lamb's most subtle criticism and most eloquent writing."]

Richard Baxter did not confine his praise to Sandys, but wrote, as we have seen, at the same time in praise of the younger poet, George Herbert. "I know," he says, "that Cowley and others far exceed Herbert in wit and accurate composure, but, as Seneca takes with me above all his contemporaries because he speaketh things by words feelingly and seriously, like a man that is past jest, so Herbert speaks to God like one that really believeth a God."

The story of his life is beautifully, if not always quite accurately told by Izaak Walton. George

Herbert belongs to a distinguished family, but
his own name stands foremost in its
annals. His eldest brother, Lord Cher-
bury, I may say in passing, has left one
of the most curious autobiographies in the language, and of the remaining five—for George was
the fifth of seven sons—all were more or less distinguished, " married plentiful fortunes and lived
to be examples of virtue." The future poet was
educated at Westminster, and at the early age of
fifteen, being a King's Scholar, he was elected for
Trinity College, Cambridge. There he soon won
a reputation for classical scholarship as well as for
the knowledge of modern languages, and in his
twenty-sixth year he was appointed public orator,
a position which he occupied for several years.

And now, in the prime of early manhood, he
formed a friendship with Bacon and Bishop An-
drewes, and also tasted some of the pleasures and
mortifications of a courtier's life, seldom looking
towards Cambridge except when the king was
there ; but " then he never failed." For a time, then,
we are to think of Herbert as a man of the world,
with a " genteel humour for clothes," and as a
courtier eager for advancement. But his hopes
from the court died with the death of King James,
and Herbert left the town for a country retreat,
where, as Walton tells us, " he had many conflicts
with himself, whether he should return to the
painted pleasures of a court life, or betake himself
to a study of divinity, and enter into sacred orders,

George
Herbert,
1593-1632.

to which his dear mother had often persuaded him." There seems to have been a long period of struggle and conflict, but "at last God inclined him to put on a resolution to serve at His altar." His life as a clergyman was as brief as it was memorable. The story of Herbert's marriage, which preceded his ordination, is quaint enough as related by Walton. A Mr. Danvers had publicly expressed a desire that he would marry any of his nine daughters, but rather his daughter Jane, who was the most beloved. This wish had been expressed to Herbert himself, and also to Jane, who "became so much a Platonic as to fall in love with Herbert unseen." Some friends brought them together, "at which time a mutual affection entered into both their hearts, as a conqueror enters into a surprised city, and love having got such possession, governed and made there such laws and resolutions as neither party was able to resist; insomuch that she changed her name into Herbert the third day after this first interview." It is a romantic story, but probably inaccurate, since there is every likelihood that George Herbert's familiar acquaintance with the father must have extended to the daughter. In 1629, Herbert, having been made deacon some years before, was appointed rector of Bemerton, in Wiltshire, a spot for ever fragrant with his memory. He was now in his thirty-sixth year, utterly frail in body, but full of energy and spiritual life. Here he lived like a saint and wrote like a poet—the most zealous of clergymen, the humblest and most

loving of men. When dying he sent his manuscript of the "Temple" to his friend, the pious
ascetic, Nicholas Ferrar, leaving him to print it or
to burn it as he might think fit.   It was published
after the poet's death, and when Walton wrote,
more than twenty thousand copies had been sold—
an enormous number considering the nature of the
poems and the character of the times.   The extreme
quaintness of the poetry often proves an offence to
the modern reader.   The external shell is rough
and hard, but there is a sound kernel within, and
the conceits of the verse never conceal its sincerity.

The "Church Porch," the introduction to the
"Temple," is full of pithy sayings ; some of them
are familiar to most readers, as for instance—

> "Kneeling ne'er spoiled silk stocking : quit thy state ;
> All equal are within the church's gate."

> "All worldly joys go less
> To the one joy of doing kindnesses."

> "He that needs five thousand pounds to live
> Is full as poor as he who needs but five."

> "A verse may find him who a sermon flies,
> And turn delight into a sacrifice."

> "God calleth preaching folly.   Do not grudge
> To pick out treasures from an earthen pot.
> The worst speak something good ; if all want sense
> God takes a text and preacheth patience."

> "Only the actions of the just
> Smell sweet and blossom in their dust,"

wrote   Herbert's   contemporary,   James   Shirley,

and a characteristic poem in the "Temple" con-
veys the same meaning. It is entitled   **James**
"Life."   **Shirley.**
                                     1596-1666.

> "I made a posy while the day ran by :
> Here will I smell my remnant out, and tie
>   My life within this band.
> But time did beckon to the flowers, and they
> By noon most cunningly did steal away,
>   And withered in my hand.
>
> "My hand was next to them, and then my heart :
> I took, without more thinking, in good part
>   Time's gentle admonition ;
> Who did so sweetly death's sad taste convey,
> Making my mind to smell my fatal day,
>   Yet sugaring the suspicion.
>
> "Farewell, dear flowers ! sweetly your time ye spent ;
> Fit while ye lived for smell or ornament,
>   And after death for cures.
> I follow straight without complaints or grief,
> Since, if my scent be good, I care not if
>   It be as short as yours."

Young readers can scarcely be expected to give
to Herbert's verse the honour it deserves, neither
are they likely to turn with much interest to the
sacred poems of Henry Vaughan, who   **Henry**
acknowledged Herbert as his master,   **Vaughan,**
                                           1621-1695.
and, with much space of time between,
may be regarded as his successor. He is less
crabbed and freer from conceits, and both have a
legitimate place in the line of English poets. Herbert is popularly known by his poem on "Sunday,"

and by the lines headed "Virtue," which begin with
the following stanza :—

> "Sweet day so cool, so calm, so bright,
> The bridal of the earth and sky !
> The dew shall weep thy fall to-night,
> For thou must die."

And Vaughan chiefly lives in the tender and
beautiful lines on the loss of friends, of which it
will suffice to quote the first four :—

> "They are all gone into the world of light,
> And I alone sit lingering here !
> Their very memory is fair and bright,
> And my sad thoughts doth clear."

This poem is to be found in the series of sacred
poems called by their author "Silex Scintillans,"
and published in the prime of life.   Strange to say,
although he lived forty years after the second
edition of his "Silex" was published, he wrote no
more poetry.   The volume is rich in noble thoughts
(read especially the poem, in six stanzas, on
"Death"), interspersed with much that is fantastical and obsolete.

[It is with more regard to similarity of purpose than to chrono-
logy that Vaughan is placed in immediate succession to Herbert,
"whose holy life and verse," he writes, "gained many pious converts of whom I am the least."

Messrs. Bell and Sons have published a dainty edition of Izaak
Walton's "Lives," and there can be read all that it is necessary to
know about Herbert.   His poetry has a place in the series of
"Aldine Poets," but it can be obtained in a variety of forms.
Vaughan's "Sacred Poems," with a memoir by the Rev. H. Lyte,
appeared in a modern dress in 1847, and has been recently
reprinted.]

Among the poets of this period, William Browne, the author of "Britannia's Pastorals," and Robert Herrick, the more famous author of the "Hesperides," deserve honourable mention.   Browne is a Devonshire worthy.   He was the contemporary of Herrick, and as the one lived at Tavistock and the other at Dean Prior, it is probable that the poets were acquainted.   The contrast between the two men is striking.   Browne published all his poems before he was thirty, and these poems, rich in fancy, luxuriant in style, and written in a coarse age, are remarkable for moral purity.   Herrick, on the contrary, published his love-poems late in life, and priest though he was, laid no restraint upon his voluptuous fancy.   Both poets abound in rural descriptions, but Browne found his whole delight in the country, while Herrick hated the solitariness of the life which he was forced to lead in "dull Devonshire."   As literary artists, the palm beyond all doubt must be awarded to Herrick, some of whose lyrics have a consummate charm, which it is more easy to enjoy than to describe ; in Browne, amidst much that is suggestive and of poetical beauty, we find little that is not marred by defect of taste and crudeness of form.

As William Browne was born a little earlier than Herrick he will engage our attention first.   In his own day he was a distinguished man, for he won the friendship and praise of Ben Jonson, Drayton, Chapman, Selden, and Wither.   Yet scarce a

William Browne, 1588-1643?

fact of his life has been preserved, and the biographer is left almost wholly to conjectures. All we know, or think we know, is that William Browne was born at Tavistock in 1588; that he was probably educated in his native town, and afterwards went up to Oxford as an undergraduate of Exeter College. From thence he moved to London and entered himself at Clifford's Inn, but soon afterwards, on the 1st of March, 1612–13, he was admitted to the Inner Temple. Like his master Spenser, Browne had apparently an early disappointment. If so, it left no ill effects on his healthy nature. He was not a man likely to " die because a woman's fair," and his marriage to the daughter of Sir Thomas Eversfield, a Sussex knight, gave him the happiness he sought. It would seem, from a letter printed by Mr. Hazlitt from the Ashmolean MSS., that Browne resided for some time at Dorking, in what he terms "his poor cell and sequestration from all business." This is an interesting fact, not only because an ancestor of Browne had resided at Betchworth Castle, afterwards the residence of the philosopher Abraham Tucker, but because Browne's name may now be added to the long list of distinguished men who have lived or sojourned in that charming neighbourhood. He, too, in common with Spenser, Drayton, Milton, Pope, and Thomson, has sung of the Mole, an insignificant stream, except for the peculiarity of its swallows, but a stream upon which has been conferred poetical immortality. The year of Browne's

death is unknown with certainty. A William
Browne, we know, was buried at Tavistock in 1643,
and this may have been the poet, but the place and
time of his death are left wholly to conjecture. For
us he lives only in his verse, and perhaps the hope
he once expressed is not altogether unrealized—

> " Each man that lives, according to his power,
>   On what he loves bestows an idle hour ;
>   Instead of hounds that make the wooded hills
>   Talk in a hundred voices to the rills,
>   I like the pleasing cadence of a line
>   Struck by the concert of the sacred Nine.
>
>   .   .   .   .   .   .
>
>   For courtly dancing I can take more pleasure,
>   To hear a verse keep time and equal measure,
>   For winning riches, seek the best directions
>   How I may well subdue mine own affections.
>   For raising stately piles for heirs to come,
>   Here in this poem I erect my tomb,
>   And time may be so kind in these weak lines
>   To keep my name enrolled past his that shines
>   In gilded marble, or in brazen leaves,
>   Since verse preserves when stone and brass deceives."

Spenser, as I have said, enjoys the just and
enviable title of "the poet's poet," but the term
may, perhaps, with some truth be applied also to
William Browne. That Milton and Keats were
indebted to him will be seen when we come to
speak of those poets. He will never again be
popular as he was unquestionably in his lifetime ;
but he will, I think, be always read by poets and
students of poetry. The task of reading his works

is not wholly pleasurable. If he charms us on one page, he wearies us on another; if he delights us one moment with a genuine bit of nature, in the next he is involved in the subtleties of allegory, and becomes unreadable if not unintelligible. When at his best his poetry is like a breath of sweet country air, or the scent of newly mown grass. His similes, drawn from what we are wont to call common objects, are often singularly happy; he gives us fresh draughts from nature, and his verse is frequently marked by an Arcadian simplicity, contrasting pleasurably with the classical conceits and forced allusions over which, in other portions, the reader is doomed to groan. On the whole, we may agree with Ben Jonson's judgment of his "truly beloved friend," that what he has written is most worthy to be read, and that his "worth is good upon the exchange of letters;" and one likes to remember that Drayton also, in his "Epistle on Poets and Poetry," places William Browne among the "rightly born poets."

[Browne's poems may be read in Chalmers' "English Poets," vol. vi. His works were also printed, in two beautiful volumes, for the Roxburghe Library, in 1868, and a cheap edition of the "Pastorals" was published in Clarke's Cabinet Series, 1845.]

Robert Herrick may be said to belong to the Shakesperians. He survived, indeed, far beyond the middle of the seventeenth century, but he was a man of five and twenty when Shakespeare died, and, living through the whole life of Milton, died in the same year,

Robert Herrick, 1591-1674.

1674. In some respects he claims kindred rather
with the poets of the Restoration than with earlier
and nobler singers.   He sings well chiefly when
he sings of love, but this love is not of the kind
which inspires our greatest poets.   He is enamoured
with the accessories of a woman's beauty—the colour
of a ribbon, the flaunting of a ringlet, with "a careless shoe-string," or the wave of a petticoat.   The
charms he sees in his mistress are likened to precious stones, and all the treasures of the lapidary
are represented in his verse.   There are few traces
of tenderness in Herrick and none of passion ;
it is probable that every pretty girl he saw suggested a pretty fancy.   To judge from his own
saying, "no man at one time can be wise and love."
Herrick was not wise.   If we may trust his verses,
the poet was perennially in love, chiefly with Julia,
"prime of all," but warmly too with Anthea, Lucia,
Corinna, and Perilla.   Making love is in Herrick's
eyes a charming amusement, and the more love-
making the more poetry.   If Julia prove unkind,
he can solace himself with Sappho ; and if Sappho
be perverse, some other mistress will charm him
with her "pretty witchcrafts."   His comparisons and
illustrations do not betray strong emotion.   They
read like the brilliant fancies of a man at ease
with himself and with the world.   He delights

> " To sport with Amaryllis in the shade,
>   Or with the tangles of Neæra's hair ; "

and his philosophy, like that of Horace, urges him

II

to secure the largest amount of pleasure out of the present moment.

> "While fates permit us, let's be merry ;
> Pass all we must the fatal ferry,"

is an argument Herrick urges again and again, sometimes in doggerel rhymes, sometimes in graceful verse. He is eminently direct in style, knows what he means and says what he means with a bluntness and coarseness which must have startled readers even in his own day as coming from the pen of a clergyman, and never attempts, as so many of his contemporaries did, to allegorize his song. In his poetical faults as well as virtues Herrick may lay claim to originality. As a lyric poet he is exquisite of his kind, and simple as many of his verses seem, it is the masterly simplicity of art. "The Night Piece : To Julia," may be quoted to illustrate Herrick's fancy and the style of his love-verses ; but this style is varied, and is perhaps seen most distinctly in the couplets and single stanzas which this poet scatters over his pages.

> " Her eyes the glowworm lend thee,
> The shooting stars attend thee ;
> 　　And the elves also,
> 　　Whose little eyes glow
> Like the sparks of fire, befriend thee.

> " No Will-o'-th'-Wisp mis-light thee,
> Nor snake or slow-worm bite thee ;
> 　　But on, on thy way,
> 　　Not making a stay,
> Since ghost there's none to affright thee.

'Let not the dark thee cumber ;
　What though the moon does slumber ?
　　The stars of the night
　　Will lend thee their light
Like tapers clear, without number.

" Then, Julia, let me woo thee,
　Thus, thus to come unto me ;
　　And when I shall meet
　　Thy silvery feet,
My soul I'll pour into thee."

The reader will notice in this lyric the modernness of the poet's language, and this peculiarity prevails throughout his poems. Several of Herrick's songs might have been sung by living poets, and where there is quaintness it is of the daintiest kind imaginable. Poets with the keenest appreciation of earthly delights will be found also to have the most vivid sense of life's brevity and vanity. This was peculiarly the case with Herrick, and in his lovely lines " To Daffodils " there is a truer vein of pathos than we often meet with in his verse.

" Fair Daffodils, we weep to see
　You haste away so soon ;
As yet the early-rising sun
　Has not attained his noon.
　　Stay, stay,
　Until the hasting day
　　Has run
　But to the even-song ;
And having prayed together, we
　Will go with you along.

"We have short time to stay, as you,
    We have as short a spring ;
As quick a growth to meet decay,
    As you or anything.
        We die
    As your hours do, and dry
        Away,
Like to the summer's rain ;
Or as the pearls of morning's dew,
    Ne'er to be found again."

Herrick professed to hate "dull Devonshire," in which, as Vicar of Dean Prior, so many years of his life were spent ; but he sings of the country, its pastimes and occupations, with singular freshness, and like a man who felt the charm of such a life. His rural pictures are delightful.   "Come," he says, describing May-day sports—

"Come, let us go while we are in our prime,
    And take the harmless folly of the time."

And he tells his Corinna how the streets are loaded with green boughs, the white-thorn covering each door, and how already, in the "childhood of the day," some have despatched their cakes and cream, while others have wooed and plighted troth, adding, with his customary and, as he deems it, conclusive argument—

"Then, while time serves, and we are but decaying,
    Come, my Corinna, come, let's go a-Maying."

Old and obsolete customs live once more on the pages of Herrick. . One of these was to dress up the "hock-cart" at harvest-home, to clothe the horses in white linen, and to follow them home with shouts of laughter, while

> "Some bless the cart, some kiss the sheaves,
> Some prank them up with oaken leaves."

Then there was the village wake, where you might see morris-dancers and mimics and players, who, though "base in action as in clothes," would please "incurious" villagers ; and in a happy poem addressed to a courtier on the delights of a country life, after recounting a farmer's duties, and noting how

> "The best compost for the lands
> Is the wise master's feet and hands,"

the poet adds, still dwelling upon country pleasures—

> "For sports, for pageantry, and plays,
> Thou hast thy eves and holy days :
> On which the young men and maids meet
> To exercise their dancing feet.
>
> .   .   .   .   .
>
> Thy wakes, thy quintels, here thou hast;
> Thy May-poles too with garlands graced ;
> Thy Morris-dance ; thy Whitsun ale ;
> Thy shearing feasts which never fail ;
> Thy harvest-home ; thy wassail bowl
> That's tossed up after Fox-i'-th'-hole ;
> Thy mummeries ; thy Twelve-tide kings
> And queens ; thy Christmas revellings ;
> Thy nut-brown mirth, thy russet wit—
> And no man pays too dear for it."

Altogether, Herrick's pictures of rural life, which represent not what it really is, but how it has

appeared to poets from the days of Theocritus to
our own, are singularly vivid and pleasing.   Herrick
tasted Devonshire cream and junkets to some purpose, and that he should have " run into rhyme " at
the sight of Devonshire girls need surprise no one.
The highest gifts of the poet were wanting to him,
but his love-verses are sometimes of the rarest
flavour, and perhaps he was not far wrong in
anticipating an earthly immortality.   Recollecting
the *non omnis moriar* of his favourite poet Horace,
he writes upon himself—

> " Thou shalt not all die ; for while Love's fire shines
>   Upon his altar, men will read thy lines ;
> And learn'd musicians shall, to honour Herrick's
>   Fame, and his name, both set and sing his lyrics."

Of Herrick, as of so many notable poets, our
knowledge is extremely slight.   He was thirty-five
years old upon taking holy orders.   He was nearly
sixty when he published his one volume of poetry,
over which it would seem that he expended much
labour ; for he requests Julia, the mistress who
inspired his most charming lyrics, if he should die
before his verses appear, to commit them to the fire.

> " Better 'twere my book were dead
>   Than to live not perfected."

Never, apparently, was there a man less fitted for
a clergyman ; the beautiful portrait of a country
pastor drawn by Goldsmith will not suit Herrick,
who is said on one occasion to have flung his
sermon at the congregation.   In London he was

in his element, and the chief object of his admiration there was "Ben Jonson;" and to this "best
of the poets," whom he calls "Saint Ben," he addresses the following characteristic lines :—

> "Ah, Ben !
> Say how or when
> Shall we thy guests
> Meet at those lyric feasts
> Made at the Sun,
> The Dog, the Triple Tun ?
> Where we such clusters had,
> As made us nobly wild, not mad,
> And yet each verse of thine
> Out-did the meat, out-did the frolic wine."

"We know," writes Mr. Palgrave, "that he shone
with Ben Jonson and the wits at the nights and
suppers of those gods of our glorious early literature. We may fancy him at Beaumanor or Houghton, with his uncle and cousins keeping a Leicester-
shire Christmas in the Manor-house ; or again in
some sweet southern county, with Julia and Anthea,
Corinna and Dianeme, by his side (familiar then by
other names, now never to be remembered), sitting
merry, but with just the sadness of one who heard
sweet music in some meadow among his favourite
flowers of springtime—there, or 'where the rose
lingers latest.' . . . But 'the dream, the fancy,' is all
that Time has spared us. And if it be curious that his
contemporaries should have left so little record of
this delightful poet and (as we should infer from the
book) genial-hearted man, it is not less so that the

single first edition should have satisfied the seventeenth century, and that, before the present, notices of Herrick should be of the rarest occurrence."

Herrick, we may add, stands alone among the poets of his time. He took his own path, and while winning, as every poet must, some grace of thought or manner from his predecessors, he belongs to no school and owns no master, unless it be Ben Jonson. He is never great, but he is always genuine, singing of what he feels, not of what, as a poet, he might be expected to feel. His music is sweet, and even when he seems to be least careful, his indifference is but apparent; indeed, throughout his poems he works in the true spirit of the artist. Truly does Mr. Palgrave say that sanity, sincerity, simplicity, lucidity, are everywhere the characteristics of Herrick. At the same time, he has grievous faults. He tells us that though his muse was jocund his life was chaste, thinking to excuse his coarseness by the statement, and forgets too often the lines written " On Himself," in which he recognizes the true end of life—

"Who by his gray hairs doth his lustres tell,
  Lives not those years, but he that lives them well :
  One man has reached his sixty years, but he
  Of all those threescore has not lived half three :
  He lives who lives to virtue ; men who cast
  Their ends for pleasure, do not live, but last." *

* These pithy couplets may remind readers of the finer lines written on the same subject by Ben Jonson—

"It is not growing like a tree
  In bulk doth make man better be ;

Herrick, like his contemporary John Donne, is so coarse a poet that his works are not fit to be read indiscriminately. The least worthy of Donne's poems, however, according to Izaak Walton, were written before the twentieth year of his age.[*] Herrick's period of verse-making covered a wider period—how wide we cannot say, nor as far as concerns our present point does it much signify ; for we know that, artist-like, Herrick kept his poems by him for careful revision, and we know also that he was in his fifty-eighth year when he published the " Hesperides." His " unbaptized rhymes " may have been written

John Donne. 1573-1631.

Or standing long an oak, three hundred year,
To fall a log at last, dry, bald, and sere.
A lily of a day
Is fairer far in May,
Although it fall and die that night—
It was the plant and flower of light.
In small proportions we just beauties see ;
And in short measures life may perfect be."

Waller, too, writes more briefly in the same strain—

"Circles are praised, not that abound
In largeness, but the exactly round ;
So life we praise that does excel
Not in much time, but acting well."

[*] Donne, as you may read in Walton's biography, lived to become a wise and good man. He took holy orders, and became eventually Dean of St. Paul's. His learning was great, his popularity as a poet immense; so, too, was his fame as a preacher. Between him and George Herbert, a man of kindred spirit, "there was a long and dear friendship." Donne, a poet by nature, was spoilt by art. His conceits, which pleased his own age, are intolerable in ours. In reading Dr. Johnson's life of Cowley, you will find some curious illustrations of Donne's "metaphysic style."

in youth, but they were printed at a very mature age, and with his full consent.*

[Mr. Palgrave's exquisite selection from the poems of this fine "pagan poet" (Macmillan and Co.) contains all that is most worthy in the "Hesperides," and the young student of our poetry need perhaps look no further. If, however, the subject attracts him, he will do well to read an essay on the poet by Mr. Gosse, in the *Cornhill Magazine* for August, 1875.]

---

* No poet was ever more careful of his fame than Herrick, and it is impossible to agree with Mr. Grosart, that in the publication of so much that had been better omitted he was "over-persuaded" by his publisher. The man who could say—

> " Better 'twere my book were dead
> Than to live not perfected "—

was not likely to leave to indifferent hands the arrangement of its contents.

CHAPTER VI.

POETS OF THE COMMONWEALTH.

ABRAHAM COWLEY—JOHN MILTON—ANDREW MARVELL.

DR. JOHNSON begins his famous work, "The Lives of the Most Eminent English Poets," with the life of Abraham Cowley. The meagre facts he has to tell of that poet are gleaned from a biography, or, as Johnson appropriately styles it, a funeral oration, written by Bishop Sprat, a small versifier, who is himself honoured with a place in Johnson's gallery of poets. Cowley, the son of a London tradesman, was born in 1618, ten years after the birth of Milton. His mother, early left a widow, is said to have struggled hard to give her son a literary education, and it is pleasant to know that she lived to see him fortunate and famous. "In the window of his mother's apartment lay Spenser's 'Faerie Queene,' in which he very early took delight to read, till, by feeling the charms of verse, he became, as he relates, irrecoverably a poet." His

Abraham Cowley, 1618-1667.

rhyming faculty was developed when a mere boy, and he published a volume of poems in the sixteenth year of his age. While at Westminster School he is also said to have written a pastoral comedy. The amazing precocity of the boy may be estimated from the following stanzas, which were written, he states, at thirteen :—

"A WISH.

"This only grant me, that my means may lie
Too low for envy, for contempt too high.
　　Some honour I would have,
Not from great deeds, but good alone ;
The unknown are better than ill known—
　　Rumour can ope the grave.
Acquaintance I would have, but when 't depends
Not on the number but the choice of friends.

"Books should, not business, entertain the light,
And sleep as undisturbed as death, the night.
　　My house a cottage, more
Than palace, and should fitting be,
For all my use, not luxury.
　　My garden painted o'er
With nature's hand, not art's ; and pleasures yield,
Horace might envy in his Sabine field.

"Thus would I double my life's fading space,
For he that runs it well, twice runs his race.
　　And in this true delight
These unbought sports, this happy state,
I would not fear nor wish my fate,
　　But boldly say each night—
To-morrow let my sun his beams display,
Or in clouds hide them ; I have lived to-day."

In 1636 he left school for Cambridge, and there,

too, he continued to show great poetical precocious-
ness. It was an age in which every Englishman had
to take a side in politics, and Cowley being a loyalist,
was forced to leave the University. He found a
home at Oxford, where he is said to have attracted
the notice of Lord Falkland. When Oxford sur-
rendered to the Parliament, Cowley followed his
royal mistress to Paris, and "was employed in such
correspondence as the royal cause required, and
particularly in ciphering and deciphering the
letters that passed between the king and queen
—an employment of the highest confidence and
honour." It would seem, from one of his charming
essays, which should be better known than they
are, that this insight into court life did not increase
his liking for it. " I saw plainly," he writes, "all the
paint of that kind of life the nearer I came to it ;
and that beauty, which I did not fall in love with,
when for ought I knew it was real, was not likely
to bewitch or entice me when I saw that it was
adulterate."

In 1656 he returned to England, and appears
to have been imprisoned for a brief period. That
year he published his poems, and in the year
following obtained a medical degree at Oxford.
" Considering botany as necessary to a physician "
—we quote once more from Johnson—" he retired
into Kent to gather plants ; and as the predominance of a favourite study affects all subordinate operations of the intellect, botany in the
mind of Cowley turned into poetry." His poems

upon plants are written in Latin, and his Latinity, wasted, according to modern judgment, in such an effort, has been highly praised. Neither Cowley's loyalty nor his verses on the Restoration obtained for him any consideration from Charles II. He complained of his treatment in some dismal lines, and got laughed at for his pains. He calls himself in these verses "the melancholy Cowley," and exclaims—

> " Kings have long hands, they say, and though I be
> So distant, they may reach at length to me."

But as the hands of Charles did not immediately reach so far, the poet retired into the country to cultivate virtue and poetry. After a time he obtained an ample income, but was not destined to enjoy it long, for he died at the Porch House, Chertsey, in 1667, in the forty-ninth year of his age. The almost unparalleled reputation Cowley had gained while living did not desert him at his death, for he was buried with great pomp near Chaucer and Spenser in Westminster Abbey. Year by year, however, his fame declined, and seventy years later Pope exclaimed—

> "Who now reads Cowley? If he pleases yet,
> His moral pleases, not his pointed wit."

We may safely say that few readers in our day gain pleasure either from his wit or his moral. This descent from brilliant fame to neglect demands the student's attention.

The poet's fame lives longer than that of other
men, but splendid though it may be for a time, it
is not always built on a sound foundation.   Verse
that utters the fantastic humours of the day dies
and is forgotten, when fresh humours are sought
for and new fashions have the power to charm.
Artificial poets necessarily live by artifice, and as
they reject Nature she repays them with oblivion.
Of this fact Abraham Cowley is a remarkable
illustration.   In his own day he was a famous poet,
praised by king and people,* and, as we have said,
the great Abbey received his dust.   One seems a
little to grudge him his place there now, and
readers of his quaintly coined and ingenious verses
will wonder at the delusion of his age concerning
him.   Probably our successors will wonder quite
as much at some of our delusions.   Of Cowley it
has been said that he was never in love but once,
and then had not courage enough to tell his passion.

---

* This is the estimate of his contemporary, Sir John Denham—

"Old mother Wit and Nature gave
    Shakespeare and Fletcher all they have ;
    In Spenser and in Jonson art
    Of slower nature got the start ;
    But both in him so equal are,
    None knows which bears the happiest share ;
    To him no author was unknown,
    Yet what he wrote was all his own.
    He melted not the ancient gold,
    Nor, with Ben Jonson, did make bold
    To plunder all the Roman stores
    Of poets and of orators.
    Horace's wit and Virgil's state
    He did not steal but emulate ;
    And when he would like them appear,
    Their garb, but not their clothes, did wear."

But Cowley, deeming love the proper theme of poetry, wrote a number of verses to an imaginary mistress, which could never have charmed any woman, and are almost as devoid of warmth and sentiment as a treatise on the mathematics. These "copies of love-verses" will now be found hard reading; but the fine gentlemen in Cowley's time had a taste for ingenuity in verse, and his fantastic turns of expression and well-hammered fancies, his laborious flights and pedantic allusions, were regarded as the proper implements and utterances of poetry. What a change from the musical songs of Shakespeare, Beaumont, and Ben Jonson, or from the dainty love-lyrics of Cowley's contemporary, Robert Herrick, to these painful and mechanical efforts! The student who wishes to see how a poetic judgment may be perverted—for Cowley unquestionably was a poet—should read the passages given in Dr. Johnson's masterly criticism, which is the more interesting inasmuch as it shows that the intellectual vice of Cowley was not peculiar to that poet. Earlier writers had been infected by it, later versemen were not wholly free from it. These quiddities and once fashionable follies proved Cowley's death-warrant as a poet, for although some of his verses have a vital force and beauty, the great body of his poetry is as dead as that of Sir Richard Blackmore, or the once popular Cleveland. Perhaps the liveliest and brightest idea of Cowley's genius may be seen in "The Chronicle," in which, with some wit and happiness of expression, he gives a long list of the ladies who had one after another succeeded to a place in his heart. Even in this poem there is no sign that the power of beauty ever stirred his pulses. Women, he declares in one of his pieces, are "most unintelligible."

> " I know not what the learned may see,
>   But they're strange Hebrew things to me."

And his best lines about women are cynical. The couplet—

> " Follies they have so numberless in store,
>   That only he who loves them can have more "—

might have been written by Pope. His love-poetry, if it deserve the name, is almost without exception rough and unmusical. Now and then, however, as if by accident, the verse moves sweetly and smoothly. Amidst the uncouth jargon and wearisome pedantry of the short pieces addressed to his mistress, the following lines occur :—

> "Love in her sunny eyes does basking play,
>   Love walks the pleasant mazes of her hair,
>   Love does on both her lips for ever stray,
>   And sows and reaps a thousand kisses there."

But such lines, which have what I may call an Elizabethan turn of expression, are by no means characteristic of Cowley, whose Muse seldom moves gracefully, but walks with an uneasy, halting gait, like a man plodding over a heavy field of stubble.

Enough of Cowley. That he once filled an important place in our literature gives us still some interest in his work, but it is an adventitious interest. He belongs to the history of English poetry, but not to the roll of famous English poets.

[There is no modern edition of Cowley's poems. A few of his best pieces, such as the "Hymn to Light," and the stanzas "On Solitude," are to be found in selections, and these will probably satisfy the curiosity of youthful readers ; but Dr. Johnson's famous life of Cowley must be read, and also Addison's essay in the *Spectator* (No. 62).]

Whether it were chance or instinct that led Johnson to begin his "Lives" with Cowley instead of Milton I do not know. Probably the order was arranged for him by his masters the booksellers. In any case, it seems fitting that the poet who carried to an extravagant extent and at the cost of much ability the worst faults of the later Elizabethans, should be criticized and dismissed before the majestic figure of Milton appears upon the scene. As we look back upon the half-century which preceded the manhood of Milton and Cowley, we find a splendid and rapid succession of poets and men of letters such as even, apart from Shakespeare, would make that period the most remarkable in our annals. Let us recall some of them for a moment. In 1628 Milton was twenty years old, and took his degree of Bachelor of Arts. Reckoning back fifty years from that event, we reach 1578, when Shakespeare was a schoolboy, when the "Faerie Queene" was as yet unpublished, when not a single Elizabethan writer of mark had printed a drama or a poem. Milton, it will be seen, was no further removed from Ben Jonson and Shakespeare, from Hooker and Bacon, than we are removed from Coleridge and Wordsworth, from Scott and Shelley. He might as a child have seen Shakespeare just as Pope when a child saw Dryden, and Scott saw Burns; he could have walked and talked with Fletcher, and long after leaving college might have spent a merry hour at the Mermaid Tavern with "rare Ben." Marlowe had been dead some years when Milton was born, but he could have shaken hands and formed an acquaintanceship with Webster, Massinger, and Ford, with Donne and Drayton, with Wither, Carew, and Herrick, with Waller, Browne, Davenant, and Crashaw, with Quarles, and with Herbert, the devout poet of "The Temple." The mention of these names will show the student of our poetry Milton's position chronologically in the history of the art; it will show him, too, that, like Cowley, he might with no great impropriety be classed with the Elizabethans. "His soul was like a star, and dwelt apart;" but great though he was, he owed fealty to his predecessors, and his earlier poems, while bearing the marks of his supreme genius, bear signs, too, of the wealth bequeathed by the lyrists who preceded him.

The prominent facts of Milton's life are well known, and they will therefore be retold here with the utmost brevity. The reader who wishes to know more about this great master will consult the list of books given at the end of this section.

John Milton was born in Bread Street, Cheapside, in 1608, five years after the accession of James. From his father, a man of high character, who was himself a composer, the future poet inherited his love of music, and from St. Paul's School and a private tutor he gained his earliest instruction in the classics. Such was the boy's eagerness in learning, that from his twelfth year he "scarce ever went to bed before midnight." At sixteen he was admitted a member of Christ College, Cambridge, where he soon gained distinction for his knowledge of Latin and skill in versification. He was nicknamed "the lady of Christ's," a title due probably to his virtuous conduct and to the beauty of his face. In 1632, after several years of college life, Milton took his final degree of M.A., and then went to his father's country home at Horton, in Buckinghamshire, where in "labour and intense study" five more years were passed. While in this retirement he put on his "singing robes," and wrote "L'Allegro," "Il Penseroso," and "Lycidas," and the noble masque of "Comus," proving himself thus early in life capable of writing poems which possess a "deathless power." Comus was written for representation at Ludlow Castle, the seat of the Earl of Bridgewater. "In that brilliant period of court life," writes Mr. Pattison, "which was inaugurated by Elizabeth and put an end to by the Civil War, a masque was a frequent and favourite amusement. It was an exhibition in which pageantry and music predominated, but in which dialogue was intro-

John Milton, 1608-1674.

duced as accompaniment or explanation ; " and he adds, "It was a strange caprice of fortune that made the future poet of the Puritan epic the last composer of a cavalier masque." In 1637, the year that produced "Lycidas," Milton's mother died, and in the year following the poet left England for Italy, where he received a generous welcome from men of genius and learning. The most interesting episode of that journey was a visit paid to the "starry Galileo," then a prisoner in the Inquisition. Milton had purposed visiting Sicily and Greece, but on hearing of the differences between king and Parliament which threatened strife at home, he shortened his tour, and turned with leisurely steps towards England, which he reached in August, 1639.

And now we hear of him in a London lodging teaching his two nephews, John and Edward Phillips, and "the sons of some gentlemen that were his intimate friends." Milton, it may be observed, was with regard to most subjects an innovator or reformer, and not least in this matter of education, about which he wrote a "Tractate," addressed to "Master Samuel Hartlib." In 1643, he went on a secret journey into the country, and returned after some weeks, bringing with him a wife, whose maiden name was Mary Powell. Never was there a more ill-assorted union. Milton was nearly six and thirty, Mary was seventeen ; Milton was a Puritan and Republican, his wife the daughter of a careless-living cavalier. The poet was far from chivalrous in his estimate of women, and the poor

girl expected, probably, more attention than she
received.   After the experience of one month she
asked permission to pay a visit to her friends, and
when her husband sent for her she refused to
return to him.   Milton's conduct at this juncture
was more characteristic than creditable.   He
appears to have written his treatise in favour of
divorce during the honeymoon, and upon his wife
declining to come back proposed taking another.
A reconciliation was ultimately effected, and afterwards, when the Powells were ejected from their
home at Forest Hill, near Oxford, Milton generously
received the family under his roof.   Mary Milton
died at the early age of twenty-six.   Of her
daughters, three in number, there will be something
to say further on.   Three years after the death of
his wife, Milton, undaunted by his former error, and
no doubt hoping to retrieve it, married again.   But
a second time his hopes of happiness were dis-
appointed, for his wife did not live a year.   That
she was worthy of the poet, and would have made
him happy, may be inferred from the sonnet dedicated to her memory.   Under the government of
Oliver Cromwell his post was that of Latin
secretary, in which he was assisted by Andrew
Marvell.   His activity during this period had been
immense, and indeed he may be said to have
devoted himself to controversial politics for twenty
years, and those years the best of his life.   "No
good man can with impunity addict himself to
party."   Milton assuredly did not come out of the

conflict without scars, but it should be remembered
to his honour that he believed intensely in the
truth of what he wrote, and that his prose works,
damaged as they are by scurrility, contain, as Mr.
Pattison truly says, "passages of the noblest English ever written." *

At forty-three, in the very prime of his energetic manhood, Milton lost his eyesight, and for all
fresh acquisition of knowledge he was therefore
dependent upon friends. These friends were few
and comparatively undistinguished. There are no
indications that he was appreciated by the chief
men of his own party. Cromwell possibly did not
know him, and men of learning amongst the
loyalists would naturally shrink from intercourse
with an advocate of regicide. Many years were
still to pass before he wrote the poem which made
Dryden exclaim, "This man cuts us all out, and
the ancients too." When the Restoration deprived
him of his Latin secretaryship, and threatened to
deprive him of liberty—and how he escaped severe
punishment is to this day a surprise to his biographers" †—Milton devoted himself to the great task

* "One virtue these pamphlets possess, the virtue of style. They
are monuments of our language, so remarkable that Milton's prose
works must always be resorted to by students as long as English
remains a medium of ideas. Yet, even on the score of style, Milton's
prose is subject to serious deductions. His negligence is such as
to amount to an absence of construction. . . . Nor is it only the
Miltonic sentence which is incoherent ; the whole arrangement of
his topics is equally loose, disjointed, and desultory" (Pattison's
"Milton," p. 69–70).

† "There is no greater historical puzzle," says Professor Masson,
"than this complete escape of Milton after the Restoration."

which many years before he had undertaken to
accomplish. He had fallen on evil days, and it was

> "In darkness, and with dangers compassed round,
>   And solitude,"

that he essayed to sing

> "Things unattempted yet in prose and rhyme."

It was well for him that he could "draw em-
pyreal air," and escape, by the help of his glorious
imagination, into heavenly resting-places, for his
home, until his third marriage, must have been
painfully desolate. He might have been happy in
his daughters had his conduct towards them been
less arbitrary. We may even use a stronger word,
and say that it was cruel. He did not allow them
to learn any foreign language, saying that one
tongue was enough for a woman ; but he taught
them to read and pronounce Hebrew, Greek, Latin,
and French, without understanding a word of what
they were reading. That they should rebel against
such treatment was inevitable, but their conduct
was nevertheless most blameworthy. His children,
we are told by Milton's nephew, Phillips, "did com-
bine together and counsel his maidservant to cheat
him in her marketings ;" and he adds that they "had
made away some of his books, and would have sold
the rest of his books to the dunghill women." *

Three years after the Restoration, the blind poet

---

* Deborah, the youngest girl, must be excused from sharing in these
unfilial acts, for she was but ten years old in 1662, when they are
said to have taken place. Aubrey says her father taught her Latin,
and in her old age she appears to have spoken of him with affection.

married a third wife, Elizabeth Minshull, a young woman of twenty-four, who is said to have regarded him with veneration, and to have acted the part of a good housewife—virtues which probably sufficed to satisfy Milton. His mental activity was not repressed by his infirmity, and the last ten years of the great poet's life proved the noblest and most fruitful. One or two accounts of this period afford a pleasing picture of Milton in his old age. You may read in every biography of the poet the story of his intercourse with the young Quaker Ellwood, who, in the Great Plague year, found Milton a retreat at Chalfont St. Giles, in a cottage which is still standing. Ellwood had been more than once sent to gaol for his créed's sake, and he was in custody when Milton reached the Buckinghamshire village. "But now being released and returned home," the honest Quaker writes, "I soon made a visit to him to welcome him into the country. After some discourses had passed between us, he called for a manuscript of his ; which, being brought, he delivered it to me, bidding me take it home with me and read it at my leisure, and when I had so done, return it to him with my judgment thereon. When I came home and had set myself to read it, I found it was that excellent poem which he entitled 'Paradise Lost.' After I had with the best attention read it through, I made him another visit, and returned him his book with due acknowledgment of the favour he had done me in communicating it to me. He asked me how I liked it, and what I thought of

it, which I modestly but freely told him ; and after
some further discourse about it, I pleasantly said
to him, 'Thou hast said much here of Paradise
Lost, but what hast thou to say of Paradise Found?'
He made no answer, but sat some time in a muse ;
then brake off that discourse and fell on another
subject."

Then we are told how he used to sit at the door
of his house near Bunhill Fields, in sunny weather,
to enjoy the fresh air ; how, after smoking a pipe and
drinking a glass of water, he would retire for the
night at nine o'clock, to rise at five in the winter
and at four in the summer ; how, after rising, he had
a chapter in the Hebrew Bible read to him, and
studied as a blind man might until twelve ; how he
would walk for hours in his garden ; how well he
loved to play the organ, the instrument which has
ever been likened to this poet's sonorous voice ;
how he frequently composed in bed, and how "his
vein never happily flowed but from the autumnal
equinoctial to the vernal." Other details of Milton's
life are to be read, which one is glad to possess of
such a poet. On these I need not dwell here, and
it will suffice to end these biographical notes with
two or three significant dates.

On the 20th of August, 1667, "Paradise Lost" was
published by Samuel Simmons, who gave the poet
ten pounds for the first edition of thirteen hundred
copies, which was exhausted in eighteen months—
a proof that there were readers, even in those evil
days, who could appreciate noble poetry. "Paradise

Regained" and "Samson Agonistes" were published in 1671.   Three years later the end came.
On the 8th of November, 1674, Milton resigned

> " This earthy load
> Of death called life, which us from life doth sever,"

and was buried near his father, in the chancel of St.
Giles's, Cripplegate.

Before studying Milton's poetry, the reader will
do well to refer to certain famous passages in his
prose works, in which the poet alludes to his great
gift, and shows under what auspices it had been
cultivated.   These noble passages are known, probably, to all adult readers ; but I am writing chiefly
for the young, and they at least will not think a
quotation or two from these significant ˙confessions
superfluous.   In "The Reason of Church Government urged against Prelacy"—a strange place, truly,
for such a communication—Milton observes that in
such writing he knows himself inferior to himself,
which is no doubt true, and then, after stating his
long course of youthful studies in England and in
Italy, he adds, alluding to the praise awarded him
by Italians—

" I began thus far to assent both to them and divers of my
friends here at home, and not less to an inward prompting
which now grew daily upon me, that by labour and intense
study—which I take to be my portion in this life—joined
with the strong propensity of nature, I might perhaps leave
something so written to after-times as they should not willingly let it die. . . . That what the greatest and choicest wits
of Athens, Rome, or modern Italy, and those Hebrews of old,

did for their country, I, in my proportion, with this over and
above of being a Christian, might do for mine, not caring to
be once named abroad, though perhaps I could attain to
that, but content with these British islands as my world,
whose fortune hath hitherto been, that if the Athenians, as
some say, made their small deeds great and renowned by
their eloquent writers, England hath had her noble achievements made small by the unskilful handling of monks and
mechanics."

And then, rising with his theme, Milton describes
the gifts and sacred calling of the poet in majestic
language.

"These abilities, wheresoever they be found, are the inspired
gift of God rarely bestowed, but yet to some (though most
abuse) in every nation ; and are of power, beside the office
of a pulpit, to imbreed and cherish in a great people the seeds
of virtue and public civility ; to allay the perturbations of the
mind, and set the affections in right tune ; to celebrate in
glorious and lofty hymns the throne and equipage of God's
almightiness, and what He works and what He suffers to be
wrought with high providence in His Church ; to sing victorious agonies of martyrs and saints, the deeds and triumphs
of just and pious nations, doing valiantly through faith against
the enemies of Christ ; to deplore the general relapses of kingdoms and states from justice and God's true worship. Lastly,
whatsoever in religion is holy and sublime, in virtue amiable
or grave, whatsoever hath passion or admiration in all the
changes of that which is called fortune from without, or the
wily subtleties and refluxes of man's thoughts from within,—
all these things, with a solid and treatable smoothness, to
point out and describe."

His noble strain of eloquence does not end here,
and at the close he promises, in these significant
words, that the intention which lives within him
shall some day be accomplished.

" Neither do I think it shame to covenant with any knowing reader, that for some few years yet I may go on trust
with him toward the payment of what I am now indebted, as
being a work not to be raised from the heat of youth or the
vapours of wine, like that which flows at waste from the pen
of some vulgar amourist, or the trencher fury of a rhyming
parasite ; nor to be obtained by the invocation of Dame
Memory and her siren daughters ; but by devout prayer to
that Eternal Spirit who can enrich with all utterance and
knowledge, and sends out his seraphim with the hallowed fire
of his altar to touch and purify the lips of whom He pleases.
To this must be added industrious and select reading, steady
observation, insight into all seemly and generous arts and
affairs ; till which in some measure be compassed, at mine
own peril and cost, I refuse not to sustain this expectation
from as many as are not loth to hazard so much credulity
upon the best pledges that I can give them."

The passages I have quoted are not only fine
prose, but they reveal to us the inner life of the poet,
and the settled purpose by which his spirit was
sustained through long years of patient waiting and
of adverse circumstance. Culture, with poetry as
its outcome, was the main purpose of his life, but
poetry with Milton was alike worship and work ;
and therefore it is not a matter of surprise that
he should have consented for a time, and even, as
it proved, for a long space of years, to engage in
the ecclesiastical and political warfare of the age.
What good came of the poet's share in that warfare ? Remembering that Milton sacrificed not
only time but his eyesight to what he regarded as
"liberty's defence his noble task," one would be
loth to believe that the sacrifice so generously

rendered was made in vain. Yet this is Mr. Pattison's deliberate judgment. "We have regarded,"
he writes, "the twenty-five years of Milton's life
between 1641 and the commencement of 'Paradise
Lost,' as time ill laid out upon inferior work which
any one could do, and which was not worth doing
by any one." This is surely too sweeping a statement. Milton may have been sometimes mistaken
in his purpose and often in his method, but much
of his work written for the age was of service to the
age, and we may say this without justifying his
amazing lack of decorum, his scurrilous language,
his perverse misrepresentation of facts, and his unworthy personalities. The age, no doubt, allowed
of much that we should consider coarse and rude,
but the higher spirits of the age—such men as
Jeremy Taylor, John Howe, and George Herbert
—would never have so debased themselves ; and
not even Milton, despite his purity of purpose, was
able to engage in party warfare without submitting
to its defilements. Unfortunately, he wallowed
for some time in this slough, and, to apply the
words of Bunyan, was "grievously bedaubed with
the dirt."

In his lifetime Milton was more admired than
loved, and even this admiration was confined within
narrow bounds. He never understood the art of
friendship ; his affection, though probably deep, was
not diffusive ; and those who knew and loved him,
by his own acknowledgment, were few. And this
"mighty-mouthed inventor of harmonies," this

"God-gifted organ-voice of England," cannot be said as a poet to have gained more than the fit audience for which he craved. His greatness is apt to repel rather than to attract young readers; and yet there is no poet whose verse is so well fitted to educate the ear for the subtle beauties of harmony, no poet who is such a master of rhythm, no blank verse in the language which in sinewy strength and majestic roll of sound can compete with Milton's; and the reader who has once felt the splendour of its music must forget the echo of that strain before he can listen with delight to the thinner notes of feebler men.* Milton is the most sublime of our poets, and next to Wordsworth, he is perhaps the most intense. I mean that every line he utters, every scene he describes, is felt and seen by the writer; that his poetry is the expression of his innermost life, and that his individuality pervades it. Unlike Spenser and Shakespeare, Milton can seldom escape from himself, but his egotism is of the noblest order. We see this egotism in the earliest poems, in the sonnets written in middle age, and again in his latest work, the " Samson Agonistes," in which,

---

* "Milton," said Keats—and the judgment of a poet on a poet is always interesting—"Milton had an exquisite passion for what is properly, in the sense of ease and pleasure, poetical luxury; and with that, it appears to me, he would fain have been content, if he could by so doing preserve his self-respect and feeling of duty performed; but there was working in him, as it were, that same sort of thing which operates in the great world to the end of a prophecy's being accomplished. Therefore he devoted himself rather to the ardours than the pleasures of song, solacing himself at intervals with cups of old wine."

as in a mirror, may be witnessed the struggles of his soul and the sorrows of his life.

How may this great poet be read with the greatest profit and delight ? He was a very learned man, and his writings teem with allusions and illustrations. Notes are therefore indispensable, but the student should not allow them to interfere too much with his first perusal of the text. Exactness of knowledge may be gained afterwards, but if the reader linger too long at first over every expression he does not understand, he will be in danger of hating Milton, for the reason that made Lord Byron hate Horace. The commentators on Milton have burdened his pages with remarks and explanations far longer than the poems themselves. Their notes are valuable, no doubt, but they are wearisome, and tend to destroy the flavour of the work to which the annotators are striving to do honour. Some notes must be read, but they should be as few as possible, and such only as are distinctly explanatory ; though it will be interesting afterwards to follow, by the help of Warton and Keightley, the parallel passages which link Milton to earlier poets.

From all sources, ancient and modern, from things new and old, this poet gained suggestions and illustrations. Milton was a consummate artist, and to trace the source and direction of his art will repay the labour bestowed on it by the student. But this examination can be postponed until he has made himself fairly acquainted with the poems. The early pieces, " L'Allegro," " Il Penseroso," " Comus," " Lycidas," and the noble "Ode on the Nativity," should be not only read and re-read, but, if possible, learned by heart. They will prove an abiding delight in after years. The two descriptive poems are remarkable as the earliest pieces of the kind we possess, and though many poems similar in character to "L'Allegro" and " Il Penseroso" have been written since, they stand at the head of their class for the vivid, if not always accurate, representation of natural objects. And it will be seen that the descriptive character of these poems is subordinate to the sentiment, which shows how Nature presents herself to the cheerful man, and how differently she affects the man of melancholy temperament. So true is it that

> " We receive but what we give,
> And in our life alone doth Nature live."

The landscape of these poems is therefore in a measure ideal, and we must not expect to find in them the exact representation of scenery which is the forte of a Cowper or a Crabbe. Milton could write charmingly about Nature, and of certain aspects no poet has written better, but his power is restricted and his imagery often conventional. He undertook many studies, and read many books, in order the better to fit himself for the poetical office. He knew well what poets had sung, and their traditional epithets were familiar to him ; but he never sought to get at the heart of Nature, and to gain from it vital heat. And yet these early

K

poems are supremely lovely, and what may seem
artificial in them was not so to the poet, for the
imagery gained from books had become a part of
his life.   The allusions to gods and goddesses, to
shepherds and sheep, belonged to the machinery of
poetry in that age, and Milton used them as a
matter of course.   They were the scaffolding by the
help of which he built his lofty rhyme.

When I have said, what has been often said
before, that "L'Allegro" and "Il Penseroso" represent two moods of mind, and must be read together
to be duly appreciated, no further remarks are
necessary upon poems so famous and so popular.
"Lycidas" calls for larger comment.   This poem is
like some of those great works of plastic art, which
need reverent study, and are not to be appreciated
at a hasty glance.   Nor is this all.   There must be
an instinct for art before we can grasp the purpose
of a great painter, and there must be an instinct for
poetry before the subtler beauties of this monody
can be felt by the reader.   Some men of great
critical sagacity have been utterly impervious to
the charms of this poem, and there is perhaps no
more glaring example of the way in which a critic
of vigorous mind may blunder in his estimate of
poetry than in Dr. Johnson's vehement and contemptuous assault on "Lycidas."   This the student
will do well to read, but not before he has discovered, as in time I hope he will, that to love
"Lycidas" is to love poetry.

Elegiac poems, expressive of fine poetical feeling

rather than of deep personal affection, have been
numerous since Milton's time, the most notable of
them being the "Adonais" of Shelley, and the
"Ave atque Vale" of Mr. Swinburne.* "Lycidas,"
however, still holds its place as the finest poem of
the kind we possess in the language, for splendour
of versification as well as for noble sentiment.
What the poem owes to classic sources the young
student will find in the notes of Masson, Keightley,
or Browne. The allusions in the same poem, and
that a Christian poem, to our Saviour and St. Peter,
and to the gods of the old mythology, is an incon-
gruity which belongs perhaps as much to the age
as to the poet. Men of letters in Milton's day
were slaves to classic story, and strong man
though he was, Milton never freed himself from
its thraldom. How often he used it with consummate art will be evident to the student, but
in "Lycidas" the art is not always satisfactory.
Possibly, however, some of the doubtful imagery
and some of the harsh passages are placed where
they are for the sake of contrast. Those rough and
mysterious lines, for instance, about the "grim wolf
with privy paw," and the "two-handed engine," are
immediately followed by a strain of superlative
beauty which fills the ear and soul, and makes one
marvel at Dr. Johnson's assertion, "Surely no

* Tickell's elegy on his friend Addison, which, as Lord
Macaulay says, "would do honour to the greatest name in our
literature," and Mr. Tennyson's "In Memoriam," on which brief
comment in a note would be impertinent, belong, on the other hand,
to the class of elegiac poems suggested by devoted friendship.

man could have fancied that he read 'Lycidas'
with pleasure, had he not known the author!"
Here, indeed, as often happens in the youthful
poems of Milton, notes of earlier poets are recalled,
but at the same time old subjects are touched with
Miltonic force and beauty.

In "Comus" we see Milton under a novel aspect.
The youthful Puritan had not displayed a Puritan's
stern dislike of "gorgeous tragedy," nor was he
averse in his cheerier moments to

> " pomp and feast and revelry,
> With mask and antique pageantry."

Masques, which at an earlier period had consisted
of dancing, music, and dumb-show, became vocal
with life at the inspiration of Ben Jonson. Gorgeous dresses, scenery, and the dance, had formed
a chief part of the court masque ; but Ben doubled
these attractions by linking them to song, and
Queen Anne of Denmark, with her maids of honour,
would sometimes act their parts in these lively
entertainments. Jonson's latest masque appeared,
we believe, in 1630; Milton's "Comus" was presented at Ludlow Castle in 1634. It was published in 1637, the year of Jonson's death ; and if,
as is most probable, the report of this great poem
had reached the ears of the Laureate, or if, which is
also probable, he had been allowed to read the
poem in manuscript, he must have acknowledged
his superior in the youthful author of " Comus."

Almost everything that Milton wrote in verse
carries with it the mark of permanence. To use

his own phrase, it is "like to live ;" and this is true, even when, as in the "Song on May Morning," the ideas are prompted by other poets.

Beyond question the following lovely stanza from the "Faeric Queene" suggested one line at least of Milton's song :—

"Then came fair May, the fairest maid on ground
Decked all with dainties of her season's pride,
And throwing flowers out of her lap around :
Upon two brethren's shoulders she did ride
The Twins of Leda ; which on either side,
Supported her like to their sovereign queen.
Lord ! how all creatures laughed when her they spied,
And leaped and danced as they had ravished been ;
And Cupid's self about her fluttered all in green."

Now read Milton's ten lines :—

" Now the bright morning-star, day's harbinger,
Comes dancing from the east, and leads with her
The flowery May, *who from her green lap throws*
The yellow cowslip and the pale primrose.
Hail, bounteous May, that dost inspire
Mirth and youth and warm desire !
Woods and groves are of thy dressing,
Hill and dale doth boast thy blessing.
Thus we salute thee with our early song,
And welcome thee and wish thee long."

Milton's sonnets, which rank with the finest in the language, were composed at different periods of life. I may be allowed, perhaps, to repeat what I have said of them elsewhere.* " Milton had an exquisite ear, and proved himself, in the 'Paradise

---

* " Studies in English Literature," p. 418.

Lost,' the most accomplished master of harmony
this country has produced.   His sonnets, while
conspicuous for majesty of thought, are lacking in
the delicate felicities of language so dear to the
sonneteer.   They have the dignity and chastity
of sculpture, the calm and serene art which is most
fitly expressed in marble or in bronze.   Some of
them are of profound interest, as uttering in severely
simple language the feelings of his heart ; some of
them are manly utterances of his political faith ;
not one, perhaps, but has a distinct value in the
history of his life.   So far from being unworthy of
his mighty genius, as Johnson thought, when he told
Hannah More that Milton 'could cut a Colossus from
a rock, but could not carve heads upon cherry-
stones,' these short poems are gems of almost priceless value, as all must own, to whom the sonnet
written 'When the Assault was intended to the City,'
that 'On the Late Massacre in Piedmont,' termed
by Savage Landor the sublimist of Psalms, that
'On his Blindness,' that 'To Mr. Lawrence,' the two
addressed 'To Cyriack Skinner,' and the beautiful
sonnet 'On his Deceased Wife,' are familiar as
household words.   'Soul-animating strains,' says
Wordsworth, and in these words describes their
character with the utmost precision."

The three immortal works written by Milton
in age, in poverty, and blindness, need to be approached with reverence.   There are places in this
world consecrated to heroic deeds and saintly
virtues which excite, and deserve to excite, the

enthusiasm of every stranger who visits them. "That man," says Johnson, "is little to be envied whose patriotism would not gain force upon the plain of Marathon, or whose piety would not grow warmer among the ruins of Iona." A similar glow of feeling and of generous emotion is felt as we survey such majestic works of art as "Paradise Lost," "Paradise Regained," and "Samson Agonistes." For these poems are the greatest achievements of one of the greatest minds England has produced. They rank with the noblest products of the human intellect; they are certain to live as long as the English language exists. Milton spoke of being content with these islands as his world, but he has won a far wider popularity, and belongs to the poets whose fame is universal.

The delight to be gained from such works is not always immediate. I mean that many youthful readers will at first, probably, turn with pleasure from Milton to poets of a homelier class. Just so are they likely to disregard the works of the greatest painters, in comparison with what they consider the more attractive pictures of inferior men. In one respect, namely, in the sincerity which actuates them, they are thoroughly right. Nothing is more enervating to the character than affectation, and the admiration given, because it is supposed proper to give it, is of course contemptible. The young student, however, should be counselled to utter no judgment hastily; he should be reminded that an artist's highest work, no matter what the depart-

ment may be, can never reveal its full meaning at
once.   He must stand long before a great picture,
and return to it again and again, before he can
apprehend the beauty of the painter's conception ;
and he must not merely read, but give patient
attention to poetry, which, like that of Milton, will
yield most to the reader who studies it most ardently.

The first thought that will strike us upon taking
up "Paradise Lost," is the profound difficulty of
the subject.   It is the only great poem in which
all the actors, with the exception of our first parents,
are either angels and devils, or the divine persons
of the Trinity.   Neither Homer nor Virgil, Dante
nor Tasso, had the obstacles to contend against
which Milton voluntarily encountered.   His sublime
theme, intended to justify the ways of God to men,
lacks the human interest so conspicuous in the
"Iliad" and in the "Odyssey."   Adam and Eve stand
far apart from ordinary mortals ; thus the want of
the life developed by the play of human passions
is strongly felt.   And even Milton's genius does
in a measure fail him when he attempts to sing
the hierarchy of heaven.   His conception of the
heavenly regions had to be shaped in a material
and tangible form, and it was inevitable that in
this adventurous flight his course should be sometimes weak and hesitating.   The impress of a great
mind is, however, visible throughout the twelve
books of the "Paradise Lost," and the student
will note a grandeur of expression and a mastery
over language even when the poet's imagination

flags. Poetical genius, remember, cannot sustain itself at the highest level throughout a long poem ; enough that even the humblest portions of the work add to the consistency and symmetry of the whole. The richness of colour, the fertilizing wealth of imagination, and even the unparalleled harmony of the versification, which enchant us in this great poem, are doubly wonderful when we remember that the beauties of nature could no longer be seen by Milton with the visible eye, and that he could not read his own verses. Never is Milton more impressive, never does he approach nearer to tenderness of feeling, than in the passages in which he alludes to his blindness. We think of him as a reserved and somewhat harsh man, but occasionally he gives utterance to his innermost and tenderest feeling. The pathos of such lines as the following is irresistible :—

> "Thus with the year
> Seasons return ; but not to me returns
> Day, or the sweet approach of even or morn,
> Or sight of vernal bloom, or summer's rose,
> Or flocks, or herds, or human face divine ;
> But cloud instead, and ever-during dark
> Surrounds me, from the cheerful ways of men
> Cut off ; and for the book of knowledge fair,
> Presented with a universal blank
> Of Nature's works to me expunged and rased,
> And wisdom at one entrance quite shut out.
> So much the rather thou, Celestial Light,
> Shine inward, and the mind through all her powers
> Irradiate : there plant eyes, all mist from thence
> Purge and disperse, that I may see and tell
> Of things invisible to mortal sight."

Milton's majestic and well-sustained verse may be sometimes said to vibrate with emotion. He does not, as many a weaker poet can do, bring tears into the eyes, but he fills the heart with tenderness and pity. Who can read, for instance, such a passage as that in book x. of " Paradise Lost," in which Eve falls a suppliant at the feet of Adam, without feeling that Milton, stern though he was, had, like all great poets, a feminine side to his nature? The sense of beauty, too, fills this great epic. It would be easy to quote superbly lovely passages, especially from the fourth and fifth books ; but the beauty to which I allude pervades the whole poem like an atmosphere, and is felt not only upon the imaginative heights where the poet breathes the air of Paradise, but also in the valleys in which it is his pleasure to rest his fancy and fold his wings.

There are portions of the sixth and seventh books which may seem dull, and might almost be termed prosaic, were it not for the perfection of language which shows everywhere the master-hand of the poet. His perception of harmony is one of his foremost charms.* His organ-notes

---

* " What other poets effect, as it were, by chance," writes Dr. Guest, the author of a " History of English Rhythms,", " Milton achieved by the aid of science and art : he studied the aptness of his numbers, and diligently tutored an ear which nature had gifted with the most delicate sensibility. In the flow of his rhythm, in the quality of his letter-sounds, in the disposition of his pauses, his verse almost ever fits the subject ; and so insensibly does poetry blend with this—the last beauty of exquisite versification—that the reader may sometimes douht whether it be the thought itself, or merely the happiness of the expression, which is the source of a gratification so deeply felt."

have never been equalled, and the more his verse
is studied, the more completely will the reader
be taken captive by its music, " to which who
listens had need bring docile thoughts and purged
ears." *   Milton is the Handel of poets.

Next to his music, if not ranking before it as a
Miltonic characteristic, is the grandeur of his imagination. The most musical of poets is also the
most sublime, and there is nothing in the English
language which can rival in this respect the first
book of " Paradise Lost ; " no poem in which
the sublimity is so long sustained upon the rolling
tide of verse.

The student will do well to read this book again
and again, and to read it aloud, for so will he best
do justice to its greatness.

What a picture is presented of the rebel angels,
" hurled headlong flaming from the ethereal sky,"
into the fiery dungeon where

> " No light, but rather darkness visible
> Served only to discover sights of woe " !

and what a picture of Satan, conquered but still
defiant, and brooding over revenge !—

> " With head uplift above the wave, and eyes
> That sparkling blazed ; his other parts besides
> Prone on the flood, extended long and large,
> Lay floating many a rood."

Lying thus chained on the burning lake, he still
retains the courage never to submit or yield, and

---

* Charles Lamb.

still resolves to wage eternal war with the Almighty ; and when, rearing from off the pool his mighty stature, he surveys the horrid clime that has been exchanged for heaven, the greatness of the arch-angel ruined is seen as he exclaims—

> " Farewell, happy fields,
> Where joy for ever dwells ! Hail horrors ! hail
> Infernal world, and thou profoundest Hell,
> Receive thy new possessor ; one who brings
> A mind not to be changed by place or time :
> The mind is its own place, and in itself
> Can make a Heaven of Hell, a Hell of Heaven.
> What matter where, if I be still the same ? "

And how sublime, too, is the image of the fiend, walking with uneasy steps over the burning marl, and leaning on his spear—

> " To equal which the tallest pine
> Hewn on Norwegian hills, to be the mast
> Of some great ammiral, were but a wand ; "

while he calls his legions, who lay entranced,

> " Thick as autumnal leaves that strew the brooks
> In Vallombrosa,"

and calls so loud that all the hollow deep of hell resounded—

> " Awake, arise, or be for ever fallen ! "

It has been said that Milton, in endowing Satan with such strength of will, with such courage never to submit or yield, excites too much our admira-tion for the spirit of evil. All force of character, whether exerted in the cause of right or wrong, must inevitably make a strong impression upon us. We admire the force while detesting the direction in which it is applied, and the heroism of Milton's Satan, although the heroism of a devil, has no doubt an attraction for the reader. But this is not the feeling which the poet's representation leaves uppermost in the mind. In the magnificent address to the sun in the fourth book Satan is made bitterly to lament his folly in warring against Heaven's matchless King, to confess the torments under which he groans inwardly, and to acknowledge that it was his own pride and worse ambition which has made him " supreme in misery."

> " Me miserable ! which way shall I fly
> Infinite wrath, and infinite despair?
> Which way I fly is Hell ; myself am Hell ;
> And, in the lowest deep, a lower deep
> Still threatening to devour me opens wide,
> To which the Hell I suffer seems a Heaven."

When the devil is rebuked by Zephon, he stands abashed, feeling how awful goodness is ; when he tempts Eve in a dream, he is made ignobly to squat like a toad close at her ear ; and his aspect after the temptation is contemptible. On returning to Hell and announcing his fatal victory achieved under the form of a serpent, Satan anticipates the high applause of his crew, instead of which he hears—

> " On all sides, from innumerable tongues,
> A dismal universal hiss, the sound
> Of public scorn ; he wondered, but not long

Had leisure, wondering at himself now more ;
His visage drawn he felt to sharp and spare ;
His arms clung to his ribs ; his legs entwining
Each other, till supplanted down he fell
A monstrous serpent on his belly prone,
Reluctant, but in vain ; a greater Power
Now ruled him, punished in the shape he sinned,
According to his doom."

Milton's estimate of woman was not the loftiest. He regarded her as the "lesser man," indeed very considerably the lesser, and this tendency to depreciate the sex leaves a few faint marks upon the character of Eve. But on the whole we may look in vain for a more consistent or more exquisite creation. The loveliness of the primal mother grows as we dwell upon it. She is so pure in her innocence, so utterly womanly in her affection, so great in noble qualities, so bewitching in feminine graces, that the reader feels she is worthy of her position as the mother of the race. From the first sight of her beauty in the fourth book, when she stands side by side with Adam in the garden, to the hour when the two, hand in hand, take their solitary way through Eden, the charm of Eve's spiritual and physical beauty pervades the work—

" Grace is in all her steps, Heaven in her eye,
In every gesture dignity and love ; "

and whatever she wills to do or say,

" Seems wisest, virtuosest, discretest, best."

From her mouth, too, proceeds, as is fitting, much of the loveliest poetry to be found in the poem.

No poetical conception could surpass in difficulty that which Milton has undertaken in " Paradise Lost ; " but in his representation of our first parents—for Adam, like Eve, is conceived with the consummate skill of a great master—he has achieved a memorable success. The weak part of the majestic poem, as I have before observed, is to be found in the description of heavenly battles and in the conversations between the Divine Father and the Son ; and that these passages should be comparatively feeble was, perhaps, inevitable. Milton could " see and tell of things invisible to mortal sight," but to say that his vision sometimes failed him is to say that he was but human. Even in his failure he is greater than many conquerors, so august and signal is his position in the hierarchy of song.

" ' Paradise Lost,' " writes Mr. Stopford Brooke, "is one of the few universal poems of the world ; imperial in the sense that the work of Homer and Virgil and Dante and Shakespeare is ; worthy to exercise command over the hearts and intellect of all ages."

Adam and Eve were tempted and fell, and so Paradise was Lost ; Christ was tempted and stood, and thus Paradise was Regained. Milton's second great epic, in range of subject, in splendour of imagination, in richness of style, will not bear a comparison with the first ; but comparison is not needed. If not so great as " Paradise Lost," it is nevertheless a poem worthy of its theme and of the poet. Two illustrious poets of our century—Wordsworth and Coleridge—have spoken of "Paradise Regained" as "the most perfect in execution of anything written by Milton," and as "in its kind the most perfect poem extant." If there be, as I venture to think, some exaggeration in these judgments, there is none in the opinion which gives to this poem a high place in the poetical literature of the country. It would suffice to immortalize any poet save Milton, and it suffers in public estimation only because the author, in his transcendent flights, has attained a higher level. It has been well said by Mr. Pattison that the patient student of "Paradise Regained" "will find himself impressed by it with a sense of power which awes all the more because it is latent." The calm strength of the Saviour contrasts finely with the wily artifices of Satan, who, as represented in this poem, has lost almost every trace of his original brightness. He is a subtle tempter, but he is no longer what we felt him to be in the first book of "Paradise Lost" —a great although fallen spirit.* There are some descriptive passages in the poem which are of the highest beauty, and the reader should note especially the picture of Rome in book iv., and the still finer picture of Athens—

"The eye of Greece, mother of arts and eloquence."

---

* Sometimes, indeed, we are reminded of the Satan that exclaimed, "Evil, be thou my good," as when in book iii. the tempter says—

"I would be at the worst; worst is my port,
My harbour, and my ultimate repose;
The end I would attain, my final good."

Milton's latest work is " Samson Agonistes," * a dramatic poem written in severely dignified language, and modelled after the style of the Greek tragedians.　It is, probably, the only English work in which the Greek drama has been closely followed and followed successfully.　The blind and aged poet found the theme congenial.　He, too, was blind ; he, too, as a politician, had dared great things and greatly failed.　His cause, like that of Samson, was, he believed, the cause of God ; yet he was, as it were, imprisoned and defeated, while the blaspheming Philistines had triumphed.　With what feeling must the blind Puritan poet have written lines like the following !—

" O loss of sight, of thee I most complain !
　Blind among enemies !　O worse than chains,
　Dungeon, or beggary, or decrepit age !
　Light, the prime work of God, to me is extinct,
　And all her various objects of delight
　Annulled, which might in part my grief have eased,
　Inferior to the vilest now become
　Of man or worm ; the vilest here excel me :
　They creep, yet see ; I, dark in light, exposed
　To daily fraud, contempt, abuse, and wrong,
　Within doors, or without, still as a fool,
　In power of others, never in my own—
　Scarce half I seem to live, dead more than half."

The whole poem, indeed, is a revelation of the poet, and has thus a biographical interest.　Noble in conception and in execution, it forms a fitting

* " There is a double sense in the word ' Agonistes.'　It may mean a striver in actual contest, or a striver in games for the amusement of the people.　Samson was both " (Henry Morley).

close to Milton's poetical life. It has been well said, that it stands alone as Milton stood alone. With the Restoration, a group of poets appear who no doubt regarded the lonely Puritan as a precisian and fanatic. Dryden, the greatest of these men, greatest in power and also in license, did indeed acknowledge in no measured words the incomparable genius of Milton. But, while declaring the "Paradise Lost" to be "one of the greatest, most noble and sublime poems" which either the age or the nation had produced, he was rash enough to turn it into a rhyming play,* and to degrade it, as he had previously altered and degraded the "Tempest" of Shakespeare. It is clear that a writer who was ready thus to debase his art had no affinity with the poet who had lived, in the great Taskmaster's eye, a life of solemn consecration.

With the words used by Samuel Johnson at the conclusion of his life of Milton, I shall close this imperfect notice of a poet who claims the reverence and admiration of all Englishmen. "His great works were performed under discountenance and in blindness, but difficulties vanished at his touch; he was born for whatever is arduous; and his work is not the greatest of heroic poems, only because it is not the first."

[There is great variety of choice in selecting editions of Milton's poetical works. They may be bought in handsome library volumes, like the edition published in three volumes, octavo, under the editor-

---

* Dryden, it is said by Aubrey, called on Milton to ask his permission to do this, and "the poet, who received him civilly, told him he would give him leave to tag his verses."

ship of Mr. Masson, or in the series of tiny and well-printed pocket volumes issued by Messrs. Kent and Co. The Clarendon Press edition, in two volumes, edited by Mr. R. C. Browne, has much to recommend it to young readers. The notes are excellent, but the text has the disadvantage of appearing in the original orthography. No lesson is learnt from this process in the case of Milton, since the spelling of a blind man, unable to read his proofs, must of necessity be uncertain. Moreover, in his age, as at a later period, there were no fixed rules of orthography, and poets, like other men, seem to have treated spelling as a matter of indifference. Do not fail to read Macaulay's essay on Milton, which has the faults of youth, but of a youth of genius ; or a little volume on Milton by Stopford A. Brooke (Macmillan and Co.). Mr. Pattison's Milton, in the series of " English Men of Letters," is well worthy of attention. Dr. Johnson's " Life " has the defects of a critic whose ear was closed to the highest harmonies of verse. He was prejudiced in one direction, as Macaulay was prejudiced in another, but there is much in the biography that is of sterling value.]

Andrew Marvell is best known as the friend and official associate of Milton, when that poet held the post of Latin secretary under Oliver Cromwell. He took part

Andrew Marvell, 1621-1678.

in the semi-political, semi-religious conflicts of that stormy age, and his course throughout life was vigorous and consistent. His honesty of purpose is unimpeachable, but, like Milton, his method of argument was often more trenchant than convincing. He first knocked his assailants down, and then, having administered a number of sound cuffs, thought that he had proved his point. But Marvell was something better than a party politician. He was a conscientious patriot, and he was a poet with a delicate fancy, a subtle sense of beauty, and a strength and elevation of thought,

which, as in the "Ode on Cromwell," entitle him to a
high place among the lesser lights of English poetry.

Marvel was born at Winestead, near Hull, of
which parish his father was the clergyman, in
March, 1621. From thence, while Andrew was
still an infant, the family removed to Hull, and no
doubt, as the child grew up, he studied under the
eye of his father, who had been appointed master
of the grammar school. In his thirteenth year,
after the fashion of those days, the boy went up to
Cambridge and entered Trinity College, where
seven years of his life were spent. Then we read of
him travelling in Spain and Italy, in France and
Holland. His tour, which produced some poetical
fruit, occupied four years. "At Rome," says Professor Rogers, "he stayed a .considerable time,
where Milton was then residing, and where in all
probability their lifelong friendship commenced."
In 1650 he became tutor to Mary Fairfax,
daughter of the great Lord Fairfax, and afterwards Duchess of Buckingham. At Nunappleton
he seems to have lived about two years, and
there he wrote, what his quaint and laborious
editor, Dr. Grosart, has called, his "Poems of
the Country," of which a few are of the rarest
quality. In 1657 Marvell obtained the appointment of assistant secretary, which Milton had
solicited for him some years before, and the two
poets, eminently congenial in sentiment, worked
together harmoniously. Marvell represented Hull
during the brief rule of Richard Cromwell, and on

through several years of the Restoration. In the
capacity of secretary to Lord Carlisle, he went on
an embassy to Muscovy, Sweden, and Denmark.
The story of his refusing a bribe of a thousand
pounds from the Lord-Treasurer Danby may or
may not be true. It is certain Marvell would have
refused such a gift had it been offered, but we have
no intimations that he was a poor man at any
period of his life, and the accessories of the story
are probably inventions. He is supposed to be
inhabiting a garret when the lord-treasurer calls
on him, and at parting slips into his hand an
order upon the Treasury for a thousand pounds.
" Marvell, looking at the paper, calls after the
treasurer, 'My lord, I request another moment.
They went up again to the garret, and Jack, the
servant-boy, was called. 'Jack, child, what had I
for dinner yesterday?' 'Don't you remember,
sir? You had the little shoulder of mutton that you
ordered me to bring from a woman in the market.'
'Very right, child. What have I for dinner to-day?'
'Don't you know, sir, that you bid me lay by the
blade-bone to broil?' ''Tis so; very right, child;
go away.—My lord, do you hear that? Andrew
Marvell's dinner is provided. There's your piece of
paper; I want it not. I know the sort of kindness
you intended. I live here to serve my constituents.
The ministry may seek men for their purpose; I
am not one.'" *

---

* It is right to say that there is another and less circumstantial
account of this interview. Both versions agree in the statement
that £1000 was offered to Marvell and refused by him.

Marvell, of whose personal appearance we can form a picture—for he is described as a round-faced, cherry-cheeked, stoutish man, with brown hair and hazel eyes—died in August, 1678, having lived faithful among the faithless during years which are perhaps the most disgraceful in English history.

He was a great genius, said Swift, thinking probably, when he said it, of his political and satirical writings. The dainty melody and quaint simplicity of such a poem as "The Nymph complaining for the Death of her Fawn," the exquisite perception of natural beauty exhibited in "The Garden," would be little appreciated by the great dean. They belong apparently less to art than nature, and yet we know that in those simply turned stanzas the pure art of the poet has been at work. Are not these lines on the dead fawn delicious?—

> "With sweetest milk and sugar, first
> I it at my own fingers nursed,
> And as it grew, so every day
> It waxed more white and sweet than they.
> It had so sweet a breath !   And oft
> I blushed to see its foot more soft
> And white—shall I say than my hand?—
> Nay, any lady's of the land.
> It is a wondrous thing how fleet .
> 'Twas on those little silver feet ;
> With what a pretty skipping grace
> It oft would challenge me the race ;
> And when 't had left me far away,
> 'Twould stay and run again and stay ;
> For it was nimbler much than hinds,
> And trod as if on the four winds.

"I have a garden of my own,
But so with roses overgrown,
And lilies, that you would it guess
To be a little wilderness ;
And all the springtime of the year
It only lovèd to be there.
Among the beds of lilies, I
Have sought it oft, where it should lie,
Yet could not till itself would rise,
Find it, although before mine eyes ;
For, in the flaxen lilies' shade,
It like a bank of lilies laid.
Upon the roses it would feed,
Until its lips e'en seemed to bleed ;
And then to me 'twould boldly trip,
And print those roses on my lip.
But all its chief delight was still
On roses thus itself to fill,
And its pure virgin limbs to fold
In whitest sheets of lilies cold :
Had it lived long it would have been
Lilies without, roses within."

The fancy and subtle simplicity of these lovely
lines form the cream of a poem, which, at its commencement and close, is less worthy of praise.
Marvell is extremely unequal, and his best thoughts
are frequently injured by crudeness of expression,
and by the quaintnesses in which they are im-
bedded. The poems of Marvell that should be
read are the roughly noble " Horatian Ode upon
Cromwell's Return from Ireland ; " " Bermudas," a
piece that has a place in selections ; " Eyes and
Tears," quaint and very suggestive, but overpraised,
perhaps, by some of Marvell's critics ; the lines

" On a Drop of Dew ; " and " The Garden," which contains the lovely and familiar couplet— .

> " Annihilating all that's made
> To a green thought in a green shade ; "

and also this richly coloured stanza—

> " What wondrous life is this I lead !
> Ripe apples fall about my head ;
> The luscious clusters of the vine
> Upon my mouth do crush their wine ;
> The nectarine and curious peach,
> Into my hands themselves do reach ;
> Stumbling on melons, as I pass,
> Ensnared with flowers I fall on grass."

All that is of choicest work in Marvell is to be found in these poems ; but he wrote also much that is to some degree felicitous, and a good deal that is far from deserving even this modicum of praise. His highest honour is that he was a friend of Milton.

[Andrew Marvell's complete works, in four volumes, edited by Mr. Grosart, were published about ten years since. There is no recent edition of his poetry, but the poems named in the text are to be met with in numerous anthologies. A life of Marvell, with selections from his works, by John Dove, appeared, in 1832. It called forth an admirable article on the poet, which was published in the *Edinburgh Review*, Jan. 1844, and reprinted in the essays by Rogers, selected from contributions to that journal, in 1855. The poems and satires of Andrew Marvell (reprint of the American edition : Alexander Murray, 1870) is, I think, the latest edition of the poetry. A selection is much needed for general reading.]

CHAPTER VII.

THE POET OF THE RESTORATION.

JOHN DRYDEN.

ACCORDING to Savage Landor, it is absurd to talk about schools of poetry. " There is only one school, the universe; only one schoolmistress, Nature." This is well John Dryden, 1631-1700. put, and may seem at the first glance unquestionable, but the remark will not bear examination. The universe is, no doubt, the poet's school, his schoolmistress Nature; but the form in which he utters what Nature teaches him, the art that moulds his verse, giving to it beauty and proportion, is due in large measure to the predecessors or contemporaries whom he regards as his masters. The history of English poetry enables us often to trace with singular distinctness this poetical succession—the links which bind poet to poet, the relationship of a son to his father in verse. Indeed, our poets have acknowledged this relationship with the utmost

frankness, and when it can be followed through
several lives, as in many instances it may be, it is
surely no fallacy to talk of a school of poetry.
Gower, with some unreasonableness perhaps, called
Chaucer his disciple; but even Chaucer, the first
great poet of England, and still, after the lapse of
four centuries, one of her greatest, was largely
indebted for the development of his genius to the
mediæval poetry of France, and while the heart of
his verse is English, it is often French in form.
How much, too, he gained from his poetical fathers
in that land of poetry—Italy—must be obvious
to every reader. To Chaucer all our poets have
been more or less indebted, but his children in
direct succession—Lydgate, Occleve, James I. of
Scotland, Robert Henryson, and William Dunbar,
for example—had not sufficient vitality to sustain
a vigorous existence. Our second master-poet
was more fortunate in his descendants, and I have
already pointed out that the vast influence exercised
by Spenser in his own age is felt as strongly in our
own. Dryden loved Spenser, but does not belong
to his school. He was not indebted to any single
writer. To Cowley and to Denham his obligations
are evident, and he owed more to Davenant. As
a dramatist he gained something from France, for
he had the open mind which takes suggestions and
assimilates ideas from many sources. His rivals
accused him of plagiarism—a fault which, in the
hands of a master like Dryden, may become a
virtue; for what he takes in silver he gives back

in gold. But he is not only, to quote the words of Robert Bell, "of all English poets perhaps the most English ;" he is also, considering the large amount of work he accomplished, by no means wanting in originality.

He was in the prime of life and in the fulness of his fame when Milton published the " Paradise Lost ;" but Milton, who, as I have already said, belongs poetically to the Elizabethans, is separated by an immeasurable gulf from the author of " The Hind and the Panther." " Glorious John," as Dryden is termed by Claud Halcro in the " Pirate," is a great poet in his way, but it is not the way of his illustrious predecessors. He stands on another platform, and wins his place in our list of poets by gifts distinguished indeed, but of a lower order. Satire is a legitimate weapon of the poet. Even Spenser, although not fond of warfare, had proved that he could use it. There had been several minor poets before Dryden's day, such as Hall and Donne, chiefly noted for satire, and there was a young satirist, John Oldham, con- temporary with Dryden, whose wit and John Oldham, 1653-1683. strength were generously acknowledged by the elder poet. He died in December, in the thirtieth year of his age, leaving the field free to Dryden ; for Samuel Butler, the brilliant author of " Hudibras," had died three Samuel Butler, 1612-1680. years before. And here I may make a digression, in order to point out that Butler's in- finitely clever but ignoble burlesque, " Hudibras,"

bristling as it does with pithy sayings, with ingenious rhymes, and with the artful contrarieties
which are the soul of wit, does not in my judgment
entitle him to rank among the poets of England.

Jonathan Swift, 1667-1745.

Like Swift, he put his wit into rhyme,
but the nature of Butler, like that of
Swift,* some of whose occasional verses
are quite the wittiest of their class, was essentially
unpoetical. Butler was a man of brilliant parts, and
Dean Swift, the greatest of prose satirists, possessed
probably the most vigorous mind and versatile intellect, in an age famous for wits and thinkers ; but,
considering what poetry is and how large are its
claims, it seems a perversion of language to call
Butler and Swift poets. Dryden, on the other hand,
with his "long-resounding march and energy divine,"
assuredly deserves the title. The exercise of .that
energy carries him swiftly along, and carries the
reader with him ; and though much of what he
wrote is often ignoble and therefore unpoetical,
enough remains to vindicate Dryden's claim to a
high place in the second order of poets.

Although this "famous poet," as John Evelyn
called him, was for forty years the most conspicuous
man of letters in London, and gained as many
enemies as friends—although he numbered among

* Swift was distantly related to Dryden, being the son of his second
cousin.   In his early days he received a rebuff from the poet which
he never forgot.   "Cousin Swift," Dryden is reported to have said,
"you will never be a poet"—a doom, says Sir Walter Scott, "which
he on whom it was passed attempted to repay, by repeated although
impotent attacks upon the fame of Dryden everywhere scattered
through his works."

his intimate acquaintances the first writers and statesmen of his time, and grew daily in reputation up to a serene old age—it is remarkable how little we know with certainty about him. When Dr. Johnson wrote his life of Dryden, he complained that, while his contemporaries reverenced his genius, they neglected to write his biography, and that " nothing, therefore, can be known beyond what casual mention and uncertain tradition have supplied." Some fresh facts about the poet have been gained since that day, thanks to the investigations of Malone and others ; but in spite of them we may still assert, with Mr. Christie, the biographer and editor of the Globe Dryden, that " the deficiency of information as to the life of one famous so long before his death is remarkable, and the names and dates and order of his publications make a large portion of his biography."

John Dryden, the eldest of a very large family, was born in 1631, at Aldwinkle, a village in Northamptonshire, of which parish his maternal grandfather was the rector. Like many a later poet, he received his school education at Westminster, the famous Dr. Busby, being at that time head master. In 1650 he gained a scholarship for Trinity College, Cambridge, and it is said he continued to reside at Cambridge until 1657. On the death of his father he came into possession of a small property, which would suffice to keep a single man in comfort. From Cambridge he removed to London. Cromwell was then in power, and Dryden's relatives were on the popular side. When the "chief of men" died on the 3rd of September, 1658, the young poet, who had early tried his hand at verse, wrote his "Heroic Stanzas"—"consecrated to the memory of his Highness, Oliver, late Lord Protector of this Commonwealth." It is a crude production, but gives intimations of the writer's future strength, and also of that disregard for the niceties of versification which marks many of his publications. The elegy closes with the following stanza :—

> " His ashes in a peaceful urn shall rest :
> His name a great example stands to show,
> How strangely high endeavours may be blest
> Where piety and valour justly go."

About seventeen months later Charles II. returned to reign, and Dryden, the future Laureate, celebrated his restoration and coronation in two poems, which may be said at least to show his skill in fiction. He tells the most disreputable of English monarchs that his goodness only is above the laws, and that the tears of joy shed on his return will work out and expiate the former guilt of his subjects. His life and blest example are to reclaim from sin, and even his pleasures are designed to noble ends. The poet's enthusiasm or flattery knows no bounds. Here is a specimen of it, characteristic alike of the times and of the poet—

> " How justly from the Church that crown is due,
> Preserved from ruin and restored by you !
> The grateful choir their harmony employ,
> Not to make greater, but more solemn joy.

Wrapt soft and warm your name is sent on high,
As flames do on the wings of incense fly.
Music herself is lost ; in vain she brings
Her choicest notes to praise the best of kings ;
Her melting strains in you a tomb have found,
And lie, like bees, in their own sweetness drowned."

Apart from his flattery of kings and courtiers—
a fault common to the time—Dryden never exhibited any high sense of honour. As a dramatist,
he prostituted his genius to suit the profligate tastes
of the age. Some of his plays are among the
basest in the language, and in his poems and translations there is much that is reprehensible and
repulsive. He was honest enough to confess the
fault he had committed in profaning the "heavenly
gift of Poesy," and debasing his noble art "to each
obscene and impious use ; " but, in spite of the confession, Dryden gave little proof of penitence, for his
latest poems are marked, like his dramas, by the
grossest improprieties. How far his life was in
accordance with his writings it is impossible to say.
One biographer calls him a libertine, another says
that his moral character was unexceptionable, and
a third declares that "though he was assuredly no
saint, there were not so very many better men then
living than John Dryden." * This is a loose kind of
writing. We are told, on the highest authority, that
we can know a man by his fruits ; and Dryden's
fruits are but too often apples of Sodom. His
great genius and many generous traits of character

* Dryden, by George Saintsbury, p. 187 (Macmillan and Co.).

should not blind us to the fact that he pandered to the lowest appetites of the people, and did this not once or twice, but throughout a long literary life. "Not so very many better men then living!" And yet, evil though the days were, the age of Dryden was the age of Barrow and of Cudworth, of Stilling-fleet and Henry More, of Sir Isaac Newton and Jeremy Taylor, and of a host of men equally good, if not equal in greatness. "Clear your mind of cant" was one of Dr. Johnson's manly sayings; and the cant of placing Dryden among the best men of his century, is just as much to be condemned as that other kind of cant, which sees no righteousness in men who do not utter the shibboleth of a sect.

The years through which Dryden laboured as a dramatist do not claim our attention. He produced twenty-eight plays. In several of them there are noble passages, marked by the strength and resonance which distinguish his poems. One or two of his dramas still retain vitality, but it is as a poetical satirist, and not as a dramatist, that Dryden holds his place in our literature. In 1665 the Great Plague broke out, and the theatres were closed. That terrible pestilence, which was followed by the equally famous fire, is described with vivid touches in the famous "Diary" of Pepys, and the so-called "History" of that eventful period by Defoe may still be read with the keenest interest.* Dryden,

* "In six months a hundred thousand Londoners died of the Plague . . . and the Plague was followed by a fire, which, beginning near Fish Street, reduced the whole city to ashes from the Tower to

like Milton, escaped into the country during this time of danger, and his poem "Annus Mirabilis" records the events of a year in which the three greatest evils that can afflict a people—plague, fire, and war—tried the courage of England. "Annus Mirabilis" deserves the attention of the student. "I have chosen," says Dryden, in a long introduction, "to write my poem in quatrains, or stanzas of four, in alternate rhyme, because I have ever judged them more noble and of greater dignity both for the sound and number than any other verse in use amongst us." His friend, Sir William Davenant, had used the same stanza in his once famous poem "Gondibert." Dryden's poem is distinguished by masterly execution and dignity of style, but it has been justly pointed out that the subject lacks variety. Indeed, the feeling with which we read it is not wholly that of pleasure; but some admiration must be given to the vigour of the writer and to his skilful manipulation of a difficult stanza. A curious feature of the poem is the pious prayer which Charles is made to offer up for his afflicted subjects, and the answer it received.

Sir W. Davenant, 1605-1668.

---

the Temple. Thirteen hundred houses and ninety churches were destroyed. The loss of merchandise and property was beyond count. The Treasury was empty, and neither ships nor forts were manned when the Dutch fleet appeared in the Nore, advanced unopposed up the Thames to Gravesend, forced the boom which protected the Medway, burnt three men-of-war which lay anchored in the river, and for six weeks sailed proudly along the southern coast the masters of the Channel" ("Short History of the English People," by J. R. Green, p. 615).

> " The Eternal heard, and from the heavenly quire
> Chose out the cherub with the flaming sword,
> And bade him swiftly drive the approaching fire
> From where our naval magazines were stored."

It will be seen that the poet, although a wit, could sometimes write in a strain which approaches to bathos. The prophecy at the end of the poem, that half of the war with Holland was over, and "the less dangerous part left behind," was painfully falsified shortly after its publication. In 1668, on the death of Davenant, Dryden was made Poet-Laureate, and obtained also the post of Historiographer-Royal. His next and far more brilliant achievement as a poet was the publication, in 1681, of "Absalom and Achitophel." He had now reached the mature age of fifty, and had he died at forty-nine would have left a comparatively insignificant name in English literature. This poem fixed his position as a satirist. To understand it the student must make himself acquainted with the history of the period—with what Scott calls the "Machiavel subtlety" of Shaftesbury, and with the ambitious designs of Monmouth. Shaftesbury was in the Tower, and was about to take his trial for high treason, when the poem appeared. He was acquitted, but assuredly owed nothing to the leniency of the poet, whose venomous satire is more creditable to his genius than to his humanity. To attack a man who had fallen was not a manly act, and to attack him, as Dryden does, through the physical and intellectual deficiencies of his son was still less manly. If it be true that satire which is not personal is power-less,* there was no failure in this respect on the part of Dryden, who not only attacked Shaftes-bury, as "Achitophel," with a force and directness which even Pope failed to surpass, but also under the name of "Zimri" produced a deathless portrait of the Duke of Buckingham, who, in a famous piece called "The Rehearsal," had held the poet up to ridicule for the inflated language of his heroic plays. A poem in which more than twenty well-known public characters were drawn with a master's hand could not fail to be popular, and it is not surprising that five editions of "Absalom and Achitophel" were required within twelve months. Dryden followed up this attack upon Shaftesbury in a satire of far less note, but perhaps of equal virulence, called "The Medal," written, it is said, at the instigation of the king. To this succeeded the shortest and most brilliant of his satires. Thomas Shadwell, a clever writer of Restoration comedies, but a dull poet, had attacked Dryden with the savage satirical weapons employed by writers in that age, and Dryden, resenting the attack, covered his adversary with shame for ever in "Mac-Flecknoe"—a poem with two hundred spear-thrusts in it, for it has about that number of lines.

Dryden's character, like that of many smaller

---

* "To attack vices in the abstract without touching persons, may be safe fighting indeed, but it is fighting with shadows" (Pope to Arbuthnot).

men, was a strange compound. His one object as
a poet was to please the public, and whatever
pleased them appeared good in his eyes. The
style of his dramas frequently approaches to bombast ; for the stage public liked big words and
sounding phrases, and he gave them what they
liked. He is constantly coarse also, because the
age liked coarseness ; and now, urged on perhaps
by the "No Popery" cry, Dryden appeared in the
novel character of a theologian, and in 1682 published his "Religio Laici." In this poem he affirms,
in accordance with the articles of our Church,
that Holy Scripture contains all things needful to
salvation, and he attacks the Papists on the one
hand, and the Sectaries, or, as he calls them, the
Fanatics, on the other. As a reasoner in verse and
as a rhetorician his genius is unrivalled. It- has
been said, and will doubtless be said again, that all
theological discussion lies outside the realm of
poetry, and this, as a general rule, is true ; but
success silences criticism, and though it may be
difficult to accept Sir Walter Scott's judgment that
the "Religio Laici" is "one of the most admirable
poems in the language," it may be allowed that
it is one of the most remarkable. Dryden's vigour
of expression and command of versification are conspicuous in this poem, which has in it the strength
that is due to eloquence rather than to poetry.
How fine, for instance, in their force and completeness are the following couplets, and yet it is obvious
that they have no claim to be called poetical :—

" Whence but from Heaven could men, unskilled in arts,
    In several ages born, in several parts,
    Weave such agreeing truths? or how or why
    Should all conspire to cheat us with a lie?
    Unasked their pains, ungrateful their advice,
    Starving their gain and martyrdom their price."

It is noteworthy that in this distinctly Protestant poem the writer does not shrink from pointing out how the exercise of private judgment, which can never be relegated to priest or pope, may be abused by fanatics—as indeed, what good gift may not?—and he also intimates that it is safest to trust to the united testimony of Scripture and the Fathers.

" In doubtful questions 'tis the safest way
    To learn what unsuspected ancients say,
    For 'tis not likely we should higher soar
    In search of Heaven than all the Church before ;
    Nor can we be deceived, unless we see
    The Scripture and the Fathers disagree."

And now occurred one of the most significant events in the life of Dryden. In February, 1685, James II. ascended the throne, and within a twelve-month Dryden became a convert to the Romish Church. Knowing what we do of the laxity of the poet's conduct, of his time-serving, of his readiness at all times to move with the tide, or, as John Bunyan quaintly puts it, to walk in silver slippers, we might feel inclined to accept Lord Macaulay's assertion, that interest and not principle was responsible for the change. Scott and Southey, on the contrary, hold the more generous view ; and Dr. Johnson, after observing that a conversion will always be suspected that apparently concurs with interest, adds, with good sense and kindly feeling, "It is natural to hope that a comprehensive is likewise an elevated soul, and that whoever is wise is also honest. I am willing to believe that Dryden, having employed his mind, active as it was, upon different studies, and filled it, capacious as it was, with other materials, came unprovided to the controversy, and wanted rather skill to discover the right than virtue to maintain it. But inquiries into the heart are not for man; we must now leave him to his Judge."

The first fruit of the change was the publication of "The Hind and the Panther," a poem in which those two beasts, the first of which represents the Romish Church, and the second the English, discuss theology with more skill than congruity. The plan of the piece was not original. Poets had used a similar machinery before Dryden's time, and have several times used it since. Chaucer, for example, makes a cock and hen quote Homer and Galen. Marvell wrote in verse a dialogue between two horses; and Burns's "Twa Dogs" is known to all readers. If the reader thinks that an artifice of this kind is a dead weight upon a poet's genius, there are few critics who will dispute the opinion. It is enough to say that Dryden mastered a difficulty well-nigh insuperable, and that the two beasts discuss theological dogmas without exciting either contempt or disgust. Of course, as is natural in such encounters, the most specious arguments come from the lips of the milk-white hind, the representative of the Church for which the poet is pleading.

If Dryden were not honest in his change of creed, his strike for worldly advancement was swiftly punished. "The Hind and the Panther" was published in April, 1687; in 1688 the Revolution not only deprived him of his official posts, but every prospect of court favour was at once destroyed. That Shadwell, "mature in dulness from his tender years," should have been made Poet-Laureate would have been galling to the great poet had not the appointment been made solely on political grounds, and by a king utterly indifferent to the claims of literature. Dryden therefore could scarcely have felt his pride hurt; but the loss of income was serious, and he was forced once more to write for the stage in order to gain a livelihood. Among the plays now written was "Don Sebastian," which is still read, and may be regarded, if we except "All for Love," as the finest of Dryden's dramas. His last play, it may be observed here, appeared in 1694, and was a complete failure.

And now Dryden entered upon a labour that might well have daunted a younger man—the translation of Virgil. In Dr. Johnson's judgment it was "the most laborious and difficult of all his works," and in some respects it is one of the most successful. The consummate charm and the elevated purity of Virgil's style have not been caught by Dryden. He is often careless, and he is even coarse. Scholars will find much to condemn in this version, but in spite of defects, it may at least be said in Dryden's praise that he has produced a translation of the great Mantuan poet that is thoroughly readable and likely always to be read.* In March, 1700, he published his translations of Boccacio and Chaucer, under the title of " Fables Ancient and Modern." They are preceded by an interesting preface — Dryden loved well to talk with his readers—in which he says that, though a cripple in his limbs, he thinks himself as vigorous as ever in the faculties of his soul. " What judgment I had," he writes, " increases rather than diminishes ; and thoughts such as they are, come crowding in so fast upon me that my only difficulty is to choose or to reject—to run them into verse or to give them the other harmony of prose." This passage is significant. The words savour more of the rhetorician than of the poet. Thoughts that may be run indifferently into verse or prose are not, in the true sense of the term, poetical. As well might you expect to have music without sound as poetry without metre, and what can be said as well in prose had better not be said in verse. Dryden, it

---

* It is on the ground of readableness that Dr. Johnson defends Dryden's Virgil, and his remarks are admirable. " It is not," he writes, " by comparing line with line that the merit of great works is to be estimated, but by their general effects and ultimate result. . . . Works of imagination excel by their allurement and delight, by their power of attracting and detaining the attention. That book is good in vain which the reader throws away. He only is the master who keeps the mind in pleasing captivity ; whose pages are perused with eagerness, and in hope of new pleasure are perused again ; and whose conclusion is perceived with an eye of sorrow such as the traveller casts upon departing day."

has been justly observed, argues more concisely and forcibly in verse than in prose. But do not therefore mistake his arguments for poetry; that is to be found in the fervid glow of intellect and in the intuitive command of language which give warmth and light even to his dullest pages.

The poet was in harness to the last. I have said that the "Fables" were published in March, 1700; on May-day he died of a mortification in his leg. The body was embalmed and lay in state, and on the 13th of the month Dryden was buried near to Chaucer and Cowley in Poet's Corner.

In appearance he is represented as more like a jolly farmer than a man whose whole life had been devoted to severe literary labour. He was short, stout, and ruddy, and Pope, who when a boy saw him at Will's coffee-house,* said that he had a "down look." And yet if the portrait by Kneller be a faithful one, Dryden's features were handsome and his look dignified.

It was the ambition of every man of letters in those days to see the poet at Will's, seated in his tavern chair—that "throne of human felicity"—and haply to gain the highly prized privilege of a pinch from his snuff-box. Dryden loved his place of honour, but he was never, if his own account may be credited, what Johnson called a "clubable man." There may be some exaggeration here, but it is probable that, like other men of letters, he was more

---

* Where it is said an armchair and a special place were kept for him by the fire in winter, and in the balcony in summer.

disposed to be confidential in the closet than in society. With the pen in hand Dryden was at home, and incidentally in his prose writings he reveals his innermost nature. His prefaces and critical essays are not likely to come before the readers for whom these chapters are written, but in later life, if a taste has been gained for fine literature, they will be read with interest.

S. T. Coleridge, an exquisite poet and a great critic, has expressed a doubt whether Dryden were a poet at all; and Wordsworth, who, like his friend, was at once a master in criticism and in poetry, has said that the only qualities he can find in Dryden that are essentially poetical are a certain ardour and impetuosity of mind with an excellent ear. It should be remembered, however, that these brother-poets lived at a period of change, and wrote under the immediate influence of what may be justly called a revolution in literature. The style of Dryden and Pope, which every poetaster of the last century imitated, had been repeated until the ear was weary of the monotony. A measure which genius had ennobled had now become an instrument of universal application. To write heroic couplets was an every-day accomplishment, like the manufacture of sonnets in the days of Petrarch. It was natural, therefore, that men of genius who felt their poetic wings growing in the early years of this century should revolt at what was tame and conventional in the art they loved. They were probably right in the main, but they failed to see that the region of poetry is wide enough to hold a Dryden as well as a Spenser, a Pope as well as a Burns.

Coming fresh from the transcendent imagination of Shakespeare, from the majestic notes of Milton, from the immortal dreams of Spenser, Dryden, who is without pathos, without passion, without the creative imagination which exhausts worlds and then imagines new, seems to occupy a very inferior position. And so he does, but it is a high position notwithstanding. Dryden's power is seen in his mastery of English, in the consummate skill with which he can turn the common affairs of life to poetic uses, in his astonishing genius as a satirist, in the fire which runs through his lines, so that the reader, whether he will or not, is forced to catch their ardour. He knew, if ever poet knew, how to say things finely ; and, indeed, Cowper's criticism is essentially just, that the beauties of this poet are numberless, and that if his faults are also numberless, they are those of a great man.

There is much in the large body of Dryden's work with which the youthful student need not concern himself—much that it is in every way better that he should avoid. He will find the best fruits of his genius in "Absalom and Achitophel," of which he should read all the first part, and the portion of part ii. from line 310 to line 509, which is known to have been written by Dryden, the remainder of the poem being the work of Nahum Tate ; in the " Religio Laici ;" in " The Hind and

the Panther ;" in "MacFlecknoe," which suggested
"The Dunciad" to Pope; and in a few shorter
poems, which, like the well-known "Alexander's
Feast," fill the measure of Dryden's fame.

There are two points of view from which this
poet's work claims attention—perhaps I ought to
mention a third aspect of his genius, for Dryden
is in some respects an admirable translator ; but it
will suffice to speak of him as a satirist and as a
lyrist. The gift of satire is a perilous one, for
it is scarcely possible to exercise it on general
themes. The satirist almost inevitably descends
to personalities. He needs a victim to impale, and
is not always careful to choose one worthy of his
scorn. Dryden, like his successor and equal, Pope,
was often thoroughly unjust. He stabbed repu-
tations and wrote as if he were doing the work
of an honest man. He does not, indeed, as Pope
did, libel women, and there was nothing underhand
in his mode of attack ; but he has no pity, and
probably looked for none. Chaucer has said that
"truth is the highest thing a man may keep."
Dryden cared but partially for truth, and was
greatly more concerned to point his couplets with
venom. The incomparable pictures of Shaftesbury
and Buckingham in "Absalom and Achitophel"
owe their origin to the interest of the time-server
and not to the indignation of the patriot, and the
attack upon Thomas Shadwell, the hero of Mac-
Flecknoe," is, of course, wholly personal. It is
impossible not to enjoy the vigour and brilliancy

of the lines in which the poet holds up these characters to laughter or to scorn, but the moralist may ask, not unreasonably, whether the action was legitimate? The sketch of Shaftesbury, indeed, is not wholly a severe one. An ambitious statesman might well bear to be told that he had

> "A fiery soul which, working out its way,
> Fretted the pigmy body to decay,
> And o'erinformed the tenement of clay;"

or to find himself compared to a daring pilot in extremity—

> · "Pleased with the danger, when the waves went high;"

but the gross attack on him in "The Medal," in which, looking back to Cromwell's time, the earl is styled

> "A vermin wriggling in the usurper's ear,
> Bartering his venal wit for sums of gold,"

and is described with absolute injustice as having

> "Groaned, sighed, and prayed, while godliness was gain,
> The loudest bagpipe of the squeaking train,"

must have been in no small measure irritating to a man like Shaftesbury.

Against the profligate and witty Duke of Buckingham, who had held the poet up to laughter in "The Rehearsal," Dryden had for some · years "nursed his wrath." The opportunity for a retort had come in writing Absalom and Achitophel, and so satisfied was the satirist with his character of

Zimri that he considered it worth the whole poem. Buckingham, the second duke bearing that title, is thus described—

> "A man so various that he seemed to be
> Not one, but all mankind's epitome :
> Stiff in opinions, always in the wrong,
> Was everything by starts and nothing long ;
> But in the course of one revolving moon
> Was chemist, fiddler, statesman, and buffoon ;
>
> .   .   .   .
>
> Blest madman, who could every hour employ
> With something new to wish or to enjoy !
> Railing and praising were his usual themes,
> And both, to show his judgment in extremes :
> So over-violent or over-civil
> That every man with him was God or devil.
> In squandering wealth was his peculiar art ;
> Nothing went unrewarded but desert.
> Beggared by fools whom still he found too late,
> He had his jest and they had his estate." *

For Shadwell, against whom the satirist levelled his shafts of ridicule in "MacFlecknoe," and under the name of Og in "Absalom and Achitophel," and for Settle, who figures in the latter poem as Doeg, the world has long ceased to care ; yet they are doomed to live an ignoble but immortal life in the pages of Dryden. This, indeed, was prophesied by the poet, who writes of them as

> "Two fools that crutch their feeble sense on verse,
> Who by my Muse to all succeeding times
> Shall live, in spite of their own doggerel rhymes."

---

* The reader should compare these powerful lines with the vivid picture of the same nobleman drawn by Pope in his "Moral Essays."

Shadwell was, to use a phrase now obsolete, a man of parts. He was a coarse but successful comedian, and one of his plays is said to have been acted with applause before the heads of houses at Oxford. It would seem, also, that Shadwell was gifted as a talker, for the Earl of Rochester is reported to have said of him that "if he had burnt all he wrote and printed all he spoke, he would have had more wit and humour than any other poet." At one time he and Dryden were friends, and the ground of quarrel between them was probably in the first place political; for Shadwell opposed the court, while Dryden was an ardent loyalist. Shadwell had not only attacked some of Dryden's opinions as a critic of the drama, but had, as Scott observes, used "very irreverent expressions" about one of his plays. He had also published a scurrilous poem against him, and had "plainly intimated that he wanted nothing but a pension to enable him to write as well as the Poet-Laureate." He was ill advised to measure swords with Dryden, and must have sorely rued the blunder when "Mac-Flecknoe, or a Satire on the True Blue Protestant Poet, T. S.," was published in October, 1682. Flecknoe had been known to the town in those days as a feeble poetaster who had at one time excited the ridicule of Andrew Marvell. He died in 1678, and the satire exhibits him in the act of laying down the sceptre which he had long held as absolute monarch of the "realms of nonsense." His first duty is to choose a successor capable of waging "immortal war with wit," and at length he decides to leave his kingdom to Shadwell—

> "Shadwell alone my perfect image bears,
> Mature in dulness from his tender years ;
> Shadwell alone of all my sons is he
> Who stands confirmed in full stupidity.
> The rest to some faint meaning make pretence,
> But Shadwell never deviates into sense."

Not content with the punishment inflicted by "MacFlecknoe," Dryden, as I have said already, "slew the slain" a second time in "Absalom and Achitophel," where Shadwell appears as Og, and where we read that

> "—though Heaven made him poor, with reverence speaking,
> He never was a poet of God's making ;
> The midwife laid her hand on his thick skull,
> With this prophetic blessing—'Be thou dull.'"

Settle was a smaller foe than Shadwell, although as a dramatist he had gained fame enough to make Dryden envious. The quarrel between them was pitiful enough, and Dryden lowered himself to Settle's level.* He could not well have sunk lower ; but the marvel is, that when these poets were living the gulf that separates them was by no means so evident as it is to us. Settle, in some of his writings, divided with Dryden, as Johnson observes, the suf-

---

* " To see the highest minds thus levelled with the meanest, may produce some solace to the consciousness of weakness and some mortification to the pride of wisdom. But let it be remembered that minds are not levelled in their powers but when they are first levelled in their desires. Dryden and Settle had both placed their happiness in the claps of multitudes " (Dr. Johnson).

frages of the nation ; yet he was both a mean poet
and a mean man. He descended so low as to
write a poem in favour of Judge Jeffreys, and it is
said that in his latter days he contrived shows for
fairs, and had a stereotyped elegy and epithalamion,
which, with some slight changes at the beginning
or end, were used on all occasions. "When any
marriage became known, Settle ran to the bridegroom with his epithalamion, and when he heard
of any death ran to the heir with his elegy." This
poor poet, who was Laureate to the Lord Mayor, has
his features drawn in these sharply defined lines—

> "Doeg, though without knowing how or why,
> Made still a blundering kind of melody ;
> Spurred boldly on, and dashed through thick and thin,
> Through sense or nonsense, never out nor in ;
> Free from all meaning, whether good or bad,
> And in one word heroically mad,
> He was too warm on picking-work to dwell,
> But faggoted his notions as they fell,
> And if they rhymed and rattled all was well.
> Spiteful he is not, though he wrote a satire,
> For still there goes some thinking to ill-nature."

Of Dryden as a satirist there may be something
more to say when speaking of Pope, the only Englishman worthy to be called his rival. Now I want
to say a few words about "glorious John" as a lyric
poet. He did not write much verse of this character, but yet enough to win, in the judgment of
some critics, a distinguished reputation. The songs
scattered through his dramas have been warmly
praised by an accomplished writer, who terms

N

them admirable, exquisite, and charming. The
truth is, Dryden's craft was such that he could do
in a measure almost everything he tried to do; but
the art of the craftsman is more visible in these
pieces than the spontaneity of the poet, and I may
add that there are sound reasons why, upon moral
as well as upon literary grounds, they should cease
to live in our literature.*   His poem on the death
of Mrs. Killigrew is, according to Johnson, "undoubtedly the noblest ode that our language ever
has produced;" and his "Alexander's Feast," on the
same authority, is "allowed to stand without a
rival;"† and more recent critics have spoken of it
in a strain almost equally flattering.   No doubt it
is a splendid poem, and proves that Dryden, at the
age of sixty-six, was still in his poetical prime.
There is no want of fire, of variety, of imperial fancy,
and of the despotic power over language, which
distinguishes this poet.   But "Alexander's Feast,"
if I rightly judge, is rather a magnificent piece of
rhetoric than a great lyrical poem.   It is the work of
an excellent artificer, not of an inspired singer; it
delights the intellect, but fails—which true lyric
poetry never does—to win its way to the heart.
Next in fame amongst Dryden's lyric pieces stands
the ode " To the pious memory of the accomplished
young lady, Mrs. Anne Killigrew, excellent in the

---

* Mr. Palgrave, in his "Golden Treasury of Songs and Lyrics,"
has not found space for a single song of Dryden's.
† This was the view taken of it by the poet himself.   "A nobler
ode," he said, "never was produced nor ever will."

two sister arts of Poesy and Painting." Even in this poem, fine though in parts it be, the student will discover, I think, more of literary ingenuity than of poetical inspiration. Some of the lines are extremely laboured, and some are disfigured by the conceits that Cowley loved. In this poem Dryden makes the well-known confession of the sins committed by poets generally, and by himself in particular.

> "O gracious God! how far have we
> Profaned thy heavenly gift of Poesy!
> Made prostitute and profligate the Muse,
> Debased to each obscene and impious use,
> Whose harmony was first ordained above,
> For tongues of angels and for hymns of love!

I have said that Dryden is without pathos, and certainly there is no pathos in this ode. Perhaps, however, it may be detected in the closing lines of the beautiful epistle addressed to his "dear friend Mr. Congreve," the wittiest, the most brilliant, and by no means the most profligate of the Restoration dramatists.

> "Already I am worn with cares and age,
> And just abandoning the ungrateful stage:
> Unprofitably kept at Heaven's expense,
> I live a rent-charge on His providence:
> But you, whom every Muse and grace adorn,
> Whom I foresee to better fortune born,
> Be kind to my remains; and oh! defend,
> Against your judgment, your departed friend!
> Let not the insulting foe my fame pursue,
> But shade those laurels which descend to you:

> And take for tribute what these lines express ;
> You merit more nor could my love do less."

Faulty though Dryden was—and few English poets have done more to degrade their genius—it is well that we should part from him remembering with gratitude the fine qualities which give him so high a place in our literature. Dryden is a master in prose as well as in verse. His intellect is robust, clear-sighted, and generous ; he is often perverse, but never feeble ; his study of French writers left his racy English unaffected ; as a man and as an author he is eminently manly ; his criticisms are full of weighty sense, and his style, like the beautiful image of the Thames which we owe to Sir John Denham, may be said to be

> "Though deep, yet clear ; though gentle, yet not dull ;
> Strong without rage, without o'erflowing full."

[The Globe edition of Dryden's poetical works, edited by the late Mr. W. D. Christie (Macmillan), contains all, and more than all, the writings of this poet which it is necessary for the student to read. Sir Walter Scott's admirable biography of Dryden will amply repay a reader for the time expended upon it. It is essential, too, that he should read Dr. Johnson's masterly life, paying especial attention to the criticism, which is none the less valuable because it differs from the broader and more general comments to which we are accustomed in the present day. The comparison between the genius of Dryden and that of Pope must also be read. It will be found in Johnson's life of the latter poet. Mr. Saintsbury's Dryden, in the series of " English Men of Letters," though open to criticism with regard to many of the opinions expressed, forms a concise and comprehensive account of the poet's work. A highly interesting essay on Dryden appeared in the *Quarterly Review* for 1878, and another critical essay will be found in Mr. Cowell's delightful volume, " Among my Books."]

CHAPTER VIII.

THE QUEEN ANNE AND GEORGIAN POETS.

ALEXANDER POPE—SAMUEL JOHNSON—OLIVER GOLD-SMITH.

WHEN Dryden was a young man, and long before he achieved reputation as a poet, Edmund Waller's fame was established. His "smooth" poems, published in 1645, were highly popular, and received a degree of praise which the judgment of a later age has not confirmed. Dryden joined in this praise, observing that he showed poets how to conclude the sense in distichs, and that "the excellence and dignity of rhyme were never fully known till Mr. Waller taught it." Four years after Dryden's death, Joseph Addison, known to us now as an incomparable humorist and essayist, gained his first laurels as a poet by the publication of "The Campaign." Waller may have known the youthful Dryden before his genius was fledged, and Addison knew him in the maturity of his powers. Viewed, therefore, chronologically, Waller may be

Edmund Waller, 1605-1687.

Joseph Addison, 1672-1719.

called Dryden's father and Addison his son ; but
both these men are now virtually dead as poets, or
if they live at all, and may not be dropped entirely
out of the succession, the life of Waller hangs upon
two lyrics, and that of Addison upon two or three
fine hymns.   It may perhaps be a question who
is entitled to be called Dryden's father in poetry,
but there can be no doubt that Pope is his legitimate son.   There were several poets or versemen
in the first half of the eighteenth century, but there
is not one who stands out so prominently as Pope.
And the fame he won in his own day can scarcely
be said to have much diminished with time.   We
cannot think of him, indeed, as his contemporaries
thought.   Greater poets than Pope had lived before
his age, and greater poets have lived since.   Modern
criticism has treated him with the utmost severity,
and not always with injustice.   Into the highest
and purest region of poetry Pope never entered,
and in his own sphere his genius has so many
flaws that the pleasure we gain from his verse is
largely mixed with pain.   His defects alike as a
man and as a poet stand out prominently, but there
is much notwithstanding, both in his life and in his
poetry, to excite the strongest interest.   I do not
know whether young students will feel this.   Pope's
treacherous and ignoble vices will disgust, as well
they may, the generous frankness of youthful
readers, and the wit and satire, the point and *verve*,
which make his lines so fascinating to older men,
may be lost in a measure on their juniors.   For

Pope wants the poetical qualities which they can best appreciate—breadth of imagination, fervour of passion, enthusiasm for what is noble, an earnest faith in what is good. With all his gifts he lacks sincerity, and whether he writes letters or poems his sentiment sounds hollow. Not that Pope was altogether a hypocrite. He meant much that he said, and probably thought that he meant much more. He may have deceived himself even in cases when the desire to deceive others appears palpable. He wished to be thought a good man ; but above all he coveted literary fame, and to gain this was content to wander in crooked paths, which led him further and further astray.

Alexander Pope was born in London in 1688, the year of the Revolution. His father, having amassed a sufficient income by trade, retired soon after his **Alexander Pope, 1688-1744.** son's birth to Binfield, about nine miles from Windsor, and there, on the skirts of the forest, the future poet was brought up by his parents with the tenderest care. Well did he repay their affection in after-years. The lonely boy began the race of life under heavy disadvantages. He was sickly and a cripple, and never knew what it was to feel the "vigorous joys of health." His genius, unlike that of Dryden, was developed at a very early period. He "lisped in numbers," and his ardour for knowledge, one of the best traits in his character, led him at an early age to

"Scorn delights and live laborious days."

Pope's father was a Roman Catholic, or, to use the term common at the time, a Papist, and this belief formed an impediment in those days not only to worldly advancement but to intellectual progress. Almost all the education the boy had which he did not gain for himself was imparted by a priest, and he said in after-years that it was "extremely loose and disconcerted." He was sent to school at Twyford for one year, but appears to have learnt nothing there. "Considering how very little I had," he observed, "when I came from school, I think I may be said to have taught myself Latin, as well as French and Greek." It appears that the precocious youth, when in his fifteenth year, went by himself to London to learn Italian and French. The adventure does not seem to have proved successful, and in a few months the boy-poet, who had already delighted his father by writing verses, returned to his country home and solitary studies. Pope had a half-sister many years his senior, but he was an only son, and enjoyed all the privileges of the position. They were never abused. His affection and reverence for his parents knew no change with the vicissitudes of years and the growth of fame and fortune. At sixteen years of age Pope was writing his " Pastorals," poems which are now unreadable, but which won no small praise when they were published some years later. They were the poet's first essays in a path which was destined to lead him to a dazzling pre-eminence in the literature of his century. In his resolution to gain a high place in the "Temple of Fame," Pope's courage never failed. There was but one field of ambition open to him, and in that he laboured with unflinching purpose. And yet there were times, before the goal was won, when he must have felt the vanity of the pursuit. Poetry, the best, and in scope the broadest of the arts, becomes degraded from its high position when it is simply made the vehicle of personal ambition. But to satisfy his over-eager craving after fame, Pope was led to write words and commit acts which even now cling to and deform his memory.

The genius of the poet was not only developed early, it was also early appreciated, and when, in 1711, he published his "Essay on Criticism," that famous piece was praised by Addison in the *Spectator*. From this time forth his career was one of unprecedented success. He won illustrious friends, and made them still more famous in his verse ; and when his superior fortune or a venomous pen stirred up against him a host of enemies, Pope had his revenge by "hitching" them into rhyme also. This was, however, work for a later period. He did not begin his career as a satirist. The " Rape of the Lock," the most exquisite effort of his fancy, the " Elegy to the Memory of an Unfortunate Lady," and the " Epistle of Eloise to Abelard," were published many years before the " Imitations of Horace " and the " Dunciad." He was still quite a young, but by no means an obscure, man, for by this time he had won the friendship of statesmen and men of letters, when he projected a translation

of the "Iliad" and the "Odyssey." Pope was never
a sound scholar, and his ignorance of Greek is said
to be undeniable ; yet his version, in spite of a thousand faults, has gained a reputation so extensive
that it has even now a wider popularity than more
recent and far more accurate translations. "A
pretty poem, Mr. Pope, but you must not call it
Homer," was the exclamation of the famous Richard
Bentley ; and Pope repaid the "mighty scholiast"
for his judgment by sneering at his dulness. Bentley,
however, was not dull, and his opinion of the
Homer has been ratified by all competent critics.
The "pretty poem" had an immediate success,
which at that period of our literary history was unexampled.   The publication of Dryden's Virgil
excited great interest.   "The nation," says Johnson,
"considered its honour as interested in the event."
For this work the veteran poet is supposed to have
received upwards of £1000.   Pope was more fortunate in the reward he obtained for his labour ; he
is said to have cleared altogether nearly £9000 ;
and although Dryden obtained generous praise,
Pope gained still more of that agreeable commodity.
One cannot but imagine the enjoyment of the
poet's parents at the reputation won so early in
life by their illustrious son.   The "Iliad," was
entirely his own work, but in the "Odyssey" he
was assisted by two small poets—Broome and
Fenton, who caught Pope's style admirably.   I am
sorry to add that, instead of being stirred to generosity or even to lavishness, which would have been

pardonable in that hour of his glory, the poet did not even treat his coadjutors with common justice. Not only did he take to himself the credit of translating some books for which Broome and Fenton were responsible, but he allowed the public to think that he had paid £130 a book instead of £50 for the help thus given. Oddly enough, Pope fooled Broome to such an extent that although he had translated eight books and Fenton four, he actually made a statement that, with the exception of five books, the whole work had been executed by Pope. The trickery of the poet at this period of his life is worthy of mention, because it affords one of the earliest illustrations of the underhand dealings which make his whole course one of perplexity and confusion to the biographer. Unfortunately, he not only endeavoured to trick the public and his enemies, but he has been convicted, as in the case of Swift, of underhand dealings even with his best friends. And here I may observe parenthetically, for the subject is not one demanding the attention of students, that the whole story of Pope's artifices with regard to the publication of his letters displays a crookedness and perverseness of nature on the part of the poet which is well-nigh incredible.*

---

* Unfortunately, there is not the shadow of a doubt about the facts, which have been laid bare by Mr. Dilke, and are admirably related by Mr. Elwin. Pope's ingenuity as an intriguer is unrivalled, and with one exception no one doubts it or excuses it. Mr. Ruskin, however, calls Mr. Elwin a "scavenger biographer," and hopes that he may live long enough to rescue Pope from his hands ; but not even Mr. Ruskin's eloquence can make black white.

He says in one of his finest poems that he "thought a lie in verse or prose the same." And so it was to Pope, for he lied in both.

The subscription to his Homer raised him to comparative affluence. He could now, as he said, "live and thrive, indebted to no prince or peer alive." The home at Binfield was given up, and the family removed to Chiswick, where not long afterwards his father died. His memory was blessed by his son many years later in the following lines :—

> "Stranger to civil and religious rage,
> The good man walked innocuous through his age.
> No courts he saw, no suits would ever try ;
> Nor dared an oath, nor hazarded a lie.
> Unlearned, he knew no schoolman's subtle art,
> No language but the language of the heart.
> By nature honest, by experience wise,
> Healthy by temperance and by exercise ;
> His life, though long, to sickness past unknown,
> His death was instant and without a groan."

And now, after a two years' residence at Chiswick, Pope removed with his mother to the villa at Twickenham, with its "little bit of ground of five acres," upon which he lavished all his skill as a landscape gardener. The garden no longer exists as Pope left it ; the house he lived in with his mother, and where he welcomed the first wits of the age, has been pulled down, and nothing is now left at Twickenham to remind us of Pope except a portion of the grotto he loved so well, and his own proud descriptions of the pretty retreat written in verse and prose. The site, cruelly as it has been

used, belongs to fame and history. There Pope
received the honour to which he was entitled as
the crowned king of wit and poetry. Princes and
statesmen, philosophers and poets, assembled at his
table. Thither came Swift and Arbuthnot, the two
greatest wits of the time; and John Gay, laziest
and most good-natured of poets; and Atterbury,
the famous Jacobite bishop; and Bolingbroke, the
famous Jacobite statesman, who affected to re-
nounce politics for philosophy. There, too, in the
poet's later years, might be seen the mild Spence,
professor of poetry at Oxford—a sort of Boswell
in miniature; and the fiery-tempered, unscrupulous
Warburton, who taught Pope to understand his
own poetry, and paid him the most ridiculous com-
pliments imaginable. Truly, Pope's position was a
proud one, and it might have been as happy as it
was proud had he not provoked a swarm of Grub
Street hornets to attack him with their stings. The
literature that centres round Pope's friends is considerable, but the literature associated with the
poet's quarrels is still more voluminous. The most
celebrated of these quarrels, and the only one I
need mention, was with the gentle but perhaps too
self-complacent Addison. The fault in this case
was, I think, wholly on Pope's side. Thomas
Tickell, a true poet if a small one,
whose beautiful lines on the death of   Thomas
Addison should be known to all readers, Tickell, 1686-1740.
published a translation of the first book of the
Iliad at the time when Pope published his first

volume. Addison was Tickell's friend and praised
the version, and there seems to have been a suspicion that he assisted Tickell in the work. Addison
had also given Pope some advice about the " Rape
of the Lock," which the poet happily did not follow,
but which was probably given in perfect good faith.
These facts, combined with one or two incidents
that need not be related, excited the jealousy and
anger of the poet, who vented his spleen in lines
which place Pope on a level with Dryden as a satirist.
The character thus drawn is probably as well known
as any satire in the language. " Its excellence,"
says Mr. Leslie Stephen, " is due in part to the fact
that for once Pope did not lose his temper."

> " Peace to all such ! but were there One whose fires
>   True genius kindles and fair fame inspires,
>   Blest with each talent and each art to please,
>   And born to write, converse, and live with ease :
>   Should such a man, too fond to rule alone,
>   Bear, like the Turk, no brother near the throne,
>   View him with scornful yet with jealous eyes,
>   And hate for arts that caused himself to rise ;
>   Damn with faint praise, assent with civil leer,
>   And without sneering, teach the rest to sneer,
>   Willing to wound, and yet afraid to strike ;
>   Just hint a fault and hesitate dislike ;
>   Alike reserved to blame or to commend
>   A timorous foe and a suspicious friend ;
>   Dreading ev'n fools, by flatterers besieged,
>   And so obliging that he ne'er obliged ; *
>   Like Cato, give his little senate laws,
>   And sit attentive to his own applause ;

---

* Pronounced in Pope's day *obleeging* and *obleeged*.

> While wits and Templars every sentence raise,
> And wonder with a foolish face of praise :—
> Who but must laugh, if such a man there be?
> Who would not weep, if Atticus were he?"

In his half-rural retirement at Twickenham Pope lived for a quarter of a century, composing poems and letters—every one of his letters is a composition—plotting as well as writing for fame, reading much—for reading was one of the choicest pleasures of his life—and nursing as best he could a weak and troublesome body. "I have learned," said Thomas Gray, "that a man can have but one mother;" and, like Gray, Pope watched over his mother with the utmost fondness and respect. No woman ever had a more affectionate son, and she lived to enjoy his love and reputation to the ripe age of ninety-two.

The poet's later years were marked by much physical weakness, but his intellectual activity continued to the last. Dr. Johnson relates that he could not dress himself without help, and that he could scarcely stand upright until supported by stays. He suffered much from headaches, and found, or tried to find, a remedy in strong coffee. Poetry, the one joy of his life—for only through poetry could he gain fame—was his best friend to the last, and by night as well as day he was eager to write down his couplets. Yet he did not fail, both in his letters and in his poetry, to maintain the vanity of the pursuit. "That man," he says in one place, "makes a mean figure in the eye of

reason who is measuring syllables and coupling
rhymes when he should be mending his own soul
and securing his own immortality;" and in the
"Epistle to Lord Bolingbroke" he expresses in
exquisite verse a similar thought.

> " Long as to him who works for debt, the day,
>   Long as the night to her whose Love's away,
>   Long as the year's dull circle seems to run,
>   When the brisk minor pants for twenty-one :
>   So slow the unprofitable moments roll,
>   That lock up all the functions of my soul ;
>   That keep me from myself, and still delay
>   Life's instant business to a future day :
>   That task which, as we follow or despise,
>   The eldest is a fool, the youngest wise :
>   Which done, the poorest can no wants endure ;
>   And which not done the richest must be poor."

Pope's life is a strange and confused story. At
one time he affects to be dissipated ; at another
he wears the mantle of a sage. No one knows
better how to moralize, and his letters abound with
expressions of exalted virtue ; but his nature was
crooked, and he descended to the most pitiful
stratagems. He was false without provocation, and
yet it is impossible to doubt that he had some of
the noble qualities which enable a man to attract
and retain friends. When the end came, we are
told that he was always saying "something kindly
of his friends, as if his humanity outlasted his
understanding ; " and Bolingbroke, weeping over the
dying poet, exclaimed to Spence, "I never in my
life knew a man that had so tender a heart for his

particular friends, or a more general friendship for mankind. I have known him these thirty years, and value myself more for that man's love and friendship than——" and his voice was lost in tears.

He died on the 30th of May, 1744, in the fifty-seventh year of his age.

For good or for evil Pope's position in our literature is unique and conspicuous, and it has been justly said that he is a landmark in the literary and social history of England. If not the greatest man of letters of his age, he took the first place as a poet. His style was imitated by a large succession of writers, and "every warbler," according to Cowper, "had his tune by heart." The tune, it must be added, had a tendency to become monotonous, and in the hands of mere versemen it became intolerably wearisome ; but Pope was a master of his instrument. His style was formed upon that of Dryden. It has not the energy or, if I may so express it, the "go" which distinguishes that poet, but Pope carried what was mechanical in the art to much higher perfection. His thoughts are sometimes scarcely better than platitudes, but the felicity with which he utters obvious truths has insured vitality to his couplets.* No poet, with the excep-

---

* "I know," writes Dr. Abbott, "few better or more valuable lessons in the choice of English words than, after reading a passage of Pope, to shut the book and to have the verses repeated, with blanks here and there for the student to fill up. By comparing one's failures with the original one learns to appreciate the unerring exactitude with which Pope elaborated every couplet till it reached absolute perfection. Pope is one of the few poets whose lines cannot be misquoted with impunity."

O

tion of Shakespeare, has written so many lines
which have passed into daily use. What he says
is expressed with so fine a sense of verbal fitness
that it is fixed in the memory for ever. His consummate skill as a writer of proverbial phrases has,
indeed, been used against him, and some great
critics have not scrupled to say that Pope is no
poet. The statement is unjust and sectarian.
Pope's verse may not be all poetry—it is sometimes
more remarkable for polish and wit; but when
stirred by passion, his words will be found instinct
with the life and light of genius.

A knowledge of the literary history of the period
is essential to the appreciation of Pope's power as
a satirist. There is no doubt much that might be
learnt which the student will do well to leave alone.
A great deal of the gossip that centres round Pope
and the names that live in his poetry, is extremely
offensive, and will simply create disgust. The more
the poet's life is laid bare, the more we see of the
men with whom he lived, the more are we struck
with the absence of true gentlemanly feeling on
Pope's part, to say nothing of Christian principle,
and at the corresponding lack of refinement and
manly honesty on the part of his associates. The
low moral tone of those days was not confined to
men of letters and Grub Street hacks. Noblemen
and statesmen were not ashamed to indulge in
the meanest vices, and to express themselves in the
coarsest language. Pope adopted as well as he
could the manners of the time, and he had some

shabby faults of his own in addition, which make much which he has written distasteful and ignoble.

Before reading Pope's poetry, it will be advisable to gain some knowledge of the literary society in which he lived and moved. In those days the London tenanted by men of letters occupied but a narrow space. Every real or would-be wit was known to all his neighbours. His personal peculiarities were noted ; his vanity, his folly, his impecuniosity, his friendships and enmities, afforded common ground for comment, and for what we should call libel. The pen was not the sole weapon employed for the redress of literary wrongs. Dryden was not only held up to ridicule on the stage, and in the rhymes of men like Shadwell and Settle, but he was brutally assailed and beaten one night in the neighbourhood of Covent Garden, by miscreants employed, it is supposed, by the Earl of Rochester, who had a literary quarrel with the poet. Daniel Defoe, the contemporary of Pope, who was known as a fierce controversialist long before he wrote " Robinson Crusoe," was twice doomed to suffer in the pillory, and was also several times assaulted. Pope, feeble though he was in frame, was in danger of similar attacks. At one time, when he walked out at Twickenham, he carried pistols and was accompanied by a large dog. It was falsely stated that he had received a whipping, and on June 14, 1728, a wag published the following advertisement in the *Daily Post :*—" Whereas there has been a scandalous paper cried aloud about the streets under the title of 'A Pop upon Pope,' insinuating that I was whipped in Ham Walks on Thursday last,—this is to give notice that I did not stir out of my house at Twickenham all that day ; and the same is a malicious and ill-founded report.—A. P."

This vulgar hoax is not without significance, since it reflects, however coarsely, the age in which it was written. Pope was no coward, and laughed at physical peril, but he felt keenly the slanders (or truths) circulated by his literary enemies. "'These things are my diversion,'" he once exclaimed with a ghastly smile ; "but as he spoke he writhed in agony like a man undergoing an operation." What Pope did not like to receive he was always ready to give, and the study of his satires, which are inspired chiefly by personal animosities, reveals in many singular features the character of the time. They must be read with notes, or half the interest will be lost ; but Mr. Pattison advises the student in the first place to read Earl Stanhope's history of the period, Mr. Carruthers' life of Pope (Mr. Leslie Stephen's admirable monograph, being much shorter, will perhaps answer the purpose still better), and some memoirs of the time. The literature connected directly or indirectly with Pope is, indeed, well-nigh inexhaustible, but the books I shall mention at the close of this chapter will suffice, probably, for the youthful student. Having gained such an amount of preliminary knowledge as will enable him to appreciate the coterie of wits popularly known in literature as the Queen

Anne men,* he will be prepared to take up the little volume of Pope's "Satires and Epistles," edited by Mr. Pattison. To his genius as a satirist there can be no better introduction than this. It contains some of the poet's best works, and the notes are at once concise and comprehensive. Pope never wrote anything finer of the kind than the "Epistle to Dr. Arbuthnot;" and the so-called "Imitations from Horace," which, as Professor Ward points out, ought rather to be called "Adaptations," are, as he rightly adds, the most enjoyable of all the poet's productions. The superiority of the "Dunciad" has been claimed by some critics. De Quincey deemed this satire the greatest of Pope's efforts ; and Mr. Ruskin, who regards Pope as the most accomplished artist in English literature, and a great moral teacher to boot, has called the "Dunciad" "the most absolutely chiselled and monumental work 'exacted' in our country." † It may seem impertinent to differ from such judgments, yet I venture to think that De Quincey and Mr. Ruskin are wrong. The way in which Pope attempts in that satire to crush a number of dullards who are not worth crushing

> "Resembles ocean into tempest tost,
> To waft a feather or to drown a fly."

The game is not worth the candle ; the genius expended upon such foes seems wasted. And much

---

* The list includes, among the friends of Pope, the names of Swift, Prior, Gay, Atterbury, Arbuthnot, and Parnell, and among men whose relations to the poet were, or seemed to be, less friendly, the equally well-known names of Addison, Steele, and Tickell.

† "Lectures on Art, delivered at Oxford," p. 70.

of the poem is eminently ignoble. As a whole, the satire is unpleasant, and smells of the sewers. Moreover, it has another fault, which few young students are likely to pardon.

"To understand the 'Dunciad' thoroughly," I have said elsewhere,* "we are forced to wade through a vast number of notes, and to read as much prose as verse. We must learn all about the men whom Pope puts into his pillory, and as most of them are but poor fellows of Grub Street notoriety, this is a sorry business. We are pulled up at almost every line by some peddling difficulty which scarcely repays the trouble it demands, and although the way is brightened here and there by inimitable flashes of wit, and by couplets that stand out like landmarks on the highways of English poetry, it is for the most part with painful steps that we travel wearily through the poem."

Probably young readers will gain a sufficient knowledge of Pope's genius as a satirist without opening the "Dunciad." In the famous "Essay on Man," which, like the "Imitations of Horace," may be read under Mr. Pattison's guidance, Pope acts the part of a poetical philosopher. In it he has endeavoured, he says, to form a temperate yet not inconsistent, and a short yet not imperfect, system of ethics. He adds, truly enough, that he might have done this in prose ; but it may be safely predicted that if he had done so the essay would have been of little value.

* " Studies in English Literature," p. 70.

Pope imbibed a taste for philosophy from his friend Bolingbroke ; but he was not a philosopher, and the interest the reader will feel in this poem is not due to the argument by which he endeavours to vindicate the ways of God to men, but to the illustrations which are scattered through the pages. If verse be a fitting vehicle for ethical discussion, Dryden, and not Pope, has used it with the greatest success. Perhaps we do not much care about the argument either of Pope or Dryden, and certainly no reader ever changed any opinion previously held in consequence of having read the " Hind and the Panther," or the " Essay on Man." The influence of poetry is felt indirectly, and its appeals reach the heart through the imagination. Common sense, an invaluable commodity, and needful alike to poets and to prosemen, is not exactly the quality we want most in poetry ; but Pope flaunts it in his reader's face as though it were the source and sustainer of the poet's genius. The faults of his character as well as the deficiencies of his genius are evident in the " Essay on Man." Elevation of tone is wanting. Pope is never great, but he is often admirable ; and here, as elsewhere, nothing can exceed the art with which he compresses obvious thoughts into couplets that, after the lapse of a century and a half, retain all their freshness.*

---

* " In Pope I cannot read a line
But with a sigh I wish it mine ;
When he can in one couplet fix
More sense than I can do in six."

(Swift.)

The poem is a mistake, for the subject was beyond the grasp of the poet ; but it is a splendid mistake, which he alone could have committed.   The Essay must be read for its style, and though, strange to say, the poem is not free from marks of carelessness, its masterly execution will attract the least critical reader.   Perhaps the charm of the verses is often due to rhetoric rather than to poetry, as, for example, in the following passage :—

> "Ask for what end the heavenly bodies shine,
> Earth for whose use? Pride answers, ''Tis for mine.
> For me kind Nature wakes her genial power,
> Suckles each herb and spreads out every flower ;
> Annual for me, the grape, the rose, renew
> The juice nectareous, and the balmy dew ;
> For me, the mine a thousand treasures brings ;
> For me, health gushes from a thousand springs ;
> Seas roll to waft me, suns to light me rise ;
> My footstool earth, my canopy the skies.'"

Another very fine passage, which, if I mistake not, is also rhetorical, will be found at the close of the first epistle, beginning at line 267.   It is too long to quote, but the student will do well to note the difference between these smooth and carefully constructed lines—there are many like them in the essay—and the richer but more carelessly ordered verse of poets like Marvell or Keats.

The reader who knows Pope only as a moralist and as a satirical poet would form a very imperfect conception of his genius. The "Rape of the Lock," as a specimen of ludicrous poetry, in which every

line is lighted up with fancy, has no equal in the
language. Mr. Lowell, a fine judge of poetry,
thinks it the most perfect poem of its kind in the
world; and Mr. Leslie Stephen, who is not an
enthusiast for Pope, allows that no more brilliant,
sparkling, vivacious trifle is to be found in our
literature. A similar judgment has been pronounced by Dr. Quincey, and it is reiterated by
Mr. Elwin, whose profound knowledge of Pope and
of the Queen Anne men generally has served to
damp instead of stimulating his enthusiasm. It is,
indeed, as Addison called it, "a delicious little
thing," written with such sprightliness and art, that
instead of serving, as pieces of this class generally
do, a temporary purpose, it must always hold its
place as the most charming effort of the poet's
fancy. The plot of this mock-heroic poem is a
simple one. Lord Petre, a young man of twenty,
had cut off a lock of Miss Arabella Fermor's hair.
The lady, a beauty of the day, considered herself
insulted, and a quarrel sprang up between the
families. It was suggested to Pope by his friend
Caryl that he might allay the discord by his art.
The first sketch of the poem was written, accordingly, and sent to Miss Fermor, who, if we may
accept Pope's doubtful statement, was pleased with
it and gave away copies. Addison recommended
Pope, reasonably enough, not to add to it, as he
proposed, by introducing the machinery of the
sylphs. The advice, as Lord Macaulay observes,
was no doubt thoroughly honest, though Pope

attributed it afterwards to jealousy. The thing as it stood was a success, and might have been spoilt by an attempt to improve it. The poet paid no attention to the well-meant counsel of the critic, and the poem as we now possess it, in its perfect form, was the growth of a happy afterthought. The piece wants delicacy; it wants what Pope, like Byron, never possessed—a proper sense of the reverence due to women; but apart from these defects, and remembering what may be called the level of the poem, it would be difficult to praise the work too highly. Nothing of the mock-heroic kind could be more felicitous than Ariel's charge to the sylphs. To one of them is assigned the lady's fan, to another her watch, to a third her earrings, to a fourth her favourite lock of hair, while fifty are entrusted to guard the "wide circumference" of the petticoat. Woe betide them if they fail in the duty!

> "Whatever spirit, careless of his charge,
> His post neglects, or leaves the fair at large,
> Shall feel sharp vengeance soon o'ertake his sins,
> Be stopped in vials, or transfixed with pins;
> Or plunged in lakes of bitter washes lie,
> Or wedged whole ages in a bodkin's eye;
> Gums and pomatums shall his flight restrain,
> While clogged he beats his silken wings in vain;
> Or alum styptics with contracting power
> Shrink his thin essence like a rivelled flower;
> Or, as Ixion fixed, the wretch shall feel
> The giddy motion of the whirling mill;*
> In fumes of burning chocolate shall glow,
> And tremble at the sea that froths below."

---

* The mill in which the chocolate was made.

The portrait of the heroine, who rejoices in the romantic name of Belinda, is equally happy.

> "On her white breast a sparkling cross she wore,
> Which Jews might kiss and infidels adore.
> Her lively looks a sprightly mind disclose,
> Quick as her eyes, and as unfixed as those ;
> Favours to none, to all she smiles extends ;
> Oft she rejects, but never once offends.
> Bright as the sun, her eyes the gazers strike,
> And, like the sun, they shine on all alike.
> Yet graceful ease, and sweetness void of pride,
> Might hide her faults, if belles had faults to hide :
> If to her share some female errors fall,
> Look on her face, and you'll forget them all."

If, in the " Rape of the Lock," Pope excels in wit and fancy, his claim to tenderness and pathos rests upon the " Elegy to the Memory of an Unfortunate Lady," and upon the epistle of " Eloisa to Abelard." Is that claim a sound one ? My own impression is that in neither poem does the poet do more than stir the surface of feeling, and that he does this by his consummate craft as an artificer rather than by the utterance of passion. We see his art distinctly ; and the emotion he wishes to produce is subordinate to it. Read the closing lines of the " Elegy," and you will, I think, agree with me in this judgment. The lines are skilfully balanced, and present a number of conventionally mournful images. . The couplet marked by italics is in Pope's best style.

> " By foreign hands thy dying eyes were closed,
> By foreign hands thy decent limbs composed,

> By foreign hands thy humble grave adorned,
> By strangers honoured, and by strangers mourned !
> What though no friends in sable weeds appear,
> Grieve for an hour perhaps, then mourn a year,
> *And bear about the mockery of woe*
> *To midnight dances and the public show ?*
> What though no weeping loves thy ashes grace,
> Nor polished marble emulate thy face?
> What though no sacred earth allow thee room,
> Nor hallowed dirge be muttered o'er thy tomb?
> Yet shall thy grave with rising flowers be drest,
> And the green turf lie lightly on thy breast ;
> There shall the morn her earliest tears bestow,
> There the first roses of the year shall blow ;
> While angels with their silver wings o'ershade
> The ground, now sacred by thy relics made."

"Weeping loves," "polished marble," "hallowed dirges," and "angels with silver wings," are a part of the machinery of verse-makers, but such imagery would be instinctively rejected by the poet swayed by a strong passion. This elegy, I must add, is not only artificial but immoral, for it contains lines in praise of suicide. "Eloisa to Abelard," which, according to Dr. Johnson, "is one of the most happy productions of human wit," is also, as that great man but unequal critic allows, distinctly immoral in tendency. "The versification of the epistle is of unrivalled sweetness, and it is easy to credit the story that Porson, whether drunk or sober, would recite, or rather sing, the poem from beginning to end." Charles James Fox, too, who called poetry "the only thing after all," spoke of "Eloisa to Abelard" with the warmest admiration, and considered it one of the most beautiful poems produced during the century.

Pope's "Satires" are his maturest work; the "Elegy," the "Epistle," the "Rape of the Lock," and the "Essay on Criticism," belong to his earlier years. He tried his hand at lyric poetry and failed. His "Pastorals," too, if judged from a modern standpoint, must be pronounced a failure. On the other hand, the poems I have mentioned can never be obsolete. There is in them a living power which defies oblivion. "A thousand years may elapse," said Johnson, "before there shall appear another man with a power of versification equal to that of Pope;" and Lord Byron, a poet of a different order, has expressed for him the most unbounded admiration.

It is not in our highest moods that we turn to Pope. He satisfies no aspiration, solves no doubt, lifts no veil from the mystery of life, infuses no courage for action or suffering. Pope is essentially a worldly poet, and in worldly hours he is a delightful companion. A consummate master of verse, a brilliant wit, a sayer of wise maxims in exquisite language, a portrait painter in indelible lines, a critic working with a fine perception of what he owes to his art,—such a poet, whatever be his deficiencies—and in Pope they are neither few nor small—can never fail to command admiration.

[The literature associated with the name of Pope is so extensive, that to grasp it thoroughly would demand the labour of years. The student would be bewildered with the mass of authorities that might readily be quoted which have a claim to be consulted. Happily it will suffice for his purpose, and for the object of this volume, to mention a few books which are alike important and accessible.

"The Poetical Works of Alexander Pope," edited, with notes and introductory memoir, by Adolphus William Ward, M.A. (Globe edition), Macmillan and Co. ; Pope, "Satires and Epistles," edited by Mark Pattison, B.D. ; Pope, "Essay on Man," edited by Mark Pattison, B.D. (Clarendon Press Series), Oxford ; "Life of Alexander Pope, including Extracts from his Correspondence," by Robert Carruthers (Bohn's Illustrated Library), Bell and Sons ; Pope, by Leslie Stephen ("English Men of Letters"), Macmillan and Co. Johnson's life of Pope, in his "Lives of the Poets" (of which there are innumerable editions), must of course be read, and several able essays might be mentioned which will add greatly to the young student's knowledge of the period. Of these the most important are—Macaulay's essay on Addison ; De Quincey's paper on Pope, in his "Leaders of Literature ;" Mr. Lowell's essay, in his "Study Windows;" and a fine article by the late Professor Connington, in the series of Oxford Essays. The interesting and invaluable edition of Pope, edited by Mr. Elwin and Mr. Courthope (John Murray), may be regarded as well-nigh exhaustive of the facts with which it has to deal.]

Among the poets who may be said to belong to the school of Pope, are two men whose names stand out prominently in the literature of the eighteenth

Samuel Johnson, 1709-1784.

century. Samuel Johnson has claims on our admiration and reverence which his poems alone would not justify. Every young reader should make himself familiar with Boswell's inimitable biography of the great moralist and critic whom he loved so well, and I need scarcely add that no student of poetry can afford to neglect the "Lives of the Poets." But Johnson's two manly satires, "London," and "The Vanity of Human Wishes," though far less known, arc also well deserving of attention. Especially do they merit it at the present time, when among our younger poets there is a tendency to trust to the charm of melodious words, and to dispense with energy and masculine thought. "London," a paraphrase of the Third Satire of Juvenal, was published anonymously, and excited the admiration of Pope, who tried to discover the author, observing, "Whoever he is, he will soon be *deterré.*" "The Vanity of Human Wishes," another and even more successful imitation of the great Roman poet—it is paraphrased from his Tenth Satire—appeared eleven years later. These poems must be read, and should be read, in an edition which will show the use Johnson made of his original, and also how the same pieces were treated by Dryden. It is always interesting to notice what poets think of poets. Byron called "The Vanity of Human Wishes" a grand poem, and Scott said he had more pleasure in reading Dr. Johnson's satires than any other poetical compositions he could mention. He loved "their deep and pathetic morality ; " and his friend Ballantyne writes : "I think I never saw his countenance more indicative of high admiration than while reciting aloud from these productions." * More than this I need not perhaps say of two satires, which, if inspired by Juvenal, possess the eminently English tone characteristic of the writer. Yet it may be well to add, what even a careless

---

* "The last line of manuscript," says Lockhart, "that Scott sent to the press was a quotation from ' The Vanity of Human Wishes.'"

reader can scarcely fail to observe, that several of Johnson's robust lines have become household words, and are constantly quoted by persons ignorant of their origin.

Oliver Goldsmith is much more distinctly and prominently a poet than the great man who wrote his epitaph. Though more than a century has gone by since he died, his name is dear to all Englishmen who love good literature. The romantic story of his life should be read in the biographies of Washington Irving and of Forster ; his books, or rather all of them that were not hack-work, are such delightful reading that it would be idle to recommend them. Who has not read " The Citizen of the World," and the immortal " Vicar of Wakefield," that enchanted the youthful Goethe ? Who has not indulged in happy, innocent laughter over " She Stoops to Conquer," and " The Good-natured Man "? And who does not hold in memory many of the delicious lines, warm from the poet's heart, and sweet as his lovable nature, that make " The Traveller " and " The Deserted Village " dear to us as the bequest of a friend. The charm of these poems is more easily felt than analyzed. There is in them the restful beauty of a serene day in summer, when the sky is cloudless ; and the very sadness of the poems is like the pleasing sadness which steals over us as we watch that day's decline. The splendour of sunshine and brightness gives place to the grey light of twilight ; but the day is not less lovely in

Oliver Goldsmith, 1728-1774.

its evening calm than in its noonday brightness. The chief element of Goldsmith's verse is sweetness, and it is a sweetness that does not pall. The inimitable ease of the poet is in reality the perfection of art; but we almost feel, as the eye glides over his smooth lines, as if to write such verse were rather a scholarly accomplishment than a poetical inspiration. This is not wholly an error. Goldsmith's genius, unlike that of such poetical seers as Coleridge and Shelley, is entirely under his own control. His Pegasus, a well-bred, ambling nag, never so misconducts himself as to get the bit between his teeth and to run away with his master. How far Goldsmith is moved poetically, and how far he writes with the feeling and art of an accomplished verseman, it is not necessary to inquire. This, at least, will be clear to the student—and it is an almost infallible mark of genius—that he occupies a distinct place in our poetical literature, and one from which no literary revolution or lapse of time is likely to remove him. His work is never great, but it is genuine, and to readers of unsophisticated taste will always give pleasure.

[Dr. Johnson's "Satires," with notes, by J. P. Fleming, M.A., B.C.L., have been published in a tiny volume by Messrs. Longmans. Goldsmith's poems are to be met with everywhere, and in every variety of form; it is therefore, perhaps, needless to mention any special edition. But the cheap Aldine series of the British poets is the best published at the price, and this, of course, includes Goldsmith's poems in one volume. Each volume, or rather the works of each poet, can be purchased separately.]

P

CHAPTER IX.

THE QUEEN ANNE AND GEORGIAN POETS
(*Continued*).

JAMES THOMSON.

THOMSON, the famous author of the "Seasons,"
gained his immense popularity in an
age that is generally thought to have
been insensible to natural beauty. The
principal characteristic of the first poet of the time
was wit; his finest writings were satires. Nature
never whispered in the ear of Pope, or if she did, he
was insensible to her voice. And Pope's poetical contemporaries, with the signal exceptions of Thomson
and John Dyer, were equally indifferent to the
charms of the mighty mother. Swift cared nothing
for her; Gay, although he wrote pastorals, was
essentially a town-made poet; and so also, to his
heart's core, was Matthew Prior. To Thomson, on
the other hand, nature was all in all; and as the
painter of what he saw, of beautiful or sublime, few
poets have surpassed him.

James Thomson, 1700-1748.

The story of his life is soon told. He was born at Ednam, in Roxburghshire, of which parish his father was the minister, on the 11th of September, 1700, four months after the death of Dryden ; and in the grammar school in Jedburgh he began an education which was more indebted to nature than to books. When the boy was fifteen years old he was sent to the University of Edinburgh, and with reference to this journey a characteristic anecdote is told. The future poet travelled behind his father's man on horseback, but was so reluctant to leave the country for a town life, that he is said to have speedily returned on foot to his home, saying he could study as well upon the braes. Of his college course nothing is told. He lost his father while at college, and his mother, a woman worthy of such a son, removed to Edinburgh. There she had to exercise the utmost thrift, for her family was large and her means small. It is satisfactory to know that, like the mother of Cowley, she reaped the reward of her care, and lived long enough to witness the reputation of her eldest son. He was intended for the Church, and no doubt it was the pious woman's most earnest wish that he should follow in his father's steps. The young man's mission, however, was otherwise ordered, and at an early age, with a bundle of manuscript in his bag, he went, like so many of his countrymen, to seek his fortune in London. His first experience of the metropolis was not auspicious, for in walking through the streets he lost the letters of introduction which he no doubt hoped would put him in the way of winning fame and fortune. A few months seem to have been spent in teaching a nobleman's child to read, which he called a low task, not suitable to his temper. The making of poems was a pursuit more congenial. The publication of his "Winter" was accompanied by a dedication addressed to the Speaker of the House of Commons, for which, after the fashion of those times, he received a present of twenty guineas. The poem soon made him famous, and there are no signs that he suffered from that "hope deferred" which has troubled so many men of genius. It is certain that before he had reached the age of thirty his poetical reputation, if not his fortune, was fixed on a sure basis. His poems, which followed one another in quick succession, gave him a national reputation, and when his first tragedy, "Sophonisba," was produced at Drury Lane, the house was so crowded that many gentlemen were forced to content themselves with seats in the upper gallery. An unlucky line nearly destroyed the fortune of the piece. One of the characters exclaims—

"O Sophonisba, Sophonisba O!"

upon which a wag in the pit cried out—

"O Jemmy Thomson, Jemmy Thomson O!"

He wrote five or six plays with a temporary measure of success; but he was not a dramatist, and at the present day these productions are neither acted nor read. The publication of the "Seasons"

in its complete form was the chief literary event of
Thomson's life, and the principal incidents in his
peaceful career, apart from his work as a poet, were
a tour in France and Italy, and a passionate love
affair. His goddess was a Miss Young, whom he
celebrated under the poetical name of Amanda.
But the lady did not return his passion ; possibly
she thought the expression of it presumptuous in a
man of forty-three. All we know is that Amanda
married an admiral instead of a poet, and that
Thomson, wanting ever afterwards what he signifi-
cantly called "a great flame of imagination," never
loved again. His long poem on " Liberty," which
he thought the finest of his works, had been published some years before this love episode. It cost
him much labour, but unfortunately it was labour
thrown away ; the readers of that day did not care
for it, and time has confirmed their verdict. Meanwhile two or more sinecures had been given to the
poet, and these, with the proceeds of his poetry,
enabled him to live in comfort.* He took a cottage
in Kew Lane at no great distance from Pope's
residence at Twickenham, and the two poets are
said to have met frequently. " Pope was," said
Thomson's hairdresser, " a strange, ill-formed little
figure of a man ; but I have heard him and Quin
and Patterson talk so together at Thomson's that I
could have listened to them for ever."

* In making this statement I follow Johnson, who states that he
lived "in ease and plenty." Smollett, on the other hand, says that
Thomson "maintained a perpetual war with the difficulties of a
narrow fortune."

The poet of the " Seasons," "more fat than bard
beseems," lived a dreamy life in his rural retreat,
where he wrote the " Castle of Indolence," the first
canto of which, to quote the words of Johnson,
" opens a scene of lazy luxury that fills the imagination."   It was published in 1748, and in the same
year, having taken a boat from Hammersmith to
Kew when fatigued and overheated, he caught a
chill, which ended in a fever that eventually proved
fatal.   He died at the comparatively early age of
forty-eight, leaving a pleasant memory behind him,
and the reputation of having never written a line
which, dying, he would wish to blot.   He was buried
in Richmond Church, and a monument to his
memory was erected in Westminster Abbey.

If fame be the darling desire of the poet, Thomson has obtained it in largest measure.   There have
been many greater poets in England, but probably
no poet, unless it be Cowper, has had so vast a
reputation among readers who have no particular
esteem for literature or poetry.   Poets like Collins
or Keats, like Coleridge or Shelley, are unknown to
the common people.   Their works are not to be
found in the parish library, nor are they seen upon
the cottage bookshelf.   But the " Seasons," like
the " Pilgrim's Progress " and " Robinson Crusoe,"
was at one time a universal favourite, and gained a
friendly welcome everywhere.   The book is far
less known in the present day than it was forty
years ago, for even poetry is subject to changes of
fashion ; but every one who loves country life, and

the natural beauty that is unaffected by time, will always find in Thomson's pictures an unfailing source of pleasure. The weak points of his truly fine poem lie upon the surface, and are obvious to every reader. The style of the "Seasons" is highly ornate ; it is sometimes almost vulgar in its tawdriness, and it is often so debased by Latinisms as to become utterly corrupt. Big-sounding words and a false construction irritate the reader who has learnt to love simplicity of language and a pure English idiom. And the poem has another but perhaps less objectionable fault, which has been pointed out by Dr. Johnson. This fault is want of method. "But for this," says the critic, "I know not that there was any remedy. Of many appearances subsisting all at once, no rule can be given why one should be mentioned before another ; yet the memory wants the help of order, and the curiosity is not excited by suspense or expectation." There can be no action in a poem designed like the "Seasons," and Thomson's episodes, the weakest portion of the work, fail to relieve it of monotony. Swift marked the defect when he wrote to Stella, that "one Thomson had succeeded the best in that way, *i.e.* blank verse in four poems he has writ on the four seasons. Yet I am not over fond of them, because they are all descriptive, and nothing is doing ; whereas Milton engages men in actions of the highest importance."

In every work, however, we must, as Pope tells us, regard the writer's end. It was Thomson's object

to describe the varied aspects of nature in the four
seasons of the year, and this he has done with a
fidelity and a poetical sensibility altogether admirable.   There are several scientific statements in the
"Seasons" which we now know to be erroneous, but
seldom, if ever, does the writer fail in accuracy of
description when representing nature as seen with
the eye of the poet.   And by this representation,
alike accurate and beautiful, he has made the rural
life of England dearer, because more familiar to us.

We sometimes meet with a note of insincerity,
of which Thomson must have been conscious; as,
for example, when he argues, or pretends to argue,
in favour of a vegetable diet, and asks the sheep
and cattle what they have done to merit death?
He does not, however, show the same regard for
fish, and describes the art of fly-fishing for trout
with the greatest gusto.

Many of his epithets and single lines are instinct
with poetic beauty, and it is noteworthy that several
of his happy touches have been imitated by Gray,
or have served him with suggestions.   If Thomson
does but describe what all of us have seen or heard,
none of us could have so represented the sight or
sound.   For that the genius of a poet is needed.
How true and beautiful is his description of the
wind in summer—

"Sweeping with shadowy gust the fields of corn;"

of the "meek-eyed morn, mother of dews;" of the
sheep-washing preparatory to shearing, when

> "The soft fearful people to the flood
> Commit their woolly sides ; "

of auriculas

> " Enriched
> With shining meal o'er all their velvet leaves ;"

and of

> "The yellow wallflower stained with iron brown."

At the risk of quoting what may be already known—although Thomson is no longer a popular poet among youthful readers of poetry—a few short passages shall be given from his famous poem illustrating the four seasons of the year.

> "In the spring a livelier iris changes on the burnished
>   dove,
> In the spring a young man's fancy lightly turns to thoughts
>   of love ; " *

and this season of love-making in the woods and fields is thus described by Thomson—

> " Up springs the lark,
> Shrill-voiced, and loud, the messenger of morn ;
> Ere yet the shadows fly, he mounted sings
> Amid the dawning clouds, and from their haunts
> Calls up the tuneful nations.   Every copse
> Deep-tangled, tree irregular, and bush
> Bending with dewy moisture, o'er the heads   .
> Of the coy choiristers that lodge within,
> Are prodigal of harmony.   The thrush
> And woodlark, o'er the kind-contending throng

---

* Tennyson.

Superior heard, run through the sweetest length
Of notes ;   .   .   .   .   .
The blackbird whistles from the thorny brake ;
The mellow bullfinch answers from the grove :
Nor are the linnets, o'er the flowering furze
Poured out profusely, silent. Joined to these
Innumerous songsters, in the freshening shade .
Of new-sprung leaves, their modulations mix
Mellifluous. The jay, the rook, the daw,
And each harsh pipe, discordant heard alone,
Aid the full concert : while the stock-dove breathes
A melancholy murmur through the whole.
'Tis love creates their melody, and all
This waste of music is the voice of love ;
That even to birds and beasts the tender arts
Of pleasing teaches. Hence the glossy kind
Try every winning way inventive love
Can dictate, and in courtship to their mates
Pour forth their little souls."

In " Summer " are many passages of the highest
beauty. From them may be chosen, thanks to its
brevity, this lovely and faithful picture of early
morning. You will observe that it begins with a
line I have already quoted.

" The meek-eyed Morn appears, mother of dews,
At first faint-gleaming in the dappled east :
Till far o'er ether spreads the widening glow ;
And, from before the lustre of her face,
White break the clouds away. With quickened step,
Brown Night retires. Young Day pours in apace,
And opens all the lawny prospect wide.
The dripping rock, the mountain's misty top
Swell on the sight, and brighten with the dawn.
Blue, through the dusk, the smoking currents shine ;

And from thc bladed field the fearful hare
Limps, awkward ; while along the forest glade
The wild deer trip, and often turning gaze
At early passenger.   Music awakes
The native voice of undissembled joy ;
And thick around the woodland hymns arise.
Roused by the cock, the soon-clad shepherd leaves
His mossy cottage, where with Peace he dwells ;
And from the crowded fold, in order, drives
His flock, to taste the verdure of the morn."

And here is an equally happy picture of high
noon.

" Around th' adjoining brook that purls along
The vocal grove, now fretting o'er a rock,
Now scarcely moving through a reedy pool,
Now starting to a sudden stream, and now
Gently diffused into a limpid plain,
A various group the herds and flocks compose ;
Rural confusion ! On the grassy bank
Some ruminating lie ; while others stand
Half in the flood, and often bending sip
The circling surface. In the middle droops
The strong laborious ox, of honest front,
Which incomposed he shakes ; and from his sides
The troublous insects lashes with his tail,
Returning still. Amid his subjects safe,
Slumbers the monarch-swain ; his careless arm
Thrown round his head, on downy moss sustained ;
Here laid his scrip, with wholesome viands filled ;
There, listening every noise, his watchful dog.
Light fly his slumbers, if perchance a flight
Of angry gadflies fasten on the herd,
That startling scatters from the shallow brook
In search of lavish stream. Tossing the foam,
They scorn the keeper's voice, and scour the plain,

Through all the bright severity of noon ;
While, from their labouring breasts, a hollow moan
Proceeding, runs low-bellowing round the hills."

Thomson's humanity, a striking feature of his poetry, verges sometimes on sentimentality. Sportsmen will object to his stern denunciation of their favourite pursuit, but some sympathy will be felt by all young readers with the following pathetic passage, transcribed from " Autumn." It is as closely true to the life as anything in Dutch painting.

" Poor is the triumph o'er the timid hare !
Scared from the corn, and now to some lone seat
Retired : the rushy fen ; the ragged furze,
Stretched o'er the stony heath ; the stubble chapped ;
The thistly lawn ; the thick entangled broom ;
Of the same friendly hue, the withered fern :
The fallow ground laid open to the sun,
Concoctive ; and the nodding sandy bank,
Hung o'er the mazes of the mountain brook.
Vain is her best precaution ; though she sits
Concealed, with folded ears ; unsleeping eyes,
By Nature raised to take the horizon in ;
And head couched close betwixt her hairy feet,
In act to spring away. The scented dew
Betrays her early labyrinth ; and deep,
In scattered sullen openings, far behind,
With every breeze she hears the coming storm.
But nearer, and more frequent, as it loads
The sighing gale, she springs amazed, and all
The savage soul of game is up at once :
The pack full-opening, various ; the shrill horn
Resounded from the hills ; the neighing steed,
Wild for the chase ; and the loud hunter's shout ;
O'er a weak, harmless, flying creature, all
Mixed in mad tumult and discordant joy."

And now, with a vivid winter scene, I will close these illustrations from the " Seasons." Slight though they are, they will perhaps suffice to show the method and style of the poet.

" Through the hushed air the whitening shower descends,
At first thin wavering ; till at last the flakes
Fall broad and wide and fast, dimming the day
With a continual flow. The cherished fields
Put on their winter robe of purest white.
'Tis brightness all ; save where the new snow melts
Along the mazy current. Low the woods
Bow their hoar head ; and ere the languid sun,
Faint from the west, emits his evening ray,
Earth's universal face, deep hid and chill,
Is one wild dazzling waste, that buries wide
The works of man. Drooping, the labourer-ox
Stands covered o'er with snow, and then demands
The fruit of all his toil. The fowls of heaven,
Tamed by the cruel season, crowd around
The winnowing store, and claim the little boon
Which Providence assigns them. One alone,
The redbreast, sacred to the household gods,
Wisely regardful of th' embroiling sky,
In joyless fields and thorny thickets, leaves
His shivering mates, and pays to trusted man
His annual visit. Half afraid, he first
Against the window beats ; then, brisk, alights
On the warm hearth ; then, hopping o'er the floor,
Eyes all the smiling family askance,
And pecks and starts, and wonders where he is :
Till, more familiar grown, the table-crumbs
Attract his slender feet. The foodless wilds
Pour forth their brown inhabitants. The hare,
Though timorous of heart, and hard beset
By death in various forms, dark snares and dogs,
And more unpitying men, the garden seeks,

> Urged on by fearless want. The bleating kind
> Eye the bleak heaven, and next the glistening earth,
> With looks of dumb despair ; then, sad-dispersed,
> Dig for the withered herb through heaps of snow."

The "Seasons" deserve to be read with care, and if allowance is made for some peculiarities of style, cannot fail, I think, to be read with pleasure.* Thomson's blank verse has the merit of originality, and in an age that acknowledged the sway of Dryden and Pope, and was accustomed to the music of the heroic couplet, it showed no small boldness and power to choose a new path to poetic fame. The only poet of much note during that period—the first half of the eighteenth century—who also employed blank verse, was Edward Young, the once famous author of the "Night Thoughts," a poem full of great thoughts, but ruined by execrable taste, of which the first three books and the ninth will best repay the labour of perusal. I cannot think Young was much indebted to Thomson for his style—the faults of it are different, and so are the merits ; but other and minor poets of that age—for example, Armstrong, in his "Art of Preserving Health," and Dyer, in "The Fleece," a poem warmly praised by Wordsworth—have felt the influence of the

Edward Young. 1684-1765.

John Armstrong. 1709-1779.

John Dyer. 1698?-1758.

---

* The hymn with which the poem closes may be compared with Adam's morning hymn in "Paradise Lost," and with Coleridge's "Hymn in the Valley of Chamouni." Thomson's hymn is inferior to Milton's and to Coleridge's, but it is an impressive poem and ends nobly.

"Seasons." Still more in matter than in style does Thomson deserve to be called the founder of a school. He brought men back to "Nature, the vicar of the Almighty Lord;" he taught them how much there is in the common sights and sounds of country life—or rather what they in their ignorance called common—that is full of beauty and of poetry; and thus he awakened a feeling of which there is no trace in the great poets—for great they are, in spite of this deficiency—who sat, in the judgment of that age, upon the highest seats of Parnassus.

A word or two must be said, before parting with this true poet, about what some critics deem his greatest achievement—"The Castle of Indolence." This poem, which, as I have stated, was published not long before his death, is written in the Spenserian stanza. As the title implies, it is a dreamy poem, full of lovely imagery and flute-like music—a poem which charms us by the sweetness of versification and of fancy, while leaving no very strong impression on the mind.* The first book especially is in every line a poet's work, and yet, unless my judgment or prejudice be at fault, the poem is too shadowy and unsubstantial to afford complete satisfaction. The reader does not care to keep it by him—does not return to it again and again, in order to secure some passage

---

* Gray's fine ear for musical verse does not seem to have been much charmed by Thomson's rhythm; for he gives to the "Castle of Indolence" the cold praise of containing "some good stanzas."

floating dimly in the memory. Yet here, too, as
in the "Seasons," there is a largeness of conception, an expansiveness of thought, which prove
that the imagination of Thomson was a faculty
by no means cabined and confined.

[The "Seasons" and "Castle of Indolence" are published in
countless editions, and may be bought for a few pence. Thomson's
poetical works, which contain much that young readers will not
care to look at, fill two volumes of the cheap Aldine series. A suggestive essay on Thomson will be found in the "Recreations of
Christopher North," and Mr. Saintsbury's appreciative criticism in
Professor Ward's "Selections" does ample justice to the special
merits of the poet. Read also Hazlitt's judgment of Thomson in
his "Lectures on the English Poets." George Bell and Sons.]

CHAPTER X.

THE GEORGIAN POETS.

Thomas Gray and William Collins.

Two years before the death of Pope, Thomas Gray first gave public proof of his genius as a poet, and the very year of Pope's death witnessed the advent in London Thomas Gray, 1716-1771. of "a literary adventurer, with many projects in his head and very little money in his pocket." No poets could be less indebted to their illustrious predecessors. They took an independent course, and gave a new impulse to English verse. Gray and Collins were great lyric poets in an age scarcely qualified to appreciate this William Collins, 1720-1756. noble gift, but to both ample justice has been done since. The bulk of their poetical works is very inconsiderable, and you may read in an hour or two all that they have written worthy of immortality. For slight as is the productiveness of these poets, the work they have left behind them

Q

is by no means wholly of the highest order.   The pure gold of their poetry occupies a tiny casket, but it is one of the rarest value.

Of the two, Gray is chronologically the foremost, and he is also the better known.   He has written the most popular poem in the language, and some charming letters, which, without being pedantic or laboured, are of the finest literary flavour.*   In his love of nature, and in his accurate observation of natural objects, Gray showed an affinity to the poets of our century ; in his careful regard to form, and in his use of what may be called the current poetical diction, he proved himself in harmony with his own.   His life was that of a laborious student. He read much but wrote little, and his vast learning, which is said to have been alike extensive and profound, had the effect perhaps of repressing his creative power.†   He felt strongly the limitation of his genius.   " If I do not write much," he said to Horace Walpole, " it is because I cannot."

Thomas Gray was born in London on the 26th of December, 1716.   He was educated at Eton, and was in due course admitted a pensioner of Pembroke College, Cambridge.   He is said to have left the university without taking a degree, and on the invitation of Horace Walpole travelled with him

---

* "Gray's letters," said Rogers, "have for me an inexpressible charm ; they are as witty as Walpole's, and have what his want— true wisdom."

† When his friend Nicholls expressed astonishment at the extent of his learning, Gray replied, " Why should you be surprised ?—for I do nothing else."

as his companion in France and Italy. A quarrel separated the friends, the fault of which Walpole generously acknowledged. He said that the poet was too serious a companion for him. " Gray was for antiquities, whilst I was for perpetual balls and plays. The fault was mine." Gray returned home by slow stages to find, on the death of his spendthrift father, that he could not afford to follow the profession designed for him—that of a lawyer. His true vocation was "to scorn delights," or rather to seek for his delights, as so many men have done, in patient and constant study. In 1741 he seems to have fixed his residence in Cambridge, and within the precincts of a university which has few worthier sons than he, the famous poet died in 1771, a few days before the birth of Sir Walter Scott. You remember that the spot which suggested the "Elegy" was Stoke Pogis churchyard, and there, appropriately enough, Gray was buried. He rests, as Mr. William Rosetti finely says, " on the scene of his greatest triumph, like a warrior on his final and victorious battle-field."

" A great wit," says Cowley, " is no more tied to live in a vast volume than in a gigantic body ; on the contrary, it is commonly more vigorous the less space it animates." The general truth of this statement is open to question—our greatest writers have almost always been prolific writers ; but it is singularly applicable to Gray and also to Collins. The " Elegy written in a Country Churchyard " has a charm which appeals to all hearts. The poet said that the popularity of the piece was due to its sub-ject, and he did not regard it as his finest work. Criticism has exhausted itself on a poem which every English reader knows and loves ; but I may observe that if Gray's muse rose, as some critics imagine, to higher flights in " The Bard " and in " The Progress of Poesy," the imperfection of those poems, as well as of his minor odes, is not less obvious than their beauty.　Gray did not venture in his lyrics to use simple words for simple things, and he too often substituted for poetical thoughts the diction that was then regarded as poetical. Thus, in his ode " On the Spring," he writes of " rosy-bosom'd hours," of " fair Venus' train," and of " cool zephyrs ; " and in his fine ode " On a Dis-tant Prospect of Eton College," the trundling of a hoop is translated into " chasing the rolling circle's speed."　His description of the hope and joy of youth, as exemplified in the careless childhood of Eton boys, is beautiful, and would be more so were it not for the error in the second line.　We cannot, as Rogers has pointed out, be said to *possess* hope.

> " Gay hope is theirs by fancy fed,
>   Less pleasing when possest ;
> The tear forgot as soon as shed,
>   The sunshine of the breast :
> Theirs buxom health, of rosy hue,
> Wild wit, invention ever new,
>   And lively cheer, of vigour born ;
> The thoughtless day, the easy night,
> The spirits pure, the slumbers light,
>   That fly th' approach of morn."

But happy schoolboys are said to be happy only
because they are ignorant, and " the little victims
play, regardless of their doom." Here is the future
in store for them as prophesied by the poet—

"These shall the fury Passions tear,
　　The vultures of the mind,
　Disdainful Anger, pallid Fear,
　　And Shame that skulks behind ;
　Or pining Love shall waste their youth,
　Or Jealousy with rankling tooth
　　That inly gnaws the secret heart ;
　And Envy wan and faded Care,
　Grim-visaged comfortless Despair,
　　And Sorrow's piercing dart."

Impersonations of this kind were at one time
highly popular in poetry, and Gray regarded them
as part of his stock when trading as a poet. Another part of a poet's business in those days was to
make classical allusions, and in this department of
his art Gray, being a master of all learning, is
often extremely happy ; these allusions, however,
are so frequent that, in the judgment of modern
readers, they are apt to appear tedious and pedantic.
Gray had in him the true feeling of the lyrist, but
his genius was not sufficiently spontaneous. It
was his misfortune to live in an age when art was
exalted at the expense of nature, and sometimes
the scholar takes precedence of the poet.

The two principal odes should be read by the
young reader in an annotated edition, so that he
may readily understand the allusions with which
those poems abound, and be reminded of parallel

passages.   Gray owes many debts to his predecessors, both ancient and modern, but the use that he
makes of their poems is legitimate.   He does not
steal his gold, but, like a skilful workman, converts
what is often a rough nugget into an exquisite
form of beauty.   Plagiarists are men who, having
few ideas of their own, pilfer from their neighbours ;
the true poet appropriates only to improve.   The
commentators describe with rather wearisome prolixity the use the poet makes of his learning in the
"Elegy," but it is none the less true that it is to his
genius and not to his knowledge that we owe that
transcendently beautiful poem.   Gray led a retired,
leisurely life.   He loved nature and he loved books ;
but to onlookers it might have seemed as if this
greatly accomplished man had buried himself self-
ishly in a cloistered cell.   What had he done for
his fellowmen ? was the question put, no doubt, and
perhaps not unreasonably, by some active workers
of his day.   A century has gone by and the answer
is not difficult.   All honour to the man who endows
a college or a hospital, but the man who writes a
noble poem like the "Elegy" has also surely done
his work in the world, and merits not our praise
alone but our gratitude.

William Collins has written no poem that has
gained the popularity achieved by Gray.   His
work is of exquisite quality, but it is too delicate,
too subtle, too remote from the common walks of
life, to win the sympathies of the general reader.
It will excite wonder rather than love, and, to quote

the words of Dr. Johnson, "may sometimes extort praise when it gives little pleasure." No student of our poetry, however, can afford to overlook Collins. If he have some of the faults of his age, he rises above the age, and may claim brotherhood with poets who, like Shelley and Keats, are the freest from prosaic qualities.

He was born at Chichester in 1720, and at the age of thirteen was admitted scholar of Winchester College. Seven years later he went up to Oxford as commoner of Queen's, where he was "distinguished for genius and indolence," and shortly afterwards was elected a demy of Magdalen. He suddenly left the university upon taking his bachelor's degree, and tried his fortune in London as "a literary adventurer." A more thankless employment for a man whose brain was teeming with bright fancies can scarcely be imagined. Like his friend Samuel Johnson, Collins had to fight for a bare subsistence. Truly and feelingly does his biographer say that "a man doubtful of his dinner, or trembling at a creditor, is not much disposed to abstracted meditation or remote inquiries." Johnson's invincible courage and untiring perseverance—qualities which, above all others, ensure success in life—were not known to Collins. He lacked resolution, and yielded too readily to the allurements of London. He is said to have been an acceptable companion everywhere, and at the coffee-houses he was welcomed by the wits of the town. Genius without strength of character is always a danger to its possessor, and

Collins failed to see that the rest and joy of life
are to be found only in the path of duty. A legacy
of £2000 removed opportunely the "unconquerable
bar" of poverty, but the poet had now a worse
enemy to encounter, a deeper suffering to bear.
He became insane, and, with rare intervals of sanity,
suffered from this direful malady for the rest of his
brief existence. "Poor dear Collins," as Johnson
affectionately called him, had his life wrecked at
the moment when it seemed most prosperous. "I
knew him a few years ago," wrote the doctor to
Joseph Warton, "full of hopes and full of projects,
versed in many languages, high in fancy and strong
in retention. This busy and forcible mind is now
under the government of those who lately would
not have been able to comprehend the least and
most narrow of its designs." Collins tried in the
first place to overcome his depression by travel,
but the attempt proved to be a vain one. After his
return from France, Johnson states that he paid
him a visit at Islington. "There was then nothing
of disorder discernible in his mind by any but
himself; but he had withdrawn from study, and
travelled with no other book than an English
Testament, such as children carry to the school.
When his friend took it into his hand out of
curiosity, to see what companion a man of letters
had chosen, 'I have but one book,' said Collins,
'but that is the best.'" Having discovered a truth
which so many fail to apprehend, it seems a folly
to deplore the broken life and early death of this

illustrious poet, who died in Chichester, the city of
his birth, at the early age of thirty-six.   A monument to his memory by Flaxman was erected in
the cathedral.

Collins has been called a minor poet, but, as
Sir Egerton Brydges has pointed out, this is a sad
misapplication of the term.   "Unless," he writes,
"he be minor because the number and size of his
poems is small, no one is less a minor poet.   In
him every word is poetry, and poetry either sublime
or pathetic. . . . He has a visionary invention of
his own, to which there is no rival.   As long as
the language lasts, every richly gifted and richly
cultivated mind will read him with intense ·and
wondering rapture."   This opinion, written many
years ago, is sanctioned by the most recent criticism.
Mr. Swinburne may justly claim to be a judge
of lyric poetry, and he has expressed his conviction
that Collins was the one man of his time who had
in him a note of pure lyric song.   "Poetry was
his by birthright; to the very ablest of his compeers
it was never more than a christening gift.   The
Muse gave birth to Collins ; she did but give suck
to Gray. . . . His range of flight was perhaps the
narrowest, but assuredly the highest of his generation.   He could not be caught singing like a finch ;
but he struck straight upward for the sun, like a
lark. . ·. . He was a solitary song-bird among many
more or less excellent pipers and pianists.   He
could put more spirit of colour into a single stroke,
more breath of music into a single note, than could

all the rest of his generation into all the labours of their lives." *

This enthusiastic praise must be accepted with some deductions. Dr. Johnson could not properly estimate the power of Collins as a singer ; but he was one of the shrewdest of critics, and has hit a blot in his friend's poetry when he writes that "his diction was often harsh, unskilfully laboured, and injudiciously selected." His imagery is occasionally obscure and his mannerism offensive, so that the reader is conscious of a want, and cannot surrender himself unreservedly to the charm of the verse. Of Collins's "Oriental Eclogues" I need say little. These Eclogues belong to an artificial form of poetry which, strange to say, possessed some attraction for writers and readers in the last century. To us the matter and the manner are alike obsolete. They are not a true picture of the life they pretend to represent, and have no charm as English verse. Perhaps, as is so often the case, the poet's simplest and least ambitious poems are those to which we turn most frequently and with the greatest pleasure. We admire "The Passions," and the still more ambitious "Ode on the Popular Superstitions of the Highlands of Scotland ;" but the incomparable "Ode to Evening," the lines, twelve in number, dedicated to the brave men who died for their country, and in a lesser degree the "Dirge in Cymbeline," and the "Ode on the Death of Thomson,"

---

* "The English Poets : Selections," edited by T. H. Ward. M.A. vol. iii.

are among the treasures of memory. Lengthened
illustrations of a poet's worth would be wholly
out of place in a volume which has neither the
merits nor the defects of an anthology, but short
poems of rarest beauty it is always an advantage
to quote, and for two reasons : they relieve the
inevitable monotony of criticism, and they exhibit
as no criticism can, the characteristics of a poet's
genius.

If there be any youthful student who has never
yet opened the little volume that contains the
masterpieces of Collins, let him, before doing so,
read with the attention they merit the two following poems. He will note that the "Ode to
Evening" is written in blank verse, and it is, as far
I know, the only instance in our literature in which
a lyric piece has been perfectly successful without
the aid of rhyme.

> "If aught of oaten stop, or pastoral song,
>   May hope, chaste Eve, to soothe thy modest ear,
>   Like thy own brawling springs,
>   Thy springs and dying gales ; .
>
> "O Nymph reserved, while now the bright-haired sun
>   Sits in yon western tent, whose cloudy skirts,
>   With brede ethereal wove,
>   O'erhang his wavy bed :
>
> " Now air is hushed, save where the weak-eyed bat,
>   With short shrill shriek flits by on leathern wing ;
>   Or where the beetle winds
>   His small but sullen horn,

" As oft he rises 'midst the twilight path,
   Against the pilgrim borne in heedless hum :
      Now teach me, Maid composed,
      To breathe some softened strain,

" Whose numbers, stealing through thy darkening vale,
   May, not unseemly, with its stillness suit ;
      As, musing slow, I hail
      Thy genial loved return !

" For when thy folding-star arising shows
   His paly circlet, at his warning lamp
      The fragrant Hours, and Elves
      , Who slept in flowers the day,

" And many a Nymph who wreathes her brows with sedge,
   And sheds the freshening dew, and lovelier still,
      The pensive Pleasures sweet,
      Prepare thy shadowy car.

" Then let me rove some wild and heathy scene,
   Or find some ruin, 'midst its dreary dells,
      Whose walls more awful nod
      By thy religious gleams.

" Or, if chill blustering winds, or driving rain,
   Prevent my willing feet, be mine the hut,
      That from the mountain's side
      Views wilds, and swelling floods,

" And hamlets brown, and dim-discovered spires,
   And hears their simple bell, and marks o'er all
      Thy dewy fingers draw
      The gradual dusky veil.

"While Spring shall pour his showers, as oft he wont,
And bathe thy breathing tresses, meekest Eve !
    While Summer loves to sport
    Beneath thy lingering light ;

"While sallow Autumn fills thy lap with leaves ;
Or Winter, yelling through the troublous air,
    Affrights thy shrinking train,
    And rudely rends thy robes ;

"So long, regardful of thy quiet rule,
Shall Fancy, Friendship, Science, smiling Peace,
    Thy gentlest influence own,
    And love thy favourite name." *

The following exquisite lines, "written in the
beginning of the year 1746," refer, no doubt, to some
skirmish with the Pretender, who seized Stirling
Castle in the month of January. It is scarcely
possible, however, that they were suggested by
General Hamley's attempt to raise the siege, for
that commander was not only defeated with much
loss, but is said to have made a hasty and disgraceful retreat to Edinburgh.

"How sleep the brave, who sink to rest,
By all their country's wishes blessed ?
When Spring, with dewy fingers cold,
Returns to deck their hallowed mould ;
She there shall dress a sweeter sod
Than Fancy's feet have ever trod.

"By fairy hands their knell is rung ;
By forms unseen their dirge is sung ;

---

* "Two of the most enchanting lyrics in our language," said
Rogers, "are Collins's 'Ode to Evening,' and Coleridge's 'Love.'"

> There Honour comes, a pilgrim gray,
> To bless the turf that wraps their clay ;
> And Freedom shall awhile repair,
> To dwell a weeping hermit there."

Had Collins written nothing beyond the two odes I have quoted, his fame as a poet would be secure. It is strange that Gray, his contemporary and rival, should have failed to discern his supremacy as a lyrist. He classes him with **Thomas Warton, 1728-1790.** Thomas Warton, a minor poet of some merit, and a critic of high reputation, and writes as if the two men occupied the same platform. This opinion was not due to any feeling of jealousy. Gray was a modest man, and if he was mistaken in his judgment of Collins, he was equally mistaken in the estimate of his own powers. He died, said his friend Bonstetten, without a suspicion of the high rank he was destined to hold amongst the poets of his country. The genius of Collins is distinct from that of Gray. The least known is the greater lyric poet, but will never be the best beloved. They are alike in learning, in their sensibility to the beauties of nature—a feeling unknown to Pope ; in the art with which they built up their lofty rhyme ; in the aspirations which lifted them into a region never to be reached by the poetical moralists of the age.

[The biographies of Gray and Collins should be read in Johnson's "Lives." Johnson knew Collins, and appreciated him as a man if not as a poet. He had no personal intercourse with Gray, and is unjust to his poetry ; but Johnson, even at his worst—and his life

of Gray is the least satisfactory of the series—has always something
to say that is worth reading. Gray's poems are to be met with in
every variety of form. His works, including the letters, and edited
by the Rev. John Mitford, were published in five volumes by the
late Mr. Pickering, who knew better than any publisher of his day
how to produce the poets in an edition worthy of their merit. The
poems, apart from the prose, can be obtained in the cheap but
beautiful Aldine series now published by Messrs. Bell and Sons, in
which series the student can also secure a Collins. Mr. Gosse,
whose competency for such a task is beyond question, has written a
masterly account of Gray in the series of " English Men of Letters ; "
and Mr. Matthew Arnold (in Ward's " English Poets ") writes an
interesting essay on the poet, taking for his text four words written
by Gray's executor a fortnight after his death—" *He never spoke out.*"
I may add that Gray's " Odes " and " Elegy," with introduction and
notes, can be bought for a few pence in Chambers's cheap reprints
of English classics.]

CHAPTER XI.

THE GEORGIAN POETS (*Continued*).

WILLIAM COWPER.

IN 1761, Charles Churchill was the most popular poet in England. In 1764 he died, and the satires which gave him such sudden popularity were as speedily forgotten. He appealed, it has been well said, "to the passion of the moment," and when that passion passed his fame died with it. His name, however, will always have some attraction for the student, since his schoolfellow, William Cowper, formed his style as a satirist upon that of the "great Churchill." Churchill was never great, although Cowper deemed him so; but there is a vigour and boldness in his lines which give them a special character, and their roughness was attractive at a time when, instead of the fine grain of poetry, the public were forced to be satisfied with the polish of veneer.*

---

* "A critic of the present day," says Cowper, "serves a poem as a cook serves a dead turkey, when she fastens the legs of it to

When this "comet of a season" disappeared, Cowper was thirty-three years old, and was suffering under the madness-cloud which made his life so pathetic. No one who knew him in that time of anguish could have imagined that he was destined to become one of the most popular of English poets. He was born at Great Berkhampstead, in 1731, of which parish his father was rector. His mother, a **William Cowper, 1731-1800.** descendant of the poet Donne, died when William was six years old, but the memory of her love clung to him through life, and fifty-three years after her death the receipt of her portrait called forth what has been well termed the most touching elegy in the language. The boy's early life was far from happy, or possibly the after-gloom coloured his remembrance of it. From a private school he was sent to Westminster, and placed under Vincent Bourne, whose Latin verses he afterwards translated. Among his schoolfellows was Warren Hastings, and when, at eighteen, he was articled to an attorney, his fellow-clerk was Thurlow, the future Lord Chancellor. "Cowper felt that Thurlow would reach the summit of ambition, while he would remain below, and made his friend promise,

---

a post and draws out all the sinews. For this we may thank Pope ; but unless we could imitate him in the closeness and compactness of his expression, as well as in the smoothness of his numbers, we had better drop the imitation, which serves no other purpose than to emasculate and weaken all we write. Give me a manly rough line, with a deal of meaning in it, rather than a whole poem full of musical periods that have nothing but their oily smoothness to recommend them."

R

when he was chancellor, to give him something. When Thurlow was chancellor, he gave Cowper his advice in translating Homer." Cowper says that he spent those days in giggling and making giggle with his cousins Theodora and Harriet Cowper ; but if he neglected law, he devoted himself to literature, and the study bore good fruit in after years. His earliest verses were written to Theodora. The two appear to have been warmly attached, but their marriage, which was forbidden by the girl's father, soon became impossible on other grounds. The affectionate Theodorà remained single, probably for the sake of her first love, in whom she never ceased to be interested. At thirty-two Cowper lost his reason, and was removed to an asylum kept by the good Dr. Cotton, who had himself considerable popularity as a verse-maker. There he remained several months, and left, not only in apparent sanity, but believing that he had undergone a great spiritual change, or, in the language of Scripture, had "passed from death unto life." He settled for a time in Huntingdon, where he made the acquaintance of the Unwins, "the most agreeable people imaginable," whose names are destined to live as long as Cowper is remembered. Under their roof the future poet lived happily for some time, and on the death of Mr. Unwin remained with his widow, whose behaviour "had always been that of a mother to a son." They resolved, unfortunately for Cowper's health and spirits, to live at Olney, in the least healthy part of an unhealthy town, and it was in some respects unfortunate also that the clergyman of Olney was the celebrated John Newton. His robust piety and courageous nature might have been of help to Cowper had not Newton expected from him more service, as a lay-curate, than he could with safety perform. He lost his reason a second time, and his insanity was of the most painful kind. Work was the one unfailing resource ; so he made rabbit-hutches, kept tame hares, built frames for hotbeds, wrote letters—the most beautiful, surely, in the language—and afterwards, at Mrs. Unwin's instigation, turned poet. He was nearly fifty years old, an age at which many poets have done with singing, when he published the series of satires known as " Table Talk," " The Progress of Error," " Truth," " Expostulation," " Hope," " Charity," " Conversation," and " Retirement." There are passages in these poems which scarcely rise above the level of prose ; there are passages which are not only weak but intolerant. Cowper was not fettered by his Christianity, but by his Calvinism, for the exposition of dogma is out of place in poetry. The poems are faulty, yet there are traces in them of the exquisite ease and charm of style that mark so many of Cowper's occasional poems, and there are satirical passages which show the hand of a master. At its best his satire is, as Christopher North called it, sublime ; and Mr. Benham, in his introduction to the Globe edition of Cowper, is, I think, right in saying that, of these poems, the stinging satire is the most telling feature. The poet's justly great reputation, however, does not rest upon these pieces.

If we owe the satires to Mrs. Unwin's suggestion, our debt of gratitude to Lady Austen is far greater, for to her we are indebted for the "Task," and for "John Gilpin." The lively friendship that sprang up between the poet and this charming woman is one of the few bright passages in a melancholy career. She inspired him as a poet and cheered him as a man, but "Sister Anne's" enthusiastic affection did not quite harmonize with the long-tried, self-sacrificing love of Mrs. Unwin, and it was found best that the lady should say farewell. Cowper was more than consoled for this loss by the arrival of his "dearest coz," Lady Hesketh, the sister of his old love, Theodora. Her presence was as refreshing as a shower on the early green of April. She came like a ministering angel, and the light she left behind her is reflected in the poet's incomparable letters. The removal from Olney to Weston, "a place in the neighbourhood, but on higher ground, more cheerful, and in better air," was her work. Here the poet occupied himself with the translation of Homer, which lightened many hours of misery, for the old foe pursued him to the new abode. "This notable job," he wrote, "is the delight of my heart, and how sorry shall I be when it is ended!" His mental fever increased rather than diminished as the end approached. Mrs. Unwin, known to all readers as "my Mary," died of paralysis, and Cowper lived on for more than three years in the profoundest depression. It was during this time of gloom, and in the belief that his life was spiritually shipwrecked, that he wrote "The Castaway," the finest and saddest of his lyrics. He died on the 25th of April, 1800.

Every one who knew Cowper spoke of him with affection, and since his death he has been always regarded with a peculiar tenderness.* "Sad as his story is," says Southey, "it is not altogether mournful. He had never to complain of injustice, nor of injuries, nor even of neglect—these had no part in bringing on his calamity ; and to that very calamity which made him leave the herd like 'a stricken deer' it was owing that the genius which has consecrated his name, which has made him the most popular poet of the age, and secures that popularity from fading away, was developed in retirement. It would have been blighted had he continued in the course for which he was brought up. He would not have found the way to fame unless he had missed the way to fortune."

As a poet Cowper's position is remarkable. He may be said to stand between the dead and the living. Whatever was of vital force in the poetry of the eighteenth century had died out ; the fulness of poetic life that enriched the early years of the present century was as yet unanticipated. Cowper came at a happy hour. His aim was to reform the world, and in trying to do this he reformed the art he practised.

---

* Read Mrs. Barrett Browning's poem, "Cowper's Grave.

His originality has never been contested. He chose his own ground, and held it without a rival. His variety is great, and whatever he did is done in a way peculiar to himself. Powerful as a satirist, he is unlike Dryden and Pope, and beyond an occasional roughness of style bears little resemblance to Churchill ; as a moralizer, he differs from Young ; as a descriptive poet, he has a rival, but not a master, in Thomson. His humour is sometimes charming, his pathos is profound ; but neither his humour nor his pathos reminds us of earlier poets. And all readers who have learnt to love Cowper, will confess with sorrow that he stands alone, also, in the narrow and rigid views he formed of life and of the Christian faith. His Calvinism, instilled into a morbidly sensitive mind, dwarfed his charity when he wrote as a theologian, but never stinted his charity as a man. His intellect is sometimes warped by his creed ; his heart is ever open as day to all humanizing influences.

Cowper wrote a great deal more verse than is likely to win attention in the present day, and much of his " poetical baggage," to quote Mr Arnold's phrase, might be thrown aside without loss. It seems strange to read his assurances that he bestowed upon his poetry the utmost care, and never allowed a slovenly line to escape him. His ear must have been in fault, or he must have mistaken carelessness for ease. His rhyming satires bear many signs of negligence, and even the " Task," full of beauty though it be, is by no means a model of

poetic art. One of its prominent charms is natural-
ness ; neither in diction nor in thought is it in the
least degree conventional. The poet may be said
to talk with his readers, and the talk is charming.
The shyest of men grew sociable and even egotistic
when he took the pen in hand, and of such egotism
one cannot well have too much. It is this that
makes the " Task " a poem so much more delightful than the " Seasons "—this chiefly, but combined
with other reasons which the student of the two
poems will not fail to discover. Thomson's instinct
for what is poetical in natural objects is as true as
Cowper's, and occasionally he rises to a height never
reached by the Olney poet, but in variety of gifts
Cowper surpasses him. He is as successful in his
lyrics as in his descriptive poetry, and writes occasional verses with inimitable ease. Thomson, on
the other hand, if we except the praise due to the
dreamy sweetness of his Spenserian poem, lives by
his descriptive work alone. He has no humour, no
lyrical power, no pathos, no genius as a satirist ; and
in a general estimate of the two men, it would be
obvious to add that while Thomson blunders when
he writes prose, there are critics who think that the
letters of Cowper are even more delightful than his
poetry.

The " Task," which consists of six books written
in blank verse, is one of the most readable of poems.
Southey says that the best didactic poems, when
compared with it, " are like formal gardens in comparison with woodland scenery." It may be called

homely poetry, appealing less to poets and to men
of large culture than to the intelligence and sympathy of the general reader.   True to the life
familiar to us all, it has few indications of the subtle
thought and lofty imagination which electrify us in
great poets.   Unlike Wordsworth, Cowper never
lifts us out of ourselves ; he has none of those
" winged words" which so haunt the memory,
that they seem to become the property of the
reader as much as of the poet.   Such gifts belong to the imperial masters of song ; but Cowper,
although occupying a lower position, has gifts of no
mean order, and in much that he has written there
is a beauty which time is not likely to wither.

Mr. Lowell has said with truth, that Cowper
"is still the best of our descriptive poets for
every-day wear."   The "Task" is his most notable
work.   It is a discursive poem needing little of
explanation or criticism.   In some passages, as I
have said, the note of prejudice and bigotry offends
the reader.   To enter a theatre, to play at chess or
billiards, is fatally to lose the creeping hours of
time ; but it is no waste of time to devote an
evening

> " To weaving nets for bird-alluring fruit,
> Or twining silken threads round ivory reels."

The astronomer, who attempts to " scale the heavens
by strides of human wisdom ;" the geologist, who
drills and bores the solid earth to discover its age,
are described as wasting

> " The little wick of life's poor shallow lamp
>   In playing tricks with nature ; "

and it would seem as if the poet thought it a more
profitable employment to wander about under trees
and to raise cucumbers. Nature, he admits, is all
enchanting and divine, but to search nature with
scientific curiosity is to spend life " all for smoke."
Foolish rant like this creates a momentary feeling
of indignation, which soon gives way to pity. The
" Task " is, however, too fine a poem to be much
injured by imperfections which are comparatively
trivial, and for the greater part of it a reader whose
taste has not been vitiated will feel the strongest
sympathy. It grows in beauty as it advances, and
the " Sofa," the " Timepiece," and the " Garden "
are distinctly inferior to the " Winter Evening," the
" Winter Morning Walk," and the " Winter Walk
at Noon." Indeed, the latter books may without
detriment be read first. They contain the cream
of Cowper's verse.

The " Winter Evening " opens auspiciously with
the familiar picture of the post-boy, who brings
" news from all nations lumbering at his back,"
and the contrast between the wintry landscape
outside and the curtains and cheerful parlour
scene within is eminently characteristic of the
poet. So, too, is the invocation to Winter that
follows, and Cowper's art in describing poetically
a scene which all of us have witnessed year after
year is displayed in the following passage—

> " How calm is my recess ; and how the frost,
>   Raging abroad, and the rough wind, endear

The silence and the warmth enjoyed within !
I saw the woods and fields at close of day
A variegated show ; the meadows green,
Though faded ; and the lands, where lately waved
The golden harvest, of a mellow brown,
Upturned so lately by the forceful share.
I saw far off the weedy fallows smile
With verdure not unprofitable, grazed
By flocks, fast feeding, and selecting each
His favourite herb ; while all the leafless groves
That skirt the horizon, wore a sable hue,
Scarce noticed in the kindred dusk of eve.
To-morrow brings a change, a total change !
Which even now, though silently performed,
And slowly, and by most unfelt, the face
Of universal nature undergoes.
Fast falls a fleecy shower : the downy flakes
Descending, and with never-ceasing lapse,
Softly alighting upon all below,
Assimilate all objects.   Earth receives
Gladly the thickening mantle ; and the green
And tender blade that feared the chilling blast,
Escapes unhurt beneath so warm a veil."

Cowper is always true when he describes natural
objects, he is often false when he moralizes.   It is
a poetical fallacy to write, as he writes in this book,
of the greater security, simplicity, and purity of a
past age.   His readers may justly ask, What age ?
And to assert that

"The course of human things from good to ill,
From ill to worse, is fatal, never fails,"

is to show not only an ignorance of history but a
distrust of Providence.*   This is a blot upon a

* Cowper's creed did not allow him to anticipate the steady
progress of the race.   The change he hoped for was one foretold by

poem that ends delightfully with an affectionate
expression of attachment to a country life.   In
the "Winter Morning Walk" the poet attains
perhaps his highest altitude.   It is altogether worthy
of him, not only for its wonderful freshness and
accuracy of description, but for the unaffected expression of devotional feeling and of a passionate
attachment to liberty.   His rural pictures here are
singularly vivid.   One, and one only, shall be trans-
ferred to these pages.   It will serve as a companion picture to the winter piece already extracted
from the "Seasons."

> "The cattle mourn in corners where the fence
> Screens them, and seem half petrified to sleep
> In unrecumbent sadness.   There they wait
> Their wonted fodder ; not like hungering man,
> Fretful if unsupplied, but silent, meek,
> And patient of the slow-paced swain's delay.
> He from the stack carves out the accustomed load
> Deep-plunging, and again deep-plunging oft,
> His broad keen knife into the solid mass :
> Smooth as a wall the upright remnant stands,
> With such undeviating and even force
> He severs it away :   .   .   .   .
> Forth goes the woodman, leaving unconcerned
> The cheerful haunts of man, to wield the axe

---

prophecy, and to be accomplished directly by the hand of God.   In
a passage rising to the high-water mark of poetry, he sees as in a
vision the glory of a world from which sorrow and sin are banished,
and in which

> "All creatures worship man, and all mankind
>   One Lord, one Father."

This noble effort of his Muse will be found in the "Winter Walk
at Noon."

And drive the wedge in yonder forest drear,
From morn to eve his solitary task.   ,
Shaggy, and lean, and shrewd, with pointed ears,
And tail cropped short, half lurcher and half cur,
His dog attends him.   Close behind his heel
Now creeps he slow ; and now, with many a frisk
Wide-scampering, snatches up the drifted snow
With ivory teeth, or ploughs it with his snout ;
Then shakes his powdered coat, and barks for joy.
Heedless of all his pranks, the sturdy churl
Moves right toward the mark ; nor stops for aught,
But now and then with pressure of his thumb
To adjust the fragrant charge of a short tube,
That fumes beneath his nose : the trailing cloud
Streams far behind him, scenting all the air."

A great portrait painter best shows his art in giving permanency on canvas to some characteristic expression ; the descriptive poet shows his art in presenting a familiar scene so that its verisimilitude is instantly recognized.   Nature has other lessons and aspects for the poet, but it is no mean power to present some of her features with the exactness displayed by Cowper in this and similar passages.   The pleasure we gain from these pictures is due to their truthfulness.   We have seen such scenes again and again, we say, and to have them fixed for us in verse gives reality and colour to our recollections.

There are critics in our day who maintain that art has nothing to do with morality, nor do they shrink from adding that, in order fully to achieve his aim, an artist is justified in being actively immoral.   We are told, for instance, by a writer of this school, that Winckelmann, who joined the Romish Church not from conviction but for his convenience as an artist, " is more than absolved at the bar of the highest criticism." * If morality be a mere matter of social compact, resting upon no divine and steadfast basis, the paramount claims of art upon the artist might allow him to act the part of a hypocrite, since this insincerity would be " only one incident of a culture in which the moral instinct, like the religious or political, was lost in the artistic." We, however, who believe that the world is under the government of an all-wise and all-holy Being, must utterly reject a principle which strikes at the root of that divine order.   At the same time, this belief does not require from painter or poet a direct and prominent inculcation of moral and religious truth.   The artist's first duty is not to preach but to paint, the poet's first duty is to sing ; and such lessons as they have to teach must be in subordination to their art, for thus only will they prove impressive and permanent.   Cowper, it may be admitted, forgetting that he was a poet, too often preached sermons in metre ; but when, instead of preaching, he is content to utter poetically what is in him, we accept his teaching with pleasure.   There is a fine passage in "Comus," in which Milton writes of Wisdom seeking for sweet-retired solitude in which " to plume her feathers and let grow her wings."   A similar thought, no doubt, suggested

---

* " Studies of the History of the Renaissance," by W. H. Pater, p. 157 (Macmillan).

these lines, which are extracted from the sixth book of the "Task." The reader must understand that they are written beneath the trees on a bright day in winter, in the silence of the snow.

> " No noise is here, or none that hinders thought.
> The redbreast warbles still, but is content
> With slender notes, and more than half suppressed :
> Pleased with his solitude, and flitting light
> From spray to spray, where'er he rests he shakes
> From many a twig the pendent drops of ice,
> That tinkle in the withered leaves below.
> Stillness, accompanied with sounds so soft,
> Charms more than silence.   Meditation here
> May think down hours to moments.   Here the heart
> May give a useful lesson to the head,
> And learning wiser grow without his books.
> Knowledge and Wisdom, far from being one,
> Have ofttimes no connexion.   Knowledge dwells
> In heads replete with thoughts of other men ;
> Wisdom in minds attentive to their own.
> Knowledge, a rude unprofitable mass,
> The mere materials with which Wisdom builds,
> Till smoothed, and squared, and fitted to its place,
> Does but encumber whom it seems to enrich.
> Knowledge is proud that he has learned so much ;
> Wisdom is humble that he knows no more."

As a lyric poet, Cowper's gifts are tenderness of feeling, simplicity of expression, and a playfulness which is all the more winning as coming from the saddest of poets.   He is never highly musical, unless it be when expressing a strong emotion, and his habit of reflection forbids the birdlike bursts of song that haunt the ear with their melody.   Read

the exquisite lines " To Mary," the sonnet addressed
to her, " Boadicea," " On the Loss of the Royal
George," " The Poplar Field," and " The Castaway," and you will be able to appreciate the
variety as well as limitation of Cowper's gifts as a
lyrist. These poems are all serious and beautiful, but Cowper—witness the " Faithful Bird," the
" Epitaph on a Hare," and the " Jackdaw "—also
wrote with incomparable ease about trifles ; and that
he could excel as a balladist needs no argument,
since everybody has read " John Gilpin." I do not
think with Mr. Goldwin Smith that Cowper took
to translating Homer under an evil star. It gave
him the steady occupation that he needed, and
lightened many an hour of sorrow. The work was
intellectual enough to occupy his mind, and at the
same time sufficiently mechanical to divert it ; and
no one who reads the poet's letters can question
the relief it afforded. But if the labour were a
benefit to the workman, was it good also for the
world ? On this point the opinions of competent
critics differ widely. Cowper was a sounder scholar
than Pope, and his version is universally allowed
to be more accurate than any which preceded it.
Mr. Goldwin Smith declares that while Pope delights schoolboys, Cowper delights nobody—an
assertion which will be vehemently contradicted by
many readers. If they want authorities to back
their favourable judgment they may refer to Thomas
Campbell, who expressed his admiration of Cowper's
Homer, and said that he used to read it to his wife,

who was moved to tears by some passages of it.
And the judgment of the author of " The Pleasures
of Hope " was expressed with equal warmth by the
author of " The Pleasures of Memory." " My father,"
said Rogers, " used to recommend Pope's Homer to
me ; but with all my love of Pope, I never could
like it.   I delight in Cowper's Homer ; I have read
it again and again."

[Southey's edition of Cowper, originally published in fifteen volumes
and reprinted in eight volumes (Bohn's Standard Library), is the
best that we possess.   It contains an interesting biography, written
in the pure style of which Southey was so consummate a master.
The poet's correspondence, and his translations of the " Iliad " and
" Odyssey," will be found in this edition.   An able and original
memoir of Cowper, by John Bruce, is prefixed to a beautiful edition
of his poems, with illustrative notes, 3 vols. (Bell and Son).

The Globe Cowper, edited with notes, contains all the original
poems and translations with the exception of the Homer, and has
a short but admirably written biography by the Rev. William
Benham.   Mr. Benham's point of view is, I think, a true one
throughout.   A biography of Cowper has also appeared in " English
Men of Letters," written by Professor Goldwin Smith.]

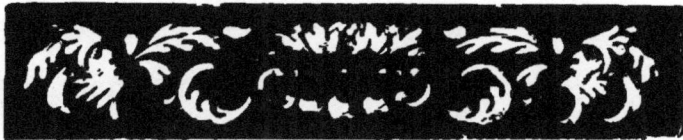

CHAPTER XII.

THE GEORGIAN POETS (*Continued*).

ROBERT BURNS.

COWPER and Burns were contemporaries, and although there was a great gulf of years between them, the poems by which both are remembered were published nearly at the same time. The "Task" appeared in 1784; Burns's first volume was published in 1786. No two men could be more unlike in temperament, in character, in the impulses which prompted their verse; but it has been rightly said that they were poetic brothers in the love of nature, in the sincerity with which they uttered what they felt, in their detestation of hypocrisy and affectation.

The peasant, who

> " Walked in glory and in joy,
> Following his plough upon the mountain-side,"

owes nothing of his fame to his position. In reading Burns we do not think of what he was, but of what

Robert Burns, 1759-1796.

S

he did.   Cowper was conscious of this when people
were treating the Scottish poet as a prodigy, and
affecting to honour him by their patronage.   In
1787 he writes, "I have read Burns's poems, and
have read them twice ; and though they be written
in a language that is new to me, and many of them
on subjects much inferior to the author's ability,
I think them on the whole a very extraordinary
production.   He is, I believe, the only poet these
kingdoms have produced in the lower rank of life
since Shakespeare (I should rather say since Prior),
who need not be indebted for any part of his praise
to a charitable consideration of his origin and
the disadvantages under which he has laboured."
Cowper adds a wish, which probably no one now
shares, that the poet had written in what he calls
pure English, and not in his native dialect.   " Poor
Burns," he says, " loses much of his deserved praise
in this country through our ignorance of his language.   I despair of meeting with any Englishman
who will take the pains that I have taken to understand him.   His candle is bright, but shut up in a
dark lantern.   I lent him to a very sensible neighbour of mine, but his uncouth dialect spoiled all ;
and before he had half read him through he was
quite *ram-feezled*."

Readers unfamiliar with the dialect will not
readily understand some of the expressions used by
Burns.   Even the "Waverley Novels," when the scene
is laid in Scotland, need a glossary, and Burns uses
his native Doric more frequently than Scott.   As a

rule, however, the difficult words in the poet's best poems can readily be mastered without any risk of the student being *ram-feezled*, which is Scottish for "fatigued." I say his best poems, since these alone the student will be advised to study. Urged by men whose lack of Christian charity was more conspicuous than their love of truth, Burns at one time debased his genius by attacking with much humour and much irreverence some of the religious customs of his country. That there is a measure of truth in his satires no one can doubt, and occasionally he struck home with tremendous power. It has been said that these poems exposed hypocrisy, but the Oxford professor of poetry says truly, that the good they may have done in this way is perhaps doubtful, while "the harm they have done in Scotland is not doubtful, in that they have connected in the minds of the people so many coarse and even profane thoughts with objects which they had regarded till then with reverence." Equally to be regretted, on account of their evil influence, are his drinking songs and some of his love songs. Nor is this all. In the exuberance of his animal spirits, and sometimes in the bitterness of his soul, Burns wrote much ranting rubbish and much coarse invective, which the unkind labour of editors has rescued from the oblivion in which the poet would fain have left it. Few men have been granted a stronger intellect than Burns ; he could judge impartially of his work, and it would have vexed him sorely could he have known that the folly, and often worse than folly, of the hour would live side by side with some of the manliest and sweetest verses ever penned by poet.

The story of his life has been frequently told, and never better told, perhaps, than by Lockhart, Scott's son-in-law and biographer, who writes of Scotland's greatest poet with discretion as well as enthusiasm. In our brief summary we shall follow his pages, correcting them here and there by the light of more recent information.

Robert Burns was born January 25, 1759, in a clay-built cottage, erected by his father, on the banks of the Doon, near the town of Ayr. It was partially wrecked by a storm a few days after the poet's birth, and the mother was carried with her infant to the shelter of a neighbouring hovel. Robert was blessed with sensible and God-fearing parents. The beautiful portrait of the father lives for ever in the " Cotter's Saturday Night ; " the mother, " a very sagacious woman," is said to have nourished the imagination of her firstborn son with ballads and traditionary tales. Robert was one of a large family, and from his earliest years became acquainted with poverty and sorrow. Every Scottish peasant, however humble his lot, gets some amount of education. William Burness (for so he spelt his name) fought " one long sore battle with untoward circumstances, ending in defeat," but he did not neglect his children. His two eldest sons, Robert and Gilbert, obtained in the few leisure hours of their young lives a fair amount of what is known to rustics as school-learning. When Robert was six years old his father took a small and poor farm, two miles from the Brig o' Doon, which never repaid the unceasing toil of the owner. At the age of thirteen the boy assisted in threshing the crop of corn, and at fifteen was the principal labourer on the farm. Yet before the close of his sixteenth year he had managed to read a considerable amount of English literature, and to acquire some knowledge of French. His passion for knowledge did not interfere with his daily work in the fields. He never feared a competitor in any kind of rural toil, and Gilbert Burns, "a man of uncommon bodily strength, adds that neither he nor any labourer he ever saw at work was equal to the youthful poet, either in the cornfield or the severer tasks of the threshing-floor." He excelled also in dancing, a recreation of which his father disapproved ; and the charm of his manners, destined afterwards to bewitch duchesses as well as country lassies, made him everywhere a welcome guest.

The sad state of the family prospects, which at length brought his father to the grave, depressed Robert extremely ; but youth has the happy faculty of casting cares beneath its feet, and Burns, with his ardent, susceptible nature, had days of the purest delight.* He tells us how, in his fifteenth year, he

---

* Mr. Carlyle, writing of the poet's residence at Irvine in his twenty-third year, observes, "We ourselves know from the best evidence that up to this date Burns was happy ; nay, that he was the gayest, brightest, most fantastic, fascinating being to be found in the world."

fell in love in the harvest-field with a " bonnie, sweet
sonsie lass ; " how love made him a poet, and how,
in the first awakening of passion, he felt a wish,
never afterwards to die out, that he—

> " For poor auld Scotland's sake,
> Some useful plan or book could make,
> Or sing a sang at least."

Domestic affection, and what he calls an " early
ingrained piety," kept him for several years " within
the line of innocence." What he lacked was the want
of an aim, and the impetuous youth, finding, despite
his grinding toil, but too much leisure for that
employment, was continually falling in love. His
heart, he says, was like tinder, and every fair face
that he saw set his fancy roaming. It was a happy
time, if not always a wise one. The genius of
poetry had touched him with her wand. Nature
with her infinite voices spoke to him, and his large
heart answered her in song.

Burns, who was always frank in acknowledging
his errors, dates the first change from a life of comparative innocence to the days when he left his
father's roof for Irvine, in order that he might learn
how to raise and dress flax. He was in his twenty-
third year when he was allured by bad company
into evil ways. A young sailor won his admiration
by many noble qualities and by his knowledge of
the world, but he spoke, says Burns ; "with levity of
illicit love, which hitherto I had regarded with
horror. Here his friendship did me a mischief."

About this time the poet's father died, and thus he was spared witnessing the dissolute course of his son, who found by the bitterest experience that vice "hardens a' within and petrifies the feeling."

A man cannot sin against his own conscience without sinning also against others. In the nature of Burns there was no cruelty; it was full of tenderness and pity for all things that are weak and suffering and dependent. Yet his selfish and evil conduct forced him sometimes to be cruel to those whom he should have cherished most tenderly. The deepest affection, probably, which he ever felt was for Mary Campbell, whose pure memory lives, and always must live, in the most pathetic lines that even Burns ever wrote. The story of the "one day of parting love" is as familiar as it is beautiful. "The lovers stood on each side of a small purling brook; they laved their hands in the limpid stream, and holding a Bible between them, pronounced their vows to be faithful to each other. They parted, never to meet again." The poor girl was on her way to meet once more her poet-lover, when she was seized with a fever and died, before Burns knew of her illness. Years afterwards he sang of his "sweet Highland Mary" in deathless verse.

> "That sacred hour can I forget?
> Can I forget the hallowed grove,
> Where, by the winding Ayr, we met
> To live one day of parting love?

" Eternity will not efface
　　Those records dear of transports past,
　Thy image at our last embrace ;
　　Ah ! little thought we 'twas our last !

"Ayr, gurgling, kissed his pebbled shore,
　　O'erhung with wild woods, thick'ning green ;
　The fragrant birch and hawthorn hoar,
　　Twined amorous round the raptured scene.

" The flowers sprang wanton to be prest,
　　The birds sang love on every spray,
　Till too, too soon, the glowing west
　　Proclaimed the speed of wingèd day.

" Still o'er these scenes my memory wakes,
　　And fondly broods with miser care !
　Time but the impression deeper makes,
　　As streams their channels deeper wear."

The Bible, in two volumes, which Burns gave to
his " ever dear Mary," is still in existence.   In the
first volume the poet has transcribed a passage from
Leviticus, " And ye shall not swear by My Name
falsely: I am the Lord;" and in the second volume
a verse from our Lord's Sermon on the Mount,
" Thou shalt not forswear thyself, but shalt perform
unto the Lord thine oath."   Alas ! the love of
Burns even for his Highland Mary was not that of
an honest man ; for we now know that a year previously he had secretly married Jean Armour, and
that while courting Mary he was the father of twin
children, and was bound in honour to cleave to the
woman he had promised to cherish for life.   No
wonder that he wrote about this time, of feeling

"stabs of remorse," and said that his gaiety was " the madness of an intoxicated criminal under the hands of the executioner." It will be enough to say here with regard to Jean, that she proved a faithful, patient, and forgiving wife, and that the love Burns felt for her, capricious though it was, drew from him one of the most beautiful of his songs.*

In the extremity of the difficulties in which Burns had involved himself, he thought of leaving the country, and to gain the means of so doing published his poems. Never was a volume received with heartier welcome, and the author at once became famous all Scotland over. Ploughboys and maidservants bought his book ; the first men of letters Edinburgh could boast of read it with delight. In the capital he was received with open arms by gentle and simple, and he is said to have conducted himself throughout this ordeal with singular dignity and independence. A prominent

---

* " Of a' the airts the wind can blaw
    I dearly like the west,
For there the bonie lassie lives,
    The lassie I lo'e best :
There wild woods grow, and rivers row,
    And monie a hill between ;
But day and night my fancy's flight
    Is ever wi' my Jean.

" I see her in the dewy flowers,
    I see her sweet and fair ;
I hear her in the tunefu' birds,
    I hear her charm the air :
There's not a bonie flower that springs
    By fountain, shaw, or green ;
There's not a bonie bird that sings
    But minds me o' my Jean."

fault in Burns's conduct was the too eager assertion of this independence before men and women of rank. He was one of the proudest of men, and was too apt to despise honours that were beyond his reach. No one could express more finely or more truly the intrinsic dignity of a man of worth apart from what we may call his artificial position; but although it be true that

> " The honest man, though e'er sae poor,
>   Is king of men for a' that,"

and that wealth and rank can never give us "ease and rest," it is equally true that the distinctions of rank and wealth are necessary to the healthy growth of a state, and that if it were possible to place all men on a level, some of the fairest and noblest virtues of the race would disappear at the same time. This was not evident to Burns, or perhaps— and this is more likely—the difficulties of his position and the consciousness of his power made him write in strong words of the precedence awarded to high birth.*

In a sketch necessarily so slight as this the details of a poet's life cannot be filled in; the most prominent incidents of his career and the stronger features of his character can alone be given. In Edinburgh we find Burns sharing a homely room

---

* " ' The rank is but the guinea's stamp;
     The man's the gowd for a' that.'
That is a word for all time. Yet perhaps it might have been wished that so noble a song had not been marred by any touch of social bitterness. A lord, no doubt, may be a 'birkie' and a 'coof,' but may not a ploughman be so too?" (Professor Shairp).

with an old Ayrshire acquaintance—and here, it may be said to his honour, he was never ashamed of his position nor of the friends that shared it—while his evenings were sometimes spent in the best society of the capital and sometimes in the worst haunts of dissipation. Hitherto "Scotch drink" had not enslaved the poet, but it now laid a hold upon him which he was never able to throw off. Those were days of hard drinking, even in what was called respectable society, and Burns fell into the snare. He had wise counsellors and true friends in Edinburgh, but seeing what was right as clearly as ever man saw it, he too often followed what was evil. His good and evil nature were in constant opposition, and the variations of his life are reflected in his poetry.

Men of high mark like Dugald Stewart thought that his powerful intellect would fit him to excel in any walk of life. His powers of conversation were extraordinary, and it would seem that in any society he was able to hold the chief place. To spend a night with Burns was the highest pleasure a tavern-frequenter could enjoy. When it was known he would sleep at a village inn, the farmers from all the district round flocked to meet him, and "the highest gentry of the country called in the wit and eloquence of Burns to enliven their carousals." The story is told of a visit to Blair Castle, where the poet spent two of the happiest days of his life. The Duchess of Athol and her two sisters, all three famed for their beauty, received him with the warmest welcome, and when he proposed leav-

ing, "they pressed him exceedingly to stay, and
even sent a messenger to the hotel to persuade the
driver of Burns's chaise to pull off one of the horse's
shoes that his departure might be delayed."

His popularity among lords and ladies did not,
however, better his position, and the loss of his most
faithful friend among the Scottish nobility, the Earl
of Glencairn, not only touched the poet's heart
deeply, but probably affected his after-life. The
last stanza of the poem dedicated to his memory is
marked by true feeling.

"The bridegroom may forget the bride
    Was made his wedded wife yestreen ;
The monarch may forget the crown
    That on his head an hour has been ;
The mother may forget the child
    That smiles sae sweetly on her knee ;
But I'll remember thee, Glencairn,
    And a' that thou hast done for me !"

Burns lost much by his visits to Edinburgh ; his
gains were an inferior appointment in the Excise
and about £500, the profit of his poetry. Part of
this sum he gave in brotherly affection to Gilbert,
and with the rest bought a farm at Ellisland, a few
miles from Dumfries, more remarkable for beauty
of position than for the quality of the soil. At this
time he openly acknowledged Jean Armour as his
wife. A cottage was built on the farm—a peasant's
cottage truly, consisting of a large kitchen, two
bedrooms, and a garret—and on this Burns entered
with many wholesome resolutions, too soon destined
to be forgotten. The happiest winter of his life

was the first in the new home. His prospects
were cheerful, and by his own ingle-nook "honest
poverty" did not make him hang his head. Before
long his own weakness of will did. As an exciseman, a post Burns detested, he was forced to ride
over a large district of country, and many were the
temptations he met with to "taste the barley bree."
The master's eye and hand were in the mean time
withdrawn from the farm, which promised at the
outset to prove a happy home, and it soon became
evident that it must be given up. "The truth is,"
writes Professor Shairp, "even if Burns ever had it
in him to succeed as a farmer, that time was past
when he came to Ellisland. Independence at the
plough-tail, of which he often boasted, was no longer
possible for him. Even if he had not been withdrawn from his farm by Excise duties, he could
neither work continuously himself nor make his
servants work. 'Faith,' said a neighbouring farmer,
'how could he miss but fail? He brought with
him a bevy of servants from Ayrshire. The lasses
did nothing but bake bread (that is, oat-cakes), and
the lads sat by the fireside and ate it warm with
ale,' Burns meanwhile enjoying himself at the house
of some jovial farmer or convivial laird. How could
he miss but fail?"

On the other hand, it is said that in the early
days of his life at Ellisland, Burns conducted himself wisely, and like one anxious for his good name
as a man and for his fame as a poet. Probably, as
things grew worse on the farm, he became reckless,

and his position as an exciseman made him irritable
and despondent. "I am now," he says, "a poor
rascally gauger, condemned to gallop two hundred
miles every week to inspect dirty bonds and yeasty
barrels;" and his jests on the subject, Lockhart
observes, are uniformly bitter. The greatest poet
of Scotland gauging beer-barrels and searching for
smuggled spirits! It seems a melancholy fate.
Much might and ought to have been done to relieve
this splendid genius from the pressure of want; yet,
as Carlyle justly observes, "it is his inward, not his
outward, misfortunes that bring him to the dust."
He was never "lord of himself," and it is due to
this cause, and not to poverty, that his life was
wrecked. There is not much to record after Burns
parted with his farm and settled in Dumfries. His
life, though not his genius, was all in shadow in
these later years. The poet's faults became more
obvious and his injudiciousness also, for he osten-
tatiously expressed his sympathy with the revolu-
tionists of France, and nearly lost his Excise appointment in consequence. In every way Burns
was ill at ease. He grew more and more reckless
and despondent, uttering wild words and doing
wild deeds. The acquaintances he had won as a
poet kept aloof from him now. To know " Robbie
Burns" was not considered respectable, and even
persons who felt kindly towards him were afraid of
his sarcasms, which were vented on friend and foe
alike. The cause of his death must be given in the
plainest words. At the beginning of 1796, soon

after recovering from a severe illness, the poet met a "jovial party" at a tavern. He fell asleep on the way home, caught rheumatic fever in consequence, and never recovered his former strength. Day by day he grew weaker, and his latest hours were troubled by anxiety for his wife and children. He had no money in the house, and it was with bitter humiliation that he borrowed fifteen pounds from friends. "Did you know the pride of my heart," he wrote to one of them, "you would feel doubly for me. Alas! I am not used to beg." He died at home, nursed by loving hands, but not by his affectionate Jean, who on the day of her husband's funeral gave birth to a son. When it was known that he was dying, "Dumfries," says Allan Cunningham, an eye-witness, "was like a besieged place. Wherever two or three people stood together their talk was of Burns, and of him alone." He died on the 21st of July, 1796, and his remains were laid in state in the Trades' Hall. Ten or twelve thousand persons followed his body to the grave. Seventeen years later a costly and hideous monument, with an inscription in Latin, was raised to his memory. Long years before he had written a pathetic epitaph, which shows that if he knew how to

> "Look through every other man
> Wi' sharpened, sly inspection,"

he had looked also with honest eyes into his own heart. Here are the closing verses :—

> "The poor Inhabitant below
> Was quick to learn and wise to know,

And keenly felt the friendly glow,
        And softer flame,
But thoughtless follies laid him low,
        And stained his name !

" Reader, attend !   Whether thy soul
Soars fancy's flights beyond the pole,
Or darkling grubs this earthly hole,
        In low pursuit ;
Know prudent, cautious self-control
        Is wisdom's root."

The most striking feature of Burns's poetry is its
intense nationality.   To the heart's core he was a
Scotchman, and his song is a home treasure to all
classes of his countrymen.   We have no English
poet, not even Shakespeare himself, who can vie
with Burns in this respect ; for Shakespeare's dramas,
though familiar on the stage and intimately known
to readers of culture, have no place in the labourer's
cottage or on the shelf of the artisan.   To Englishmen of this class, Spenser and Milton, Wordsworth
and Shelley, are but names, while Burns has a hold
upon his countrymen which he gained at once,
and is never likely to lose.   Another point worth
noting is the limitation and, at the same time, the
elasticity of his genius.   The concentration of purpose and the sustained poetical inspiration needed
to build up a great poem were denied to him.   The
emotion of the day produced the poem of the day,
and a widely different impulse prompted the verses
of the morrow.   The versatility of the poet's moods
is wonderful.   Pathos, wit humour, satire, and

sparkling fancy are all at his command, and to
these gifts is added a peerless voice for song. We
must not forget that he owed much to his predecessors. Scotland, even in the eighteenth century,
had many singers of sweet songs whose birdlike
notes filled the heart and ear of Burns. In early
youth a book of such songs was, he says, his *vade
mecum*, and from the collections made by Allan
Ramsay, the poet of "The Gentle Shepherd," to
the poetical pieces of Robert Ferguson, his "elder
brother in misfortune," there was not a nook of
Scottish song which Burns had not explored. It
is to his infinite credit that as a result of this search
he purified the literature of his country. He has
written much that is objectionable, but he has
swept away far more that had become intolerable,
substituting new and exquisite words for the gross
expressions linked to the national melodies of
Scotland. The hearty zeal with which he entered
on this labour during the last four years of his life
is the one gleam of light that relieves their dark-
ness. He would take no money for the work, for
his songs were "either above or below price," and
many of his loveliest or most humorous pieces
were produced under this condition. As a song-
writer Burns touched every chord of the lyre.
His sympathy is universal, his tenderness like that
of a woman. Here and there we may meet with a
song equal to any which Burns wrote, but what
other singer can compete with him in the compass
and richness of his notes? You will be able to

T

measure his worth in this respect if you read the
following pieces, remembering that to this list many
a song might be added of almost equal worth.
"Auld Lang Syne," "John Anderson my Jo," "My
Nanie O," "Tam Glen," "Mary Morison," "Dun-
can Gray," "A Man's a Man for a' that," "Ye
Banks and Braes o' Bonie Doon," "Highland
Mary," "The Soger's Return," "Bannockburn," "To
Mary in Heaven," and "O wert thou in the Cauld
Blast?" which was the last song Burns wrote.

It is not, however, wholly as a song-writer that
this poet deserves his fame.   He has proved in
some of his poems also

> "How Verse may build a princely throne
> On humble truth."

The "Cotter's Saturday Night" (which opens with
the most prosaic of couplets and ends with a generous burst of patriotism) shows the best and purest
side of the Scotch character, and is a picture of
what the poet had seen in his own family.*   The
sympathy of Burns with his "fellow-mortals," his
pity for the meanest thing that breathes, is expressed with consummate beauty in the address
"To a Mouse, on turning her up in her Nest with
the Plough."   The poet places himself for the time
on an equality with the "timorous beastie" whose
"wee bit housie" he has laid in ruin, and who sees
all her hopes of comfortable winter quarters destroyed in a moment ; and then, thinking of his own

---

* It is curious, by the way, that this poem, written in the
Spenserian stanza, should contain two quotations from Pope.

state, he points the moral with as much humour as pathos.

> " But, Mousie, thou art no thy lane,*
> In proving foresight may be vain ;
> The best-laid schemes o' mice an' men
> Gang aft a-gley,†
> An' leave us nought but grief an' pain
> For promised joy.

> " Still thou art blest, compared wi' me !
> The present only toucheth thee ;
> But, och ! I backward cast my e'e
> On prospects drear !
> An' forward tho' I canna see,
> I guess an' fear ! "

Of a similar character is " The Death and Dying Words of Poor Maillie, the Author's only Pet Yowe " (ewe). Read also the poem " To a Mountain Daisy, on turning one down with the Plough." It expresses the same tender feeling, and ends with the same moral as the verses " To a Mouse." " An Epistle to a Young Friend " shows the serious side of the poet's character. And no one could be wiser or more serious than Burns when giving advice to others ; witness, for example, the " Epistle to Davie," in which he writes that the source of happiness is not in our possessions but in a good conscience, and in " joys that riches ne'er could buy."

> " If happiness ha'e not her seat
> And centre in the breast,
> We may be wise, or rich, or great,
> But never can be blest."

---

* Not alone.   † Go often wrong.

"Tam o' Shanter" is, perhaps, his finest effort as a humorist. The fiery haste of Tam's flight when followed by the witches—

"Wi' monie an eldritch skreech and hollow"—

is scarcely exceeded by the speed with which this wonderful poem was written. Burns composed it in one day, and in such a state of ecstasy that the tears were "happing down his cheeks." It was, he considered, his greatest poem, and the best critics have confirmed the judgment.

Here we must part from Burns, and can we do so better than in the words of a yet greater poet, who had hailed his light "when first it shone," and in more than one noble poem has done honour to his memory?

> "Through busiest street and loneliest glen
> Are felt the flashes of his pen ;
> He rules 'mid winter snows, and when
> 　　Bees fill their hives ;
> Deep in the general heart of men
> 　　His power survives.

> ·　　·　　·　　·　　·

> "Sweet Mercy ! to the gates of Heaven
> This Minstrel lead, his sins forgiven ;
> The rueful conflict, the heart riven
> 　　With vain endeavour,
> And memory of Earth's bitter leaven
> 　　Effaced for ever.

> "But why to Him confine the prayer,
> When kindred thoughts and yearnings bear

On the frail heart the purest share
With all that live?
The best of what we do and are,
Just God, forgive !"

(Wordsworth.)

[Lockhart's life of Burns is a beautiful piece of biography. Professor Shairp has written a judicious narrative of the poet's life in "English Men of Letters"—too judicious and impartial to suit some of his admirers. In the third volume of Professor Wilson's "Critical and Imaginative Essays," one will be found worthy of the writer on "The Genius and Character of Burns," and another on a still higher level is to be found in Carlyle's "Miscellaneous Essays." Do not fail to read this paper. It is written in vigorous, eloquent English, and is without any mark of the author's later style. There is a cheap Globe edition of Burns, edited by the late Alexander Smith.]

CHAPTER XIII.

POETS OF THE NINETEENTH CENTURY.

WILLIAM WORDSWORTH.

MR. JOHN STUART MILL made an unfortunate statement when he called Wordsworth "the

**William
Wordsworth,
1770-1850.**

poet of unpoetical natures, possessed of
quiet and contemplative tastes." On the
contrary, we should be inclined to say that Wordsworth makes larger demands on a man's capacity for
receiving the highest poetic truth than any poet of
this century. He never meets his readers half-way,
makes no attempt to allure them to his side, but is
content to sow his poetic seed, and, like the farmer,
to leave its growth and fruit to the influences of
nature.

William Wordsworth, the second son of John
Wordsworth, an attorney, was born at Cocker-
mouth, in Cumberland, on April 7, 1770. His
mother died when the child was eight years old,

and his father when he was thirteen.   Thus it will be seen that neither parent took an active part in moulding the character of their son.   Of his school days at Hawkesworth, an interesting account is given in the "Prelude." If ever "the child is father of the man" it was so in Wordsworth's case, and while still a boy he received joyously, but unconsciously, the lessons taught by the common face of nature.   The simple ways, he tells us, in which his childhood walked, first led him to the love of rivers, woods, and fields.   The vivid impressions of those happy days were never lost.   From school, thanks to the kindness of two good uncles, he went up to St. John's, Cambridge, where he does not seem to have made much progress in the special studies of the place.   A vacation spent in a walking tour through Switzerland, an enterprise quite unusual in those days, marked a characteristic in Wordsworth which continued through life.   De Quincey calculates that long before the close of it he had walked nearly two hundred thousand miles.   He had more faith in his legs than in a carriage, and not without justice, for he knew nothing of horses ; and his sister relates how, upon having to unharness one from a cart, he was unable—and Coleridge was in the same dilemma—to lift the collar over the horse's neck.   Wordsworth took his degree at Cambridge, without honours, in 1791, and after a delay of some months went to France, spending the greater portion of a year at Orleans and Blois. The fever of the times infected the youthful poet

as it infected Coleridge and Southey. He trusted
in the Revolution to regenerate society, not having
yet learned that by the soul only can a nation be
great and free. The massacres of October, 1792,
dismayed him ; but he would have offered his ser-
vices as a leader of the Girondist party had not the
want of money brought him back to England—

> " Forced by the gracious providence of Heaven."

With defeated hopes and a loss of faith in human
nature, Wordsworth fell into a sea of doubt, and
was tempted, as he tells us, to yield up moral
questions in despair. His sister Dorothy came at
this time like a guardian angel, and her influence
saved him, keeping him

> " True to the kindred points of heaven and home."

The entire sympathy of taste between William
and Dorothy, the warmth and constancy of their
affection, what each did for the other, the poems
Dorothy inspired, the love William gave her in
return,—all this must be read at large, and can only
be alluded to here. In 1795, Wordsworth, then
twenty-five years old, had neither profession nor
prospects. Early in the year his friend Raisley
Calvert died, leaving the poet, who had already
published a small volume, a legacy of £900. This
sum, coming thus opportunely, enabled Wordsworth to devote himself to poetry as his life's work.
Some years afterwards he wrote : " Upon the interest of the £900, £400 being laid out in annuity,
with £200 deducted from the principal, and £100,

a legacy to my sister, and £100 more which the " Lyric Ballads " have brought me, my sister and I have contrived to live seven years, nearly eight."

Together they settled at Racedown, in Dorsetshire, and there for the first time Coleridge and Wordsworth met. Each was the inspirer of the other, and at Nether-Stowey, in Somersetshire, whither the Wordsworths removed in order to be near Coleridge, the genius of that poet produced its ripest fruit, and there Wordsworth also wrote some of his most characteristic poems.* The " Lyrical Ballads," for which the good Cottle, of Bristol, gave Wordsworth thirty guineas, was published in 1798. A visit to Germany followed, and the brother and sister, instead of learning the language by intercourse with the natives, shut themselves up with books and dictionaries ; and the winter being unprecedently severe, were almost frozen for their pains. In the spring of 1799 they returned to England, and, after travelling with Coleridge in the Lake district, settled at Grasmere. Several happy and busily poetical years were spent in the tiny Grasmere cottage, to which, in 1802, the poet brought his wife, whose maiden name was Mary Hutchinson. She inspired Wordsworth's lovely lyric " She was a Phantom of Delight," and doubled the happiness of what was already one of

---

* " I think," says Sara Coleridge, " there was never so close a union between two such eminent minds in any age. They were together, and in intimate communion at the most vigorous, the most inspired periods of the lives of both."

the happiest of lives. Children were born here, and in the course of these years Wordsworth published more volumes of poetry.

A tour in Scotland, made for ever memorable by his sister's diary, is also noteworthy as the occasion of the poet's first introduction to Scott, then living in his pretty cottage at Lasswade. Soon after returning to Grasmere, where, to quote from Dorothy's notes, they found "Mary in perfect health, and little John asleep in the clothes-basket by the fire," Wordsworth went over the mountains to Greta Hall, Keswick, Coleridge's temporary home, and the residence for life of the more constant Southey. "Southey," he writes, "whom I never saw much of before, I liked much; he is very pleasant in his manner, and a man of great reading in old books." Wordsworth, it may be observed, could not sympathize with the keenest enjoyment of his friend. He cared little for books, and his study, as a servant once observed to visitors, was in the open air. He was always "booing about," to use the words of a country neighbour, and the beauty of the scenery he knew so well is reflected in his poetry.

The Wordsworths took possession of Rydal Mount in 1813, leaving behind them two children in Grasmere churchyard. This change of residence is the most prominent event for many years in his happily eventless history, unless we may give precedence to his appointment as distributor of stamps for the counties of Westmoreland and

Cumberland—a pleasant office for a poet, since it removed all pecuniary anxiety and demanded little labour. We may think of Wordsworth, then, living his fruitful life with wife and sister and children, amidst the loveliest of English scenery, finding every day some new incident for verse, or brooding with deep joy over his own thoughts, while the breeze of nature stirred within his soul. His life had always been pure ; it was now serenely pious. He regarded God as a Judge in whose eye

> "A noble aim,
> Faithfully kept, is as a noble deed,
> In whose pure sight all virtue doth succeed ; "

and his faith

> "in Heaven's unfailing love
> And all-controlling power "

was strong enough to keep his spirit calm in those dark moments of mental conflict or domestic bereavement which almost every man has to face in his passage to the tomb. The life led at Rydal was of the simplest kind—so simple, indeed, that one might be excused for deeming it a little uncomfortable. Of high thinking there was plenty, but perhaps the "great bread-and-butter question" was not sufficiently regarded. "The Wordsworths never dine," said a literary gossip ; "when they are hungry they go to the cupboard and eat ;" and the story runs that upon a visit Scott paid, either to Rydal or Grasmere, he found Mrs. Wordsworth's lenten fare a little unattractive, and was wont to step out to the inn for a glass of good ale.

Wordsworth's concentration of purpose and the strength of his attachment to nature made him unfitted for London society. We can picture him on Helvellyn better than in the drawing-room of a fashionable lady. But wherever he went he carried the air of the mountains with him, and people felt they were in the presence of a great man. It is possible this feeling was not wholly and always pleasurable. A pigmy does not like to stand beside a giant, and Wordsworth could not, like Scott, entirely forget his greatness. His love for his own poetry was a little too absorbing. Yet Samuel Rogers, who lived in society, speaks of him as joyous and communicative, and if not eminently social, he was certainly not a recluse. One of his most intimate friends describes him as the most humble and loving of men ; and as his long life drew towards its end, a lady who knew him says, " The gentle, softened evening light of his spirit is very lovely, and there is a quiet sublimity about him, as he waits on the shores of that eternal world, which seems already to cast over him some sense of its beauty and its peace."

Thirty-seven years were spent at Rydal Mount, and in this dear home, filled with a thousand memories, and intimately associated with the inner life of the poet, he breathed his last. A few years before the end, his beloved daughter, Mrs. Quillinan, died under her father's roof, and he never recovered the shock. When his own time came, his wife said to him, " William, you are going to Dora." He made no reply at the time, and the words seem to have passed unheeded; indeed, it was not certain that they had been heard. More than twenty-four hours afterwards one of his nieces came into his room, and was drawing aside the curtain of his chamber, and then, as if awakening from a quiet sleep, he said, "Is that Dora?" He died on the 23rd of April (Shakespeare's death-day), and was buried by the side of those he loved best in Grasmere churchyard.

> "Keep fresh the grass upon his grave,
>   O Rotha! with thy living wave.
>   Sing him thy best! for few or none
>   Hears thy voice right, now he is gone."

"I am myself," said Wordsworth, "one of the happiest of men; and no man who does not partake of that happiness, who lives a life of constant bustle, and whose felicity depends on the opinions of others, can possibly comprehend the best of my poems."

There is a truth in these words which will grow more and more evident in proportion to our knowledge of this great poet. He demands much from the reader, and in return gives him a new life of thought, a new impression of humanity, and a love of Nature which brings him into closest fellowship with her simplest charms. Wordsworth describes natural objects with accuracy, but he looks at them with the "inward eye" by which alone we can "see into the life of things." He is, perhaps, the most uniformly truthful of poets, never uttering what he does not feel, never telling what he does not know.

With him imagination is a faculty used for the apprehension of truth, and if in one sense he may be called a high priest of Nature, in another sense he is the most reverent of her servants. He resembles Milton in the high resolve with which he dedicated his life to poetry and in the unfaltering courage with which he pursued his calling; like Milton, too, his self-reliance and want of humour lead him sometimes to write what literature could readily dispense with. "Wordsworth's ship," said Landor, "would sail better for casting many loose things overboard;" and Mr. Matthew Arnold expressed the same idea in another form, when he wrote that he "needs to be relieved of a great deal of the poetical baggage which encumbers him." While admitting this, Mr. Arnold maintains, and I think justly, that Wordsworth is the greatest poet this nation has produced since the days of Shakespeare and Milton.* Yet his sway is even now but partially acknowledged. There are critics, and readers too, who prefer Byron; there are more

---

* How deeply Mr. Arnold has felt Wordsworth's power will be seen in the following lines :—

> "Time may restore us in his course
>   Goethe's sage mind and Byron's force,
>   But where will Europe's latter hour
>   Again find Wordsworth's healing power?
>   Others will teach us how to dare,
>   And against fear our breast to steel;
>   Others will strengthen us to bear ;—
>   But who—ah ! who will make us feel ?
>   The cloud of mortal destiny,
>   Others will front it fearlessly—
>   But who, like him, will put it by ?"

who give the precedence to Shelley.   When, however, Wordsworth "finds" a man, his influence is
more profound than theirs.   For his words may be
said to feed the soul, and he has done for those
who love him what his sister did for him.

> " She gave me eyes, she gave me ears,
> And humble cares and delicate fears,
> A heart the fountain of sweet tears,
> And love and thought and joy."

There is a stanza in another poem in which, while
describing the character of the shepherd, Lord
Clifford, he unconsciously portrays his own.

> " Love had he found in huts where poor men lie ;
> His daily teachers had been woods and rills,
> The silence that is in the starry sky,
> The sleep that is among the lonely hills."

Owing to his dislike of what is called "poetical
diction" Wordsworth fell into the error of supposing
that the highest poetry might be expressed in the
common speech of rustics.   His theory is explained
with much elaboration in a celebrated preface, and
is full of interest for the student, since it is eminently
useful to know a poet's design and to compare it
with the work he achieves.   He will find, upon
reading Wordsworth, that the homely speech used
in the least imaginative poems is generally, if not
always, discarded in the higher efforts of his genius.
As the thoughts rise the language rises, and form
and substance are alike changed.   Now and then,
however, he falls ignominiously from a great height,

and a poem is damaged by a fatally prosaic expression. A remarkable instance of this occurs in
the lovely lyric, "She was a Phantom of Delight,"
where in a fatal line he views "the very pulse of
the machine"! And there are instances of it also
in a few pieces the ludicrous character of which the
poet's entire want of humour prevented him from
seeing.

Another fault must be mentioned. Wordsworth
said he was either a teacher or nothing, and undoubtedly he was a great teacher, opening up
new springs of thought, new aspirations, new
affections; but when he does this effectually, he
does it as all poetry must do it, indirectly. On
the other hand, in attempting to dogmatize he
forgets his calling and loses his power. Youthful
readers of Wordsworth, upon their first introduction
to his works, are apt to lose patience. His defects
are obvious to them; his transcendent merit as an
interpreter of nature and of life is unperceived.
He has passion, but the fire glowing in his pages
never bursts into a blaze; he has the tenderest love
for every simple object in nature, but his feelings
are always uttered with reserve. His largest and
most imaginative thoughts will escape the reader
who is not also a student of his verse. But there
is no poet who will better repay study, none more
capable of affording exquisite delight. He said it
was Burns who first set him on the right track;
and inasmuch as the Scotch poet taught Wordsworth to find poetry in the lowliest objects of

nature and human life, this is no doubt true, but Wordsworth's power lies in a totally different direction to that of Burns. The one poet is profoundly meditative, full of self-restraint, and of what Mr. Hutton justly calls "thriftiness" in the expression of his emotions; the other writes from the impulse and passion of the moment. The one is heavily weighted with the affluence of poetic thought; the other sings his song with a rapturous thrill of feeling, which reminds us of the quivering of the lark's wing as he rises into the blue. Wordsworth's sense of responsibility was great. In his eyes poetry is a divine art, never to be lightly touched by profane hands. "It is an awful truth," he writes, "that there neither is nor can be any genuine enjoyment of poetry among nineteen out of twenty of those persons who live, or wish to live, in the broad light of the world—among those who either are or are striving to make themselves people of consideration in society. This is a truth and an awful one; because to be incapable of a feeling of poetry, in my sense of the word, is to be without love of human nature and reverence for God." And then, alluding to the indifference with which his poems were received, he adds, "Of what moment is that compared with what I trust is their destiny?—to console the afflicted, to add sunshine to daylight, by making the happy happier, to teach the young and gracious of every age to see, to think, and feel, and therefore to become more actively and sincerely virtuous. This is their office, which I trust they will faithfully perform, long after we (that is, all that is mortal of us) are mouldered in our grave." The character of the man is seen in these words. They form a key to his verse. They account for the fact that he occasionally falls into prose, and is more intent on the lesson he has to teach than on his way of teaching it. His teaching, whether prosaic or poetical, is essentially Christian. He rarely composes what is commonly known as religious poetry—indeed, he shrunk from so doing —but the pure spirit of Christianity sustains and invigorates him throughout.

Between 1799 and 1809 almost all Wordsworth's finest work was done. His long life was dedicated to poetry, but in these few early years his power was at its height, for it was then he produced the poems that live in the memory and heart of all lovers of his verse. The four eminently characteristic poems on " Lucy," " The Affliction of Margaret," " Michael," " To the Cuckoo," " Yew Trees," " Nutting," " She was a Phantom of Delight," " The Daffodils," " Resolution and Independence," " Ode to Duty," " Song at the Feast of Brougham · Castle," the incomparably lovely lines written near Tintern Abbey, " The Solitary Reaper," " The Old Cumberland Beggar," " The Fountain," the great " Ode on Immortality," and many more poems which, like " Peter Bell " and the " White Doe of Rylstone," are of equal merit in the eyes of Wordsworth's disciples, were composed within the ten years I have mentioned. So also were the " Prelude" (finished in 1805), and the finest portion of the first book of the "Excursion." The former poem, however, remained in manuscript forty-five years, and was not published until after the poet's death. Other poems there are of great significance, written at a later period—notably, "Dion," "Laodameia," "Yarrow Revisited," "The Eclipse of the Sun," "The Primrose of the Rock," and "Devotional Incitements;" but these may be said to have confirmed his fame rather than to have made it. Had Wordsworth died at the age of forty, his reputation as the greatest poet of his century would have been sufficiently secured.

All the poems just mentioned should be read. The larger number of them are wholly unlike any poetry previously written, and while unlike, are on a level with the noblest verse England has produced. He has more than one manner, but he is always Wordsworth, never catching the tone of earlier singers, unless perhaps in a few elaborately constructed passages which remind us of the stately verse of Milton. A significant example of Wordsworth's ballad style may be read in the "Reverie of Poor Susan."

> "At the corner of Wood Street, when daylight appears,
> Hangs a thrush that sings loud, it has sung for three years :
> Poor Susan has passed by the spot, and has heard
> In the silence of morning the song of the bird.

> "'Tis a note of enchantment ; what ails her ? She se
> A mountain ascending, a vision of trees ;
> Bright volumes of vapour through Lothbury glide,
> And a river flows on through the vale of Cheapside.

" Green pastures she views in the midst of the dale,
    Down which she so often has tripped with her pail ;
    And a single small cottage, a nest like a dove's,
    The one only dwelling on earth that she loves.
" She looks, and her heart is in heaven : but they fade,
    The mist and the river, the hill and the shade :
    The stream will not flow, and the hill will not rise,
    And the colours have all passed away from her eyes."

There was a poet living when Wordsworth wrote this poem whose peculiar genius might have been equal to its production. William Blake, the artist and poet, was called by Charles Lamb "one of the most extraordinary persons of the age." The simplicity of his verse is delightful, for it is due to imaginative power. He might have equalled Wordsworth in poetry of the class to which " Poor Susan " belongs, but there are heights in Wordsworth infinitely beyond Blake's power of attainment. Indeed, he stands alone, on land never owned before by poet, one of the wisest and most imaginative interpreters of nature, and also one of the humblest. For Mr. Ruskin is, I think, wrong in saying that Wordsworth had " a vague notion that nature would not be able to get on well without him," though it must be confessed that, while humility and reverence lay at the basis of his character, its surface was a little marred by self-consciousness. That he was lowly in heart, especially in later years, is testified, as I have already said, by those who knew him best ; that he felt in early life how noble this virtue was, is testified by the following lines :—

William Blake,
1757-1828.

> " The man whose eye
> Is ever on himself doth look on one,
> The least of nature's works, one who might move
> The wise man to that scorn which wisdom holds
> Unlawful, ever.   O be wiser, thou !
> Instructed that true knowledge leads to love,
> True dignity abides with him alone
> Who, in the silent hour of inward thought,
> Can still suspect, and still revere himself,
> In lowliness of heart."

A critic has said, with great justice, that there are many passages in Wordsworth's writings that seem, ever since we first read them, to be our special property.   Being thus special in character, every reader must, of course, find them for himself; but it may be observed here that no English poet, with the sole exception of Shakespeare, has written so many single lines, couplets, and short passages which are alive with imagination.   It is wit, or some quality nearly allied to it, with an unequalled conciseness of expression, that makes Pope's lines so familiar ; it is poetry of the finest order that gives vitality to Wordsworth's.

There is a good deal of what one may call barren ground in the " Excursion," but how frequently are we cheered and gladdened by the joyous imagination that floods the path with sunshine !   In the second book you will find the description of a spot of hidden beauty among the mountains, a sweet recess lying tenderly protected in rugged arms—

> " So lonesome and so perfectly secure ;
> Not melancholy—no, for it is green,
> And bright and fertile."

" Peace is here or nowhere," adds the speaker, as he throws down his limbs at ease upon a bed of heather ; and this hidden beauty and this restful peace—peace to the intellect and tranquillity to the heart—are the gifts Wordsworth offers us in the great poem which Lord Jeffrey so flippantly asserted would " never do." The wealth it yields, however, is not likely to be appreciated by the readers for whom this volume is written. They will turn with greater pleasure, and reasonably so, to the poet's shorter poems, and, learning the beauty of these, will be prepared in later years to study the " Prelude," the " Excursion," and the two great " Odes." One of the most tenderly imaginative of the lyrics is also probably among the most familiar, but I quote " The Solitary Reaper " the more readily because I think that, like Wordsworth's " Daffodils " and Keats's "Ode to the Nightingale," it is a poem that will test the reader's poetical sensitiveness.

> " Behold her, single in the field,
> Yon solitary Highland lass !
> Reaping and singing by herself ;
> Stop here or gently pass !
> Alone she cuts and binds the grain,
> And sings a melancholy strain ;
> Oh, listen ! for the vale profound
> Is overflowing with the sound.

> " No nightingale did ever chant
> So sweetly to reposing bands
> Of travellers in some shady haunt,
> Among Arabian sands ;

A voice so thrilling ne'er was heard,
In springtime, from the cuckoo-bird,
Breaking the silence of the seas
Among the farthest Hebrides.

" Will no one tell me what she sings ?
Perhaps the plaintive numbers flow
For old, unhappy, far-off things
And battles long ago.
Or is it some more humble lay,
Familiar matter of to-day ?
Some natural sorrow, loss, or pain
That has been and may be again ?

" Whate'er the theme, the maiden sang
As if her song could have no ending.
I saw her singing at her work,
And o'er the sickle bending ;—
I listened till I had my fill,
And when I mounted up the hill,
The music in my heart I bore,
Long after it was heard no more."

As yet nothing has been said of Wordsworth as
a writer of sonnets. Of this form of the poetic art
he was pre-eminently a master. No poet ever
loved liberty more truly, but this love was tempered,
as it ever must be in thoughtful men, with a profound reverence for the " patrimony of experience."
He loved well the freedom that " broadens slowly
down from precedent to precedent ;" he shrank,
with the disgust of one who had lived through the
French Revolution, from every political movement
which he deemed destructive rather than progres-
sive. Among the noblest sonnets that ever Wordsworth wrote are the series dedicated to Liberty. He

saw, as Burke also saw, that the vaunted freedom of France was no freedom at all, since to be free a people must be virtuous and wise ; and, feeling this, he exclaims in a moment of despondency—

> "O friend ! I know not which way I must look
> For comfort, being, as I am, opprest,
> To think that now our life is only drest
> For show ; mean handy-work of craftsman, cook,
> Or groom !—We must run glittering like a brook
> In the open sunshine, or we are unblest :
> The wealthiest man among us is the best ;
> No grandeur now in nature or in book
> Delights us. Rapine, avarice, expense,
> This is idolatry ; and these we adore ;
> Plain living and high thinking are no more ;
> The homely beauty of the good old cause
> Is gone ; our peace, our fearful innocence,
> And pure religion breathing household laws."

This mood is not lasting, for hope and faith inspire the patriot and the poet. So he is ashamed of his unfilial fears for England—fears caused by his affection—and, taking heart, refuses to believe that the flood of British freedom can perish in bogs and sands.

> " In our halls is hung
> Armoury of the invincible knights of old :
> We must be free or die, who speak the tongue
> That Shakespeare spake: the faith and morals hold
> Which Milton held. In everything we are sprung
> Of earth's first blood, have titles manifold."

Of Wordsworth as a sonnet-writer I have written elsewhere, and it will suffice, perhaps, to transcribe the following passage :—

" There is no intensity of passion in Wordsworth's sonnets, and herein he differs from Shakespeare and Mrs. Browning, for whose sonnets the reader may feel an enthusiastic admiration that Wordsworth's thoughtful and calm verse rarely excites ; neither has he attained the dignified simplicity which marks the sonnets of Milton ; but for purity of language, for variety and strength of thought, for the *curiosa felicitas* of poetical diction, for the exquisite skill with which he associates the emotions of the mind and the aspects of nature, we know of no sonnet-writer who can take precedence of Wordsworth. In his larger poems the language is sometimes slovenly, and occasionally, as Sir Walter Scott said, he chooses to crawl on all fours ; but this is rarely the case in the sonnets, and though he wrote upwards of four hundred, there are few, save those on the " Punishment of Death," and some of those called " Ecclesiastical " (for neither argument nor dogma find a fitting place in verse), that we could willingly part with. Wordsworth's belief that the language of the common people may be used as the language of poetry, was totally inoperative when he composed a sonnet. He wrote at such times in the best diction he could command, and the language, like the thought, is that of a great master. The sonnets embrace almost every theme except the one to which this branch of the poetical art has been usually dedicated. Some of the noblest are consecrated to liberty, some describe with incomparable felicity the personal feelings of the writer ; some might be termed simply descriptive, were it not that even these are raised above the rank of descriptive poetry by the pure and lofty imagination of the poet. ' The light that never was on sea or land ' pervades the humblest of these pieces, and throughout them there is inculcated a cheerful because divine philosophy."*

These few hints about Wordsworth will suffice,

---

* " English Sonnets," a selection collected and arranged by John Dennis. 2nd edition. Kegan Paul and Co.

if they lead the student to his poetry and to the masterly criticisms of which that poetry has been the theme. It claims patience and a mind free from low desires and petty cares. "There are writings," says Landor, "which must lie long upon the straw before they mellow to the taste, and there are summer fruits that cannot abide the keeping." Wordsworth's poetry takes some time, perhaps, to "mellow to the taste," but if it be true that in our best and purest moments we turn to it most eagerly, then must it be true also that the fruit it yields is of no common growth.

[Wordsworth's power was acknowledged in his lifetime by the greatest critics of the period ; notably by Coleridge, in his "Biographia Literaria ;" by Professor Wilson, who said that his genius had exercised "a greater influence on the spirit of poetry in Britain than was ever before exercised by any individual mind" (see "Essays Critical and Imaginative," vol. i., Blackwood); by De Quincey, who has written much about Wordsworth, in his "Autobiographic Sketches," that will attract and amuse the reader (De Quincey's statements must not be accepted without reserve, but there are vivid touches and curious reminiscences in his essays not to be found elsewhere) ; by Hazlitt, who considered many of the lyrical ballads and sonnets of "inconceivable beauty," and declared that they "open a finer and deeper vein of thought and feeling than any poet in modern times has done or attempted."

A life of Wordsworth, by his nephew, the present Bishop of Lincoln, appeared in 1851. It contains much valuable matter, and will always be consulted by students ; but it is not and never was intended to be a full and final biography of the poet. Wordsworth was of opinion that the sanctities of domestic life ought not to be exposed to the public, and would probably, had he lived in our day, have held the opinion more strongly still. Mr. F. W. H. Myers has written a short biography of Wordsworth in the series of "English Men of Letters ;" and the reader, as he pursues his study of the poet, should read Professor Shairp's " Studies in Poetry," the " Essays " of Mr. R. H. Hutton and of the late George Brimley, and the brief essay by the Dean of St. Paul's, in "The English Poets," edited by Professor Ward (Macmillan and Co.). " Poems of Wordsworth," chosen and edited by Matthew Arnold (Macmillan and Co.), is a volume to be commended above all others, as an introduction to the study of the poet.]

CHAPTER XIV.

POETS OF THE NINETEENTH CENTURY
(*Continued*).

SIR WALTER SCOTT.

WALTER SCOTT'S name is a household word with
Englishmen as well as Scotchmen. No
author belonging to the first half of this
century has won so much love and admiration. Wherever English is spoken Scott is a
cherished writer, and the delight he affords is shared
by the young and the old ; by men of the highest
genius, and by men who turn to his pages for an
hour's happy forgetfulness of the cares of life. This
" beloved writer," says George Eliot, "has made a
chief part in the happiness of many young lives."
"Walter Scott," says Goethe, "is a great genius; he
has not his equal.   He gives me much to think of,
and I discover in him a wholly new art with laws
of its own."   Dean Stanley, addressing the students
of St. Andrew's in 1875, spoke of " the far-seeing

Sir Walter
Scott,
1771-1832.

toleration, the profound reverence, the critical insight into the various shades of religious thought and feeling, the moderation which turns to scorn 'the falsehood of extremes,' the lofty sense of Christian honour, purity, and justice that breathe through every volume of the 'Waverley Novels;'" and the present Dean of Westminster has said, that of all the great names of literature none was so dear to his predecessor as that of Scott. "To Sir W. Scott," it has been said of Dr. Pusey, " he remained faithful to the last, and knew him as Fox and Grenville knew Homer, and as Lamb knew Shakespeare." S. T. Coleridge's verdict in favour of Scott's novels is equally strong, for he said that when ill they were the only books he could read. Nathaniel Hawthorne, the most original of American novelists, is said almost to have worshipped Sir Walter's romances, and was accustomed to read them aloud in his family ; and Robertson of Brighton, alluding to more recent fictions, says, " From those of Scott you rise with a vigorous, healthy tone of feeling ; from the others with that sense of exhaustion and weakness which comes from feeling stirred up to end in nothing."

Similar judgments might readily be quoted, but these will serve as an illustration of the high esteem in which Scott has been ever held by the wise and good. No one but a poet could have written the splendid novels which Scott poured forth so rapidly. Later novelists appeal to feelings untouched by the great magician, who acknowledged that the delicate workmanship of his contemporary, Jane Austen, was beyond the reach of his pen ; but where, save in the Waverley series, will you find so much variety of action and life, such skilful management of plot, such wealth of knowledge and resources, such an out-of-door freshness, such accurate descriptions of nature, such breadth of charity, such humour combined with purity, and pathos so free from sentimentality? I must not dwell, however, on this subject, tempting though it be. I hope that Scott's tales are known to all my readers and loved as they deserve to be ; but it is as a poet, using his proper instrument, metre, that the author of the Waverleys asks now for our attention.

With the exception of Boswell's life of Dr. Johnson, there is perhaps no biography that admits us more completely into the presence of its hero than Lockhart's life of Scott. It contains passages of merely temporary interest, and others that it would have been wiser to omit, but in spite of slight flaws such as these, the book acts upon the reader with the fascination which Sir Walter himself exercised upon all who came within his circle. If not already acquainted with the beautiful narrative, read it on the earliest opportunity, and by way of alluring you to a task which is sure to prove a pleasure, take up in the first instance Mr. Hutton's admirable monograph of Scott in the series of "English Men of Letters," or Mr. Palgrave's shorter narrative in the Globe edition of Scott's poetry.

"An eminently good and noble-hearted man,"

writes Mr. Palgrave, "tried by almost equal extremes of fortune, and victorious over both,—the life
of Scott would be a tragic drama in the fullest
sense, moving and teaching us at once, through pity
and love and terror, even if he had not else in many
ways deserved the title of greatness." This tragedy,
which is not without many scenes of joyousness
and beauty, must be read at large, and I shall content myself with giving a few facts and dates in
accordance with the plan of this volume.

Like all Scotchmen who are blessed with one,
Scott was proud of his pedigree, which he traced
from Auld Wat of Harden, known in border legend,
up to the ducal house of Buccleugh. His father,
a writer to the signet in Edinburgh, is pictured not
unfilially in "Red Gauntlet." His mother—a woman
worthy of such a son—was the daughter of a
physician. She had twelve children, of whom six
died in early childhood. Walter was the ninth of
the family. An early fever made him lame for life,
and for years he was not strong ; but by degrees,
thanks to the free air of the hills, he overcame this
weakness, and in spite of his lame leg he became
not only an accomplished horseman, but a vigorous
climber. A bright picture is given of his youth
and early manhood. His sweetness of disposition,
his power of attaching friends, his immense capacity
for work as well as sport, his love of poetry, and
especially of the border ballads of his country, and
that passionate feeling for nature which led him to
say he thought he should die if he could not see

the heather once a year, were as characteristic of Scott in youth as in old age.

On leaving school, where he acquired a fair knowledge of Latin, but none of Greek—a loss he greatly deplored afterwards—Scott was in the first instance apprenticed to his father. Ultimately he became an advocate, but he had little success at the bar, and accepted an appointment as Sheriff of Selkirkshire. He had previously married, after a disappointment in love, which called forth some stanzas of great beauty ; * and now, with the prospect of a permanent income as Clerk of Session, he devoted all his leisure—and Scott knew how to make the leisure he needed—to the studies he loved best.

He was upwards of thirty when he published the "Border Minstrelsy," by which he gained fame if not money. The collection of these ballads had been the labour of years, and the volumes contained also some original poems, whose trumpet-notes take a lasting hold of the memory. Then followed the "Lay of the Last Minstrel," written "in a light-horseman sort of style." It was received

---

* "The violet in her greenwood bower,
   Where birchen boughs with hazels mingle,
 May boast itself the fairest flower
   In glen, or copse, or forest dingle.

"Though fair her gems of azure hue,
   Beneath the dewdrop's weight reclining,
 I've seen an eye of lovelier blue,
   More sweet through watery lustre shining.

"The summer sun that dew shall dry
   Ere yet the day be past its morrow ;
 Nor longer in my false love's eye
   Remained the tear of parting sorrow."

with acclamation, and from that moment the name
of Scott was popular throughout the country.   And
now one splendid achievement followed another
in swift succession. "Marmion," his finest poem, was
followed in about two years by the " Lady of the
Lake," which gained still higher popularity.   The
next venture, somewhat less successful, was
" Rokeby," and in addition to the poems, which
seemed scarcely to tax his powers — much of
" Marmion " was composed on horseback, and
the clang of his horse's hoofs is echoed in the
verse—he undertook an amount of editorial
labour which might well have daunted the most
diligent man of letters.   In a few years comparatively, Scott produced a series of imaginative works unequalled, when we weigh quantity
with quality, by any writer of his age ; and he did
this, remember, in spite of his official duties as Clerk
of Session and Sheriff of Selkirkshire.   Not one of
his contemporaries, excepting Southey, worked so
hard at the desk ; and yet the impression conveyed
by his biography is that of the daring rider, of the
eager sportsman, of the man who loved all health-
ful recreations, and had always leisure for hospi-
tality, for charity, and for that true courtesy which
made a poor man once say, "Sir Walter always
talks to us as if we were blood-relations."   The
impression is a true one.   Scott was too large-
hearted, too full of human interests, perhaps I may
add, had too keen a sense of humour, to be a slave
to books.   He loved literature well, but he loved

X

men more, and his great modesty and good sense
kept him wholly free from the foibles which we are
so often asked to forgive in poets and men of letters.

"Waverley," Scott's first romance in prose, was
published anonymously in 1814, when the poet
was forty-three years of age, and two years after
he had bought the "mountain-farm" at Abbotsford,
which was destined to become so famous. And
from this period up to 1829, or to 1831, if we include
the novels published when the stream of his genius
was dried up, the "Great Unknown," as he was
now called, poured forth one romance after another
with a rapidity that seems magical. Nor was this
all, for in these years not only did Scott produce
additional poetry, but he published a history of
Scotland, a life of Napoleon, in nine volumes, a
biography of Swift, including an edition of his
works, in nineteen volumes, the delightful "Tales
of a Grandfather," and other works which would
have made the reputation of an ordinary man.
Money poured into his coffers, and Sir Walter, who
wished above all things to found a family, spent
freely what he earned. Unfortunately, his affairs
were mixed up with those of his printers and
publisher. He had taken upon himself the respon-
sibilities of a man of business without troubling
himself much about the way in which the business
was conducted. The result was bankruptcy. And
now the true heroism of Scott's nature appeared.
He was fifty-five years old, and had signs of failing
health ; his wife was dying, his obligations amounted

to £117,000, and the prospects of his family seemed to be ruined. He felt the blow profoundly, but it did not stagger him; scarcely, indeed, did it hinder him in his work. Within two years he repaid his creditors nearly £40,000. Within five years his debt was lessened by £63,000. But his health gave way, and one paralytic stroke after another showed the cost of the stupendous effort he was making. "Like the headland stemming a rough sea," Mr. Hutton says finely, "he was gradually worn away, but never crushed." Before the end came, Sir Walter, having had a vessel placed at his disposal by the king, sailed for the Mediterranean. He visited Malta, Naples, and Rome; but it was too late for enjoyment, and a strong yearning for home came upon the poet. For some time he lay ill in London, but recovered sufficiently to reach Abbotsford, where he died, on the 21st of September, 1832.

"It was a beautiful day," writes Lockhart; "so warm that every window was wide open, and so perfectly still that the sound of all others most delicious to his ear, the gentle ripple of the Tweed over its pebbles, was distinctly audible as we knelt around the bed, and his eldest son kissed and closed his eyes." He was buried at Dryburgh Abbey, but it may be said of Scott, as Milton said of Shakespeare, that he has built himself "a livelong monument."

> "And so sepulchred in such pomp doth lie
> That kings for such a tomb would wish to die."

The day before Sir Walter left Abbotsford for the Mediterranean, carrying with him "the might of the whole world's good wishes "—

> "Blessings and prayers in nobler retinue
> Than sceptred king or laurelled conqueror knows "—

Wordsworth, from whose noble sonnet on his friend's departure these lines have been taken, visited Scott for the last time. Together they wandered on the banks of Yarrow, and the sweet influences of nature felt in such a presence, and at a time when pain must have been largely mixed with pleasure, inspired a tribute from Wordsworth which deserves to last as long as the stream of which he sings. It must suffice to refer to this celebrated poem, "Yarrow Revisited," without quoting from it, since the student either of Scott or of Wordsworth will naturally turn to these stanzas —a golden link binding together the two greatest spirits of their time.

And now a few words about Scott's poetry. The source of its inspiration is to be found in the border ballads he loved so well and recited with such spirit. One of the earliest anecdotes we have of the future poet is characteristic. He relates that, having learned the ballad of " Hardyknute,"* he shouted it forth so vigorously that a visitor exclaimed, "One may as well speak in the mouth of a cannon as where that child is." Scott's genius

---

* Written by Lady Wardlaw, and in Scott's judgment, expressed the year before his death, a noble imitation of the best style.

as a poet was that of the ballad-writer, and this may be the best place to make a few remarks upon the ballad, a form of verse which takes no mean place in the history of English poetry. The ballad is a lyrical narrative, and the tale told in it, sometimes humorous, but far oftener tragical, is of a direct character, and appeals to popular sentiment. The singer or the reciter (and we must remember that all the old ballads were recited or sung long years before they appeared in print) deals with the primary feelings of the race—with the passions, hopes and fears in which all can more or less sympathize. The old ballad is the simplest style of poetry we possess, and the charm of it to modern ears lies in its pathos, its arch quaintness of expression, in the occasional sweetness of the music, in the manly strength of the thought. It has been said that the ballad is the true springhead of history; with greater truth it may be called the source of the drama and the epic; and it is impossible to study the works of our great poets without seeing how largely they stand indebted to their predecessors the balladists. Bishop Percy, who in Wordsworth's judgment possessed a genius for this kind of poetry superior to that of any modern writer, was the first to bring together in a readable form the finest of our British ballads. His "Reliques of Ancient English Poetry" (1765) produced a poetical revolution, and the effect of the work upon Coleridge, Wordsworth, and Scott was so great that it is scarcely an exaggeration to call

Percy their poetical father. Walter Scott was a schoolboy when the work fell into his hands. The influence it exercised was magical, and it was permanent.

"I remember well," he wrote, "the spot where I read these volumes for the first time. It was beneath a large platanus tree, the ruins of which had been intended for an old-fashioned arbour. The summer day sped onward so fast that notwithstanding the sharp appetite of thirteen I forgot the hour of dinner, was sought for with anxiety, and was found entranced in my intellectual banquet. To read and to remember was in this instance the same thing, and henceforth I overwhelmed my schoolfellows, and all who would hearken to me, with tragical recitations from the ballads of Bishop Percy. The first time, too, I could scrape a few shillings together I bought unto myself a copy of these beloved volumes; nor do I believe I ever read a book half so frequently or with half the enthusiasm."

No editor can pretend to fix a date for what may be justly called the people's poetry. We can trace several of the ballads back to the fifteenth century, but there is every likelihood that they were old ballads then. Nor is it possible to discover the origin of a large number of the romantic ballads, since the same subjects have been treated in popular verse by the early poets of Scandinavia and Germany. It has been justly observed that this strong family likeness to ancient foreign ballads is in itself no bad testimony to the age of ours. Other evidence may be found in incidental allusions, made by early authors, to manners and customs, to religious rites and ceremonies, which passed away many centuries ago. Sir Philip Sidney, for example, wrote of "Chevy-Chace" as an ancient ballad in his day. And, again, the use of a ballad by an old poet shows to some extent its antiquity. Scattered through the plays of Shakespeare are many lines or stanzas from popular ballads. It was in all probability the ballad of Geruntus that suggested to the dramatist the plot of the "Merchant of Venice ; " it was apparently from a ballad also that he gained important hints with regard to the plot of "King Lear." Three hundred years, however, is comparatively a short life for a ballad, and we may be sure that many of our best pieces of this kind date from an earlier age.

The old English ballad first assumed a place in literature in the last century, partly by the help of Allan Ramsay, the author of a lovely pastoral, "The Gentle Shepherd," but Allan Ramsay. 1686-1758. chiefly through the labours of Percy. Walter Scott's own famous work, "The Minstrelsy of the Scottish Border," appeared at the beginning of this century. It was a splendid success, for it contained, in addition to a large amount of valuable information, a great number of ballads never before published, some of these being among the most valuable we possess. Several collections of ballads have been edited since Scott's day, and in any one of them the characteristics of this early poetry may be readily traced. There is in it abundance of coarse humour, but the balladist delighted still more in tragic incidents, and it may be said without much exaggeration that a track of blood is visible over the wide field of ballad poetry. The old ballads, indeed, abound in acts of barbarous cruelty, in atrocious crimes and extravagant incidents. The nature exhibited in these poems is the nature belonging to a turbulent, unsettled time, when brutal passions were unrestrained by law, and when the people's poets uttered what they had to say in the plainest language they could use. Simplicity of diction and directness of purpose are the unfailing marks of the ancient ballad, and later imitations, so far as they are successful, bear the same features.

Of all modern writers, Scott retains in the largest degree the force and picturesqueness of style which distinguish the old minstrels. He sees what he sings about, and makes his readers see it also. The description of Flodden Field in "Marmion," while exhibiting an artistic skill unknown in earlier times, has the vividness and spirit which delight us in the balladists; and it has been justly said that his "Bonnie Dundee" is, of all Jacobite ballads, one of the most spirited and soul-stirring. In "Young Lochinvar," a modern version of an old story, Scott gives another fine specimen of rapid and vigorous narrative which would have delighted the wandering singers of an earlier age.*

---

* Lord Macaulay, too, caught with singular art the strain of the ballad-singers, and there is not a schoolboy in England who has not read, I had almost said who cannot recite, " The Battle of Naseby," or the glorious story of

"How well Horatius kept the bridge
In the brave days of old."

Perhaps " Cadyow Castle " is a still finer specimen of
his art.   Listen to the following stanzas, Thomas Campbell, 1777-1844.
which the poet Thomas Campbell was
wont to shout upon the North Bridge
at Edinburgh, until, as he said, the whole fraternity
of coachmen knew him by tongue as he passed :—

> " Through the huge oaks of Evandale,
>   Whose limbs a thousand years have worn,
> What sullen roar comes down the gale
>   And drowns the hunter's pealing horn.

> " Mightiest of all the beasts of chase
>   That roam in woody Caledon,
> Crashing the forest in his race,
>   The mountain bull comes thundering on.

> " Fierce on the hunter's quivered band
>   He rolls his eyes of swarthy glow ;
> Spurns, with black hoof and horn, the sand,
>   And tosses high his mane of snow."

As a war-lyrist, whose trumpet-notes send the
blood bounding, Scott has no modern rival, unless
it be Campbell.* "I am sensible," Scott wrote,
" that if there be anything good about my poetry,
it is a hurried frankness of composition which

---

* Campbell's reputation in the very early years of this century
was extraordinary, but time has considerably dimmed its lustre,
and not unjustly. The "Pleasures of Hope," which pushed him
into fame at twenty-one, is little better than a first-class prize poem,
and not wholly free from the plagiarisms natural to youth ; his
" Gertrude of Wyoming," although sweet in its Spenserian versification, is comparatively feeble, and his fame is now chiefly sustained
by his fine war-lyrics—" The Battle of the Baltic," " Ye Mariners of
England," and " Hohenlinden." Far distant be the day when these
spirit-stirring verses are forgotten !

pleases soldiers, sailors, and young people of bold and active dispositions."

He is too modest. His poetry, owing perhaps to the force of contrast, wins the love of readers who are neither active nor bold ; and once won, it is a love that abides for life. The memory holds his verse tenaciously, and none the less because the heart finds its principal nourishment in poetry of a higher order.

It is easy to say what the reader will not find in the poetical works of Scott. There are in them no profound depths ; no lofty heights up which we can ascend, "dazzled and drunk with beauty ; " no daring metaphors ; none of that subtle felicity of language which Mr. Tennyson so justly finds in Virgil, and possesses himself—

"All the charm of all the Muses often flowering in a lonely
      word."

Scott loves Nature with a manly love, and his descriptions of what he sees are unrivalled for accuracy, but he does not reach her heart as Wordsworth does. The life breathing through his pages is that outward life which, though it needs a poet's pen to describe, requires no inspiration to enjoy. I do not think Scott is often conventional or commonplace, but through long pages there is sometimes little sign of strong poetical emotion ; yet there is not one in which you do not feel the winds of heaven blowing on your cheeks, and enjoy the exhilarating sense of freedom. His poetry is the

reverse of all that is effeminate and enervating.
The instrument he loves best is the trumpet, but he
can play sweetly too upon the flute, and some of
his love-lyrics have a unique charm.   Their tenderness and beauty show the true nature of the man,
whose pathetic depth of feeling is apt to escape the
casual observer.   His songs are unlaboured, and
occasionally, as in the following lines, the voice of
the singer reminds us of our early lyrists :—

> " Proud Maisie is in the wood,
>   Walking so early ;
> Sweet Robin sits on the bush,
>   Singing so rarely.
>
> " 'Tell me, thou bonny bird,
>   When shall I marry me ?'—
> ' When six braw gentlemen
>   Kirkward shall carry ye.'
>
> " ' Who makes the bridal bed ?
>   Birdie, say truly ?'—
> ' The grey-headed sexton,
>   That delves the grave duly.
>
> " ' The glow-worm o'er grave and stone
>   Shall light thee steady ;
> The owl from the steeple sing,
>   Welcome, proud lady.' "

And now let me give one illustration of Scott's
martial notes.   There is an old Gaelic melody,
" The Pibroch of Donald Dhu," which is supposed
to refer to an expedition of a chieftain belonging
to Clan MacDonald, who invaded Lochaber, and

at Inverlochy defeated the Earls of Mar and Caith-
ness. This old melody inspired the rapid verses
of the poet—

> " Pibroch of Donuil Dhu,
>   Pibroch of Donuil,
> Wake thy wild voice anew,
>   Summon Clan Conuil.
> Come away, come away,
>   Hark to the summons !
> Come in your war array,
>   Gentles and commons !
>
> " Come from deep glen, and
>   From mountain so rocky ;
> The war-pipe and pennon
>   Are at Inverlochy.
> Come every hill-plaid, and
>   True heart that wears one ;
> Come every steel blade, and
>   Strong hand that bears one !
>
> " Leave untended the herd,
>   The flock without shelter ;
> Leave the corpse uninterred,
>   The bride at the altar.
> Leave the deer, leave the steer,
>   Leave nets and barges ;
> Come with your fighting gear,
>   Broadswords and targes.
>
> " Come as the winds come, when
>   Forests are rended :
> Come as the waves come, when
>   Navies are stranded.

Faster come, faster come,
   Faster and faster :
Chief, vassal, page, and groom,
   Tenant and master.

" Fast they come, fast they come ;
   See how they gather !
Wide waves the eagle plume,
   Blended with heather,
Cast your plaids, draw your blades,
   Forward each man set !
Pibroch of Donuil Dhu,
   Knell for the onset ! "

I need not say much about the separate poems.
Of the "Lay of the Last Minstrel," forty-four
thousand copies are said to have been sold in
twenty-five years. It is a spirited, ballad-like
piece, loose in construction, and not always consistent ; but full of fire, of picturesque incident, and
of patriotic feeling. The passage commencing—

" Breathes there the man with soul so dead,
   Who never to himself has said,
   ' This is my own, my native land ' ? "—

is one of the most familiar in the poem. The spirit
of these lines breathes through all the poet's works,
whether in rhyme or prose, for happily he had not
reached the height of wisdom attained by some
modern philosophers, who have discovered that
patriotism is no virtue.* It has been said by a

---

* Not so thought Scott's countryman, the "Chelsea Philosopher," Thomas Carlyle. In his essay on Burns, he writes :—

well-known critic that the night ride of William
of Deloraine to Melrose Abbey, in the "Lay," is
as fine a piece of descriptive poetry of its kind as
could be found anywhere; and this is true, or was
until Mr. Browning produced his famous ride from
Ghent to Aix.

A considerable portion of "Marmion," Scott's
second poem, was composed, as I have already
said, in the saddle, when Edinburgh, like the rest
of the island, was threatened with an invasion by
the first Napoleon. It is not entitled to be called
a great poem, but it has great and, indeed,
unequalled passages, one of which—the battle of
Flodden—is worthy of the poet who has written
his own character, or rather one aspect of it, in
the following stanza :—

> "Sound, sound the clarion! fill the fife!
> To all the sensual world proclaim,
> One crowded hour of glorious life
> Is worth an age without a name."

The epistles prefixed to the different cantos of
"Marmion" may be read separately. Some readers
will look upon them as the choicest portion of the
work, nor will they be far wrong. Scott was not

"We hope there is a patriotism founded on something better than
prejudice, that our country may be dear to us without injury to our
philosophy, that in loving and justly prizing all other lands, we may
prize justly and yet love before all others our own stern Motherland,
and the venerable structure of social and moral life which mind has
through long ages been building up for us there. Surely there is
nourishment for the better part of man's heart in all this; surely
the roots that have fixed themselves in the very core of man's being
may be so cultivated as to grow up, not into briers, but into roses, in
the field of his life."

an egotist like Byron, but in these poetical letters we see something of his healthy and lovable nature.

The "Lady of the Lake" followed "Marmion," in little more than two years. According to Lockhart it is "the most interesting, romantic, picturesque, and graceful of his great poems." It was certainly the most popular at the time, and brought a vast swarm of tourists to Loch Katrine and the Trosachs. Through this poem, and still more by his Scotch novels, Sir Walter opened his country to the civilized world. No Scotchman has indirectly conferred such benefits on the land of the mountain and the flood. "It is stated as a fact, that from the year in which the 'Lady of the Lake' was published, the post-horse duty in Scotland rose in an extraordinary degree, and continued to do so regularly for some time afterwards, as successive editions of the poem appeared, and as the circle of readers grew wider." * The story is charmingly told, but it is not for its story that we judge a poem, and in poetical qualities the "Lady of the Lake" is inferior to "Marmion." On the other hand, nowhere in Scott's verse will you find such picturesque scenes, more sensibility, which, however, is sometimes in danger of verging on sentimentality, or sweeter snatches of song.

An anecdote characteristic of Scott may be given here. His little daughter Sophia was asked how she liked the "Lady of the Lake." Her answer was given with perfect simplicity: "Oh, I have not

* F. T. Palgrave.

read it. Papa says there is nothing so bad for young people as reading bad poetry." Here is another. His son Walter came home from the High School one day with signs that he had been fighting. He had been called a lassie, he said, and would not bear the imputation. The fact was his companions had dubbed him " The Lady of the Lake," a phrase the bold boy naturally resented, for he had never heard of the poem.

To return to Scott's poetry. The young student must read, and is sure to enjoy, the three poems upon which the author's reputation rests as a verse-man. " Rokeby " and the " Lord of the Isles," though full of spirited passages, have not the merit of the earlier poems, and one notices a still greater decline in the strength and freshness of his song when reading the " Bridal of Triermain " and " Harold the Dauntless." His " Field of Waterloo " does not do justice to the subject, but there is a passage in it scarcely to be surpassed for energetic force. It is too long to quote, but you will turn to the volume. The lines to which I refer begin with the eleventh section of the poem and end with the twelfth. In verse as in prose this "wondrous Potentate," as he is justly called by Wordsworth, shows the fine moral qualities which make us love the man while admiring the artist. What he has done for his country is inestimable, what he has done for literature, by the scorn of what is base, and the honour paid to all that is pure and noble, is of even greater value. It was not Scott's design to be a teacher, but his work has taught the world lessons it is not likely to forget.

[The best editions of Scott's poems and novels are published by Messrs. Black, in every variety of form. Of late years, owing to the expiration of copyright, other publishers have reproduced the poet's works, and the editions are innumerable. Lockhart's life, in ten volumes, was abridged by the author, and another abridgement also, published by Messrs. Black, was made a few years ago by Mr. Jenkinson. I have already referred to Mr. R. H. Hutton's biography, and to Mr. Palgrave's critical memoir prefixed to the Globe edition. Both these books are issued by Macmillan and Co.]

CHAPTER XV.

POETS OF THE NINETEENTH CENTURY
(*Continued*).

SAMUEL TAYLOR COLERIDGE—ROBERT SOUTHEY—
WALTER SAVAGE LANDOR.

SAMUEL TAYLOR COLERIDGE, whose extraordinary influence has been felt by men
ranking with the intellectual rulers of the century, was Wordsworth's most intimate friend in the early years of his poetic life. His mind, unlike that of Wordsworth, ranged over a vast field of philosophy and of literature. He read immensely, and made use of what he read with a happy forgetfulness of the original sources of his knowledge. His genius was receptive of ideas from every quarter, and without apparent effort he made these ideas his own. It is neither as a philosopher nor as a profoundly suggestive critic that Coleridge claims our attention. He was a poet also, and one who in his own department is

Samuel Taylor
Coleridge,
1772-1834.

unrivalled.   He lived to be an old man, but with a
few exceptions his best poetry was the produce of
five or six youthful years.   It is unique of its kind,
"musical as Apollo's lute," magical in beauty, perfect in imaginative conception.   "The highest lyric
work," writes Mr. Swinburne, "is either passionate
or imaginative.   Of passion Coleridge has nothing,
but for height and perfection of imaginative quality
he is the greatest of lyric poets.   This was his
special power, and this is his special praise."

The pathetic narrative of his life has been written
only in fragments.   He was born at Ottery St.
Mary's, Devonshire, in 1772, and was therefore two
years younger than Wordsworth, one year younger
than Scott, and the senior of Southey by two years.
Educated at Christ's Hospital, he was the schoolfellow of Charles Lamb, and the friendship begun
in those early days lasted for life.   Coleridge was
a dreamy boy, as he continued to be through life a
dreamy man, and a story is told of his plunging
his hands into a gentleman's pockets in Cheapside,
under the belief that he was Leander swimming
the Hellespont.   At school he gained distinction
enough to be made a deputy Grecian, and to win a
scholarship to Jesus College, Cambridge.   At college,
however, he did not take a degree, and we read of
his suddenly enlisting as a private soldier under
the name of Titus Comberback.   After this curious
escapade he returned for a brief interval to Cambridge.   At this period he had no settled views
nor any distinct purpose in life.   Already his clo-

quence was extraordinary, and bewitched every one who came under its spell. He became a Unitarian preacher and political lecturer, and a friendship formed with Southey, then equally unsettled and visionary, but high-minded, generous, and enthusiastic, led to the proposal of a settlement on the banks of the Susquehanna, where, according to "the minutest calculation," the demand on their labour for absolute necessaries would not exceed two hours a day. At this time Coleridge and Southey were engaged to two sisters, and their friend Lovell to a third. Nothing, as it seemed, was lacking to their felicity but money, and money sufficient for such an enterprise was not forthcoming. A gleam of unexpected fortune, however, awaited the two friends, for Joseph Cottle, a bookseller at Bristol, and a writer of verse on an extensive scale, after experiencing the "unmingled pleasure" of lending Coleridge five pounds, followed up this kindness by offering him thirty pounds for the copyright of his manuscript poems—an offer which was also made to Southey, and joyfully accepted by both. On the strength of a promise from Cottle of one guinea and a half for every hundred lines of verse he might write, Coleridge married Sarah Fricker (1795), and took a little cottage at Clevedon, where "the tallest rose peeped at the chamber window." But if there was a rose outside there were neither provisions nor kitchen utensils within, and these, at the poet's request, were supplied by his faithful friend and publisher.

The cottage, with its modest rent of five pounds a year, was speedily exchanged by its restless tenant for Bristol, and afterwards for Nether Stowey. And now he projected a review, and travelled over a large part of England to secure subscribers. A few numbers appeared, and then, as was the case with most of Coleridge's projects, the publication proved a failure. Southey wished he were free to write innumerable epics. Coleridge projected one on a vast scale. He should require ten years, he said, to warm his mind with universal science, five years for the composition of the poem, and five for its correction. "So would I write," he adds, "haply not unhearing of that divine and nightly whispering voice which speaks to mighty minds of predestined garlands starry and unwithering." The aspiration was noble, but the courage and force of purpose which such a work demanded were wanting, and we hear no more of the epic.

His first volume of poems, chiefly interesting as being the first, appeared in 1796. The following year (1797) produced the finest fruit of Coleridge's genius. In that year he and Wordsworth met apparently for the first time at Racedown, in Dorsetshire. The acquaintance soon warmed into friendship, and when Wordsworth and his sister removed to Alfoxden, he was within walking distance of his friend, who was then living at Nether Stowey. The result of this acquaintance, which led to close intimacy, was the publication of a little volume which contained among its treasures " The

Rime of the Ancient Mariner" and Wordsworth's immortal "Lines written above Tintern Abbey." The poets, accompanied by Miss Wordsworth, went in the autumn of that year to Germany, where, however, they parted company. To Coleridge the earliest result of his German studies was a translation of Schiller's "Wallenstein." It contains some beautiful lines not to be found in the German text, but this poet's version of a poet's work—the labour of six weeks—will not satisfy a reader familiar with the original. Yet it is probably one of the finest translations we possess of a foreign drama.

Soon after returning to England, Coleridge took up his residence at Keswick, where Southey was already living; but before long, leaving his wife under Southey's care—an arrangement made, apparently, by her husband with entire equanimity—Coleridge went abroad, and for one year acted as secretary to the Governor of Malta, Sir Alexander Ball. Then we find him once more at Keswick, or with Wordsworth at Grasmere, until the year 1810, when he finally left the Lake district, handing over his wife and children to the generous care of Southey, but not without some slight provision for their support. According to Southey he never wrote to them, and never opened a letter from them. It is a miserable story. Coleridge had become a slave to opium, and this vice, without destroying his sense of right and wrong, had so weakened the moral power, that all capacity of resistance seemed destroyed. Few men have been more gifted, but the want of resolution not only hindered great achievements, but prevented Coleridge from performing the common duties of life. Owing to what he calls "the worse than death that opium entailed," his transcendent gifts were squandered, and the best years of his life lost. His remorse in lucid moments was profound, but his vice held him captive. "He promises and does nothing," are the words of his truest friend. "He leaves his family," Southey adds, "to chance and charity. With good feelings, good principles as far as the understanding is concerned, and an intellect as clear and as powerful as was ever vouchsafed to man, he is the slave of degrading sensuality, and sacrifices everything to it."

The narrative is told, with perhaps unnecessary details, by the generous, warm-hearted Cottle. Coleridge never rejoined his wife and family ; but he did succeed eventually in overcoming his "one cunning bosom sin," and during the last eighteen years of his life lived under the friendly roof of Mr. Gillman, of Highgate. Long before this time he had renounced the cold creed of his youth, and the influence of his half-theological, half-philosophical writings was widely felt. As a talker he has been pronounced unrivalled, but his ideas were not always expressed with clearness, and even Wordsworth came away on one occasion confessing his inability to understand anything that had been said. Carlyle, too, in his cynical account of a visit to the Highgate philosopher, while admitting him to be the most surprising talker extant in the world,

adds that his flood of utterance was " confused and
unintelligible," and although " piercing radiances of
a most subtle insight came at intervals," he is
reminded of Hazlitt's sarcasm : " Excellent talker,
very, if you let him start from no premisses and
come to no conclusion."   Against this opinion
of a writer who states frankly his want of sympathy
with Coleridge's religious views, must be set the
statements of men who knew him better than
Carlyle, and had listened to him in his brightest
hours of inspiration.*   Carlyle, no doubt, hit upon
a real blot when he said that Coleridge wanted
will.   " He never straightens his knee-joints," he
writes.   " He *would* do with all his heart, but he
knows he dares not."

The latter years of Coleridge's life were years of
great suffering.   His virtues were passive rather
than active ; his patience was exemplary, and his
temper seldom ruffled.   Living out of the world,
his great fame brought men of the highest mark to
the Grove at Highgate.   To have seen and heard
Coleridge was an event in a man's life.   His flow
of talk was unceasing, and might sometimes have
been monotonous.   Possibly it was too much like
preaching.   "Have you ever heard me preach " said
Coleridge to Lamb one day.   " I never heard you
do anything else," was the reply.

He died on the 25th of July, 1834, and was
buried in the old and now disused churchyard

* Read the preface to " Specimens of Coleridge's Table Talk,"
by his son-in-law, H. N. Coleridge, and read that " Talk " itself.

of Highgate.   "When I heard of the death of
Coleridge," Lamb wrote, " it was without grief.   It
seemed to me that he had long been on the con-
fines of the next world—that he had a hunger for
eternity.   I grieved then that I could not grieve ;
but since, I feel how great a part he was of me.
His great and dear spirit haunts me.   I cannot
think a thought, I cannot make a criticism on men
or books, without an ineffectual turning and reference to him.   He was the proof and touchstone
of all my cogitations."   Mr. Ainger, * who quotes
this passage, adds—

"The death of his friend was Charles Lamb's
death-blow.   There had been two persons in the
world for whom he would have wished to live—
Coleridge and his sister Mary.   The latter was now
for the greater part of each year worse than dead
to him.   The former was gone, and the blank left
him helplessly alone.   In conversation with friends,
he would suddenly exclaim, as if with surprise that
aught else in the world should interest him, 'Coleridge is dead !'   And within five weeks of the day
when the touching tribute just cited was committed
to paper, he was called to join his friend." †

---

* " English Men of Letters : Charles Lamb," by Alfred Ainger
(Macmillan and Co.).

† Charles Lamb (1775–1834) is one of the most delightful
humorists in the language—the most delightful, not excepting
Addison, who has given us in essays the best fruits of his genius.
No man could have written " Elia " who had not a poet's heart ;
but Lamb also expressed some of his deepest and tenderest feelings
in verse, and although not a giant among them, belongs to the race
of poets.   What reader, indeed, can dispute his title who is ac-

An imagination fantastic and subtle, and an exquisite ear for melody, are the chief characteristics of the poetry of Coleridge. He has been charged with plagiarism as a prose-writer; in poetry his originality is undoubted.* The marvellous story of the "Ancient Mariner," the still stranger story of "Christabel," hold the reader by a spell which is due to Coleridge alone. There is nothing like these poems in our literature. They are unrivalled for imaginative charm, as well as for the lovely music of the rhythm. The "Ancient Mariner" is the worthier of the two, because it is complete, while "Christabel" remains a fragment. Prosaic critics complain that the penalty inflicted on the mariner for merely shooting an albatross is so disproportionate to the offence as to mar the concep-

---

quainted with "Hester," "The Old Familiar Faces," and the lines which have the flavour of a seventeenth-century poet, "On an Infant dying as soon as born." It was fitting that Wordsworth should couple the old schoolmates and friends, who were also his friends, in one regretful stanza—

> "The rapt one of the godlike forehead,
> The heaven-eyed creature sleeps in earth;
> And Lamb, the frolic and the gentle,
> Has vanished from his lonely hearth."

* Strange to say, Coleridge owed his poetical birth to the Rev. William Lisle Bowles (1762–1850), Canon of Salisbury, a writer of plaintive sonnets, marked by sensibility and sweetness. There is, however, no sign in them of that living power which would be likely to stimulate a mind like Coleridge's. Goethe in like manner confessed his early obligations to the "Vicar of Wakefield;" but that story, although in Carlyle's judgment it is "nothing more" than the best of modern idyls, has a charm which takes every reader captive. The gentle verse of Bowles, on the contrary, one would have thought, is too deficient in impressiveness to affect any intellect strongly.

tion of the "Rime," but a poem that carries us at once into the region of the marvellous must be read with a belief in the supernatural element. It is enough that the poet's conception hangs together, and that the idea which prompted the poem is congruous throughout. In this respect the execution of the "Rime of the Ancient Mariner" is masterly.

The vividness of the whole representation is wonderful, and we seem to see, with the very eyes of the mariner himself, all that happened on that eerie voyage when the dead men, two hundred in number, navigated the ship in silence.

> "The helmsman steered, the ship moved on,
>   Yet never a breeze up-blew ;
> The mariners all 'gan work the ropes,
>   Where they were wont to do ;
> They raised their limbs like lifeless tools—
>   We were a ghastly crew !
>
> "The body of my brother's son
>   Stood by me knee to knee ;
> The body and I pulled at one rope,
>   But he said nought to me."

Observe, in reading the poem, the effect caused by the introduction of the Wedding Guest, whom the mariner holds with his glittering eye until his tale is told ; and note, too, the lovely touches of natural beauty and the pictures of familiar objects which prevent the atmosphere of the poem from growing too oppressive. The happy living things darting through the water "with a flash of golden fire;" the little birds filling sea and air "with their sweet jargoning;" the pleasant noise of the sails—

> "A noise like of a hidden brook
> In the leafy month of June,
> That to the sleeping woods all night
> Singeth a quiet tune "—

the wind that fanned the mariner's cheek like "a meadow-gale of spring;" the bride and bridesmaids singing in the garden-bower;—these are pleasant images used by the poet with consummate art.

"Christabel," had the poet fulfilled his purpose, might have proved a still higher illustration of his genius. Yet, although a tale half told, it remains one of Coleridge's highest efforts—a poem no other poet could have written.* Scott heard it read in manuscript, and the movement of the verse suggested the metre of his "Lay;" but fresh and spirited as that metre is, Scott had not Coleridge's unerring sense of melody, which is still more striking in the poem he professed to have dreamed, called "Kubla Khan." This is a musical play of words. Of a far higher order of poetry, since, in language not easily to be surpassed, it appeals to human feelings, is "Love"—a poem of youth and hope; a poem fitted to make life more beautiful, even in its most beautiful season. There is not space here for quotation, and such a poem cannot be broken into fragments; but room may be found for

---

* "The thing attempted in 'Christabel' is the most difficult of execution in the whole field of romance—witchery by daylight—and the success is complete" (*Quarterly Review*, No. ciii.).

a short piece called "Youth and Age," written at a later period of the poet's life. The concluding lines are omitted, as the poem is complete without them.

"Verse, a breeze 'mid blossoms straying
Where Hope clung feeding like a bee—
Both were mine! Life went a-maying
With Nature, Hope, and Poesy,
    When I was young!
When I was young? Ah, woful When!
Ah! for the change 'twixt Now and Then!
This breathing-house not built with hands,
This body that does me grievous wrong,
O'er aery cliffs and glittering sands
How lightly then it flashed along:
Like those trim skiffs, unknown of yore,
On winding lakes and rivers wide,
That ask no aid of sail or oar,
That fear no spite of wind or tide!
Nought cared this body for wind or weather
When Youth and I lived in't together.

"Flowers are lovely, Love is flower-like;
Friendship is a sheltering tree;
O! the joys that came down shower-like
Of Friendship, Love, and Liberty,
    Ere I was old!
Ere I was old? Ah, woful Ere,
Which tells me Youth's no longer here!
O Youth! for years so many and sweet
'Tis known that Thou and I were one;
I'll think it but a fond conceit—
It cannot be that Thou art gone!
Thy vesper-bell hath not yet tolled,
And thou wert aye a masker bold!
What strange disguise hast now put on
To make believe that thou art gone?

I see these locks in silvery slips,
This drooping gait, this altered size ;
But Springtide blossoms on thy lips,
And tears take sunshine from thine eyes !
Life is but Thought ; so think I will
That Youth and I are housemates still."

It is possible that Mrs. Barbauld's beautiful lines on " Life," which may be read below,* suggested to Coleridge his still more beautiful poem. The thought of one poet is often the inspiration of another, and there can be no doubt that Coleridge's great " Hymn before Sunrise in the Vale of Chamouni," owes its origin to a little German poem of twenty lines, written by Frederica Brun— a fact which does not lessen its beauty or diminish its greatness.

We have said that all, or nearly all, Wordsworth's best work was written before he was forty years old.   Of Coleridge, his most recent biographer

---

* " Life ! I know not what thou art,
   But know that thou and I must part ;
   And when, or how, or where we met,
   I own to me's a secret yet.
   Life ! we've been long together,
   Through pleasant and through cloudy weather ;
   'Tis hard to part when friends are dear—
   Perhaps 'twill cost a sigh, a tear :—
   Then steal away, give little warning,
      Choose thine own time ;
   Say not ' Good night '—but in some brighter clime
   Bid me ' Good morning.' " [1]

[1] " Sitting with Madame D'Arblay," says Rogers, " some weeks before she died, I said to her, ' Do you remember those lines of Mrs. Barbauld's " Life," which I once repeated to you ?' ' Remember them !' she replied ; ' I repeat them to myself every night before I go to sleep.' "

observes with truth, that "in any estimate of
modern poetry, the rank and importance of
Coleridge's contributions to it can never be
adequately or duly estimated without remembering that all the essential part of them had been
produced long before Byron, Shelley, Keats, or
even Scott, had begun to write." He was a leader
among the poets of his century, and he was one of
the leaders of modern thought. Let us write his
faults on the sand ; what he has done for England
deserves to be chronicled in letters of gold.

[The memoir from which we have quoted is prefixed to an edition
of Coleridge's poetical and dramatic works, four vols., 1880 (Macmillan and Co.). Gillman wrote, or rather tried to write, a life of
Coleridge, and the first volume was published in 1838. The second
failed to appear, and to this day no biography has been written
worthy of the name. In the works of Leigh Hunt, of Lamb, of
Hazlitt, and of De Quincey, the reader will find constant allusions
to Coleridge, and also criticisms of his works. Turn especially to
Leigh Hunt's "Imagination and Fancy," and see also Shairp's
"Studies in Poetry." Joseph Cottle's "Reminiscences of Coleridge
and Southey," garrulous and injudicious, but not unkindly in purpose, will assist the future biographers of the poet.]

Sara Coleridge, the poet's beautiful and gifted
daughter, thought Southey the best
man she had ever known. After saying
how greatly her mind had been moulded

Robert
Southey.
1774-1843.

by Wordsworth's conversation and intellect, she
adds that in matters that concerned the heart and
the moral being she was still more deeply indebted
to the character and conduct of her admirable
uncle Southey. There was, indeed, a daily beauty
in his life which attracted every one who knew

him. He was a true hero of literature, and ennobled a great profession by his signal virtues.

To read his life properly it is necessary to be
acquainted with all its details. His happy home
at Keswick, happy for so many years, but destined
to be sadly overclouded, his vigorous persistent
labour, his joy in books, his firm attachment to
friends—and some of England's noblest men were
friends of Southey—his charming letters, which
show, as few of his works do, the innermost heart
of the man, his vast acquisitions and the joyous
energy he put into his work, his unbounded
generosity and freedom from low aims,—all this
cannot be told at all, much less told satisfactorily
in a few brief pages. Some prominent dates and
incidents must suffice here.

Robert Southey was born at Bristol, August 12,
1774, and was educated at Westminster and Balliol
College, Oxford, where his college course was de-
frayed by his uncle, the Rev. Herbert Hill. He
took no honours at Oxford, and after vainly trying
to study medicine and law, discovered, with an un-
alterable conviction, that his success and happiness
in life were to be found in literature alone. Before
reaching this conclusion, however, he had written
and burnt innumerable verses; had made the acquaintance of Coleridge in 1794 (three years before
the meeting of Wordsworth and Coleridge); had
planned with them the alluring scheme of Panti-
socracy, a vision of the golden age; and at his uncle's
request and cost had visited Spain and Portugal.

Mr. Hill hoped that this tour would wean Southey
from an imprudent attachment. It only served to
make that attachment binding. On the day fixed
for the departure he was married to Edith Fricker.
"They parted immediately, and Edith went to
reside with Joseph Cottle's sisters, preserving her
maiden name, and wearing the wedding-ring hung
round her neck." Truly does Mr. Dowden say
that "never did woman put her happiness in more
loyal keeping." In six months he returned to
England and to Edith, and after some delay made
the "one happy choice" of a profession which few
writers have done more to dignify.

Landor called Southey, Coleridge, and Wordsworth "three towers of one castle." Looked at as
poets, there is little connection between them, and
the absurdity of linking these friends together as
the "Lake School" is obvious, but as friends the
three names are inseparable. They were alike, too,
in their rejection, as life advanced, of the political
and religious opinions formed in youth. The flame
of their early zeal burnt itself out, but not before
their hearts and intellects were illuminated by a
clearer and more steadfast light. In the expression
of his ultimate opinions of Church and State
Southey was not always judicious; he was sometimes intolerant and sometimes illogical; but to
write, as some critics have done, of him or of his
friends as renegades and turncoats, is to pervert the
meaning of words. Southey was ultimately made
Poet-Laureate, and Wordsworth, who "uttered

Z

nothing base," succeeded him ; but neither of them was indebted for success in life to his change of opinion, and to Coleridge worldly success was a boon denied altogether.

At Greta Hall, near Keswick, Southey lived for forty years, composing epics which he believed would be immortal, editing books, writing quarterly reviews and biographies for bread, in his limpid and forcible English, and portioning out his days, hour by hour, with marvellous regularity. His books did not bring much gold to the family till, and when Sir Robert Peel wished to make Southey a baronet, the Prime Minister was surprised to learn that he could not support the title. He might have been a wealthy man had he wished, but he loved his freedom too well. At one time he was offered £2000 a year and a share in the profits to write the leading article in the *Times ;* and he declined, also, the more congenial office of librarian to the Advocates' Library at Edinburgh. His happiness was found in reading books and writing them, in the love of wife and children, in noble and, considering his position, unparalleled charity. His heart was in his home ; there he found the greatest joys of life and its bitterest sorrows. The loss of a son made him feel an old man. While still in his prime he lost a daughter, too, and in 1834 he had to tell his oldest friend, Grosvenor Bedford, " I have been parted from my wife by something worse than death. Forty years she has been the life of my life, and I have left her this day in a lunatic asylum." Mrs.

Southey died, happily in her own house, in the following year. Before his life ended, Southey's active brain was worn out. Had Landor feared this when, in the beautiful address to his friend, he writes?—

"The dance of youth, O Southey, runs not round,
But closes at the bottom of the room,
Amid the falling dust and deepening gloom,
Where the weary sit them down,
And Beauty, too, unbraids, and waits a lovelier crown.

"We hurry to the river we must cross,
And swifter downward every footstep wends;
Happy, who reach it ere they count the loss
Of half their faculties and half their friends."

In 1840 Wordsworth writes that Southey did not recognize him till he was told. "Then his eyes flashed for a moment with their former brightness; but he sank into the state in which I had found him, patting with both hands his books affectionately, like a child." This was written in 1840. In 1843 Wordsworth stood beside his grave. He is buried in Crosthwaite churchyard, his "long home" being within sight of Greta Hall. In the church a recumbent marble effigy preserves, as well as marble can, the handsome features of the poet, and a monument has been also raised to his memory in Westminster Abbey. Never were such honours less needed or more deserved.

A distinguished living poet has recently placed a wreath upon the tomb of Southey. Sir Henry Taylor, in the laureate's later years, was his youth-

ful friend and admirer, and it is a matter of lasting
regret that he was not permitted to write his life.
In his old age, and after the lapse of many years,
his final and deliberate judgment on Southey is
thus recorded :—

> "Of what he did accomplish, a portion will not soon be
> forgotten.   There were greater poets in his generation, and
> there were men of a deeper and more far-reaching philosophic
> faculty ; but take him for all in all—his ardent and genial
> piety, his moral strength, the magnitude and variety of his
> powers, the field which he covered in literature, and the
> beauty of his life—it may be said of him justly, and with no
> straining of the truth, that of all his contemporaries he was
> the greatest MAN." *

Southey had no doubt that he should live as a
poet, and live also as an historian.   The time perhaps has not yet come to fix his position in our
literature.   His style as a prose-writer is nearly
faultless.   In poetry he stands alone, and has no
affinity either with Coleridge or Wordsworth, unless
it is to be found in the great simplicity, reminding us
occasionally of the latter exhibited in some of his
shorter pieces.   In Southey's vast epics his descriptions are frequently beautiful ; he delights in the
picturesque, and great art is often displayed in the
composition of his pictures.   Something we seem
to miss even in his most perfect work, "Roderick;"
and that something is the living soul of poetry

---

* "The English Poets," edited by T. H. Ward, M.A., vol. iv. p.
164.   A still more glowing eulogy of Southey as a man and as an
author will be found in the first volume of Coleridge's "Biographia
Literaria."

which gives, as it were, breath and being to the immortal creations of great poets. His metrical eccentricities, displayed especially in "Thalaba," were unfavourable to the immediate success of his verse, and must always stand in the way of its popularity. Southey had not the ear for harmony which would justify experiments, and Landor probably felt this when he wrote : "Are we not a little too fond of novelty and experiment, and is it not reasonable to prefer those kinds of versification which the best poets have adopted and the best judges have cherished for the longest time ?" Many of his shorter poems are humorous, but the humour, when not grotesque, as in the "Old Woman of Berkeley," is boyish in character. He wrote capital nonsense verses, and doubtless found a relief in this recreation from the severe strain upon his mind. Southey's pathos, if not more genuine than his humour, is more attractive, and poems like the "Holly Tree," and the "Stanzas written in his Library," touch every heart, and are not likely to be forgotten. Who does not remember, too, his "Battle of Blenheim"?

[To know truly what Southey was as a man and as an author would need far more leisure than most readers have to bestow. There is a "Life" by his son, in six volumes ; there is a selection from his letters by his son-in-law ; there are ten volumes of poetical works, and a vast number of volumes in prose. His best lyrics and ballads are to be found in selections, but the epics which he built up with such hope and such labour do not appeal to the young. An exception may be made, perhaps, in favour of the "Curse of Kehama."]

Walter Savage Landor has a great name in
literature due principally to his noble
prose.   There is a dignity in his style,
a loftiness of purpose in his aims, a
wealth of thought, and an harmonious completeness
in his work, which strike us with admiration.   Some
of his " Imaginary Conversations " are models of
art, perfect in construction as a Grecian temple, but
like that temple wanting the less sharply defined
but more romantic features of a Gothic cathedral.
The man was in some respects singularly unlike
his work.   Probably no modern writer has given
utterance to statelier wisdom.   His words are suggestive of mental tranquillity, and a freedom from
the passions and fretful cares that agitate mankind ;
yet Landor from early youth to extreme old age
was one of the most irascible and turbulent of men.
His outrageous temper embittered his own life and
that of others.   His course was that of a tempestuous day, but it had its gleams of sunshine as well
as its storms, and the true heart of the man is seen
in the friends he clung to, and who loved him
warmly in return.   I shall not attempt to relate
even in the most concise way the narrative of Landor's ill-regulated life.   It may be read at large in
Forster's biography—a book which, though loosely
written, is of great interest ; or more tersely in
the appreciative biography of Professor Colvin.
When the young reader comes to know Southey
and Landor he will see how fitting it is that
their names should be linked together.   In some

Walter Savage Landor, 1775-1864.

respects no two men could be less alike, and it might almost seem as if they belonged to different worlds. Yet from the poetical standpoint they had much in common, and Southey did not exaggerate when he said he would go a hundred miles to see the author of "Gebir," neither did Landor wilfully overstate his admiration when he said of "Roderick," "There is no poem in existence that I shall read so often." "Gebir," thus dear to Southey, won also the high admiration of Shelley. It is splendid in parts but not as a whole, and its obscurity, due to extreme condensation of style, will repel a reader whose purpose is not fixed enough to support him in the study. The same criticism may be passed on his "Count Julian," a subject which in different forms has been treated by Scott and Southey. Milton said that in writing prose he was using his left hand, and this was Landor's position in writing verse. And yet, although this be true, it seems almost unjust to say it, as we recall many of the short poems through which this strong, passionate-natured man uttered the tenderness of his heart.

[Selections from the writings of Landor, arranged and edited by Sidney Colvin (Macmillan and Co.), belongs to the Golden Treasury Series, and is worthy of it. Landor is the original of Boythorn in Dickens's "Bleak House.]

CHAPTER XVI.

POETS OF THE NINETEENTH CENTURY

(*Continued*).

LORD BYRON.

DURING the lifetime of Lord Byron and for a considerable time after his death there was

George Gordon Byron, 1788-1824.

no English poet who could compete with him in popularity. He was praised lavishly and without discrimination, and the critics who blamed him most severely as an immoral writer had no hesitation in admitting that the author of "Childe Harold" and "Don Juan" ranked with the greatest poets of the world. And this position Byron holds still upon the Continent, where he is placed next to Shakespeare in the roll of English poets.

In England, however, he has fallen, and I venture to think has fallen permanently, from this high estate.* Time, one of the most trustworthy of critics, has not proved altogether in favour of this passionate poet. It has taught us that much of his pathos is spurious, that much of what looked like gold is pinchbeck. His egotism fails to create sympathy, his dramatic characters have lost the little vitality which they once possessed, his voice is unmusical, and his grave moral faults repel rather than fascinate a generation that has never felt the glamour of his name. How strong it once was may be made evident by a single illustration. Thomas Carlyle, though he loved heroes, did not care to look for them in the men of his own age. He had never seen Byron, and perhaps this fact may account for what he wrote on hearing of his death. "Poor Byron!—alas, poor Byron! The news of his death came upon my heart like a mass of lead; and yet the thought of it sends a painful twinge through all my being, as if I had lost a brother." And Miss Welsh, Carlyle's future wife, wrote: "If they had said the sun or the moon was gone out of the heavens, it could not have struck me with a more awful and dreary

---

* In what I have to say of Byron in this chapter I know that I run the risk of being called hard names. There is a school of criticism which esteems withering contempt the fittest reply to writers who see defects in the gods of their idolatry—especially when these idols are looked at from a moral standpoint. To say a word against Shelley's conduct, to discover a weak side in his poetry, or to hint that the impurity of Byron's life has fatally injured the quality of his verse, is to run the risk of being assailed with a shower of scornful adjectives—

"Thick as autumnal leaves that strow the brooks
In Vallombrosa."

blank in the creation than the words, 'Byron is dead.'"

A similar feeling would probably have been expressed by three-fourths of the educated men and women who appreciated literature and loved poetry in 1824. We cannot share the feeling now, but it is possible to understand it. The youthful imagination of those days had made Byron a hero. His birth, his misfortunes, his physical beauty, his glaring faults, and his habit of letting the public into his confidence, fixed attention upon him. The man as well as the poet had very impressive qualities. We shall see what those qualities were when I have sketched in barest outline the painful incidents of his life.

George Gordon Byron had a long and famous pedigree, but his immediate ancestors were not men to be proud of. The fifth lord, known as the "wicked lord," who died about the end of the last century, fought a duel with a kinsman, killed his antagonist and was convicted of manslaughter; the poet's father led a life utterly vicious and unprincipled; and his mother had a temper so unbridled, that she gave way to the most furious bursts of passion, one of which ultimately caused her death. Her treatment of George Gordon, her only child, was injudicious in the extreme; sometimes it was brutal, as when she taunted the boy for being "a lame brat," or flung at his head the first object of which she could lay hold. Never had a poet worse training; and when we remember the vices of his life, we must also remember how infinitely worse off is the child of bad parents than if he were born into the world as one of God's orphans. The boy had warm feelings, and the friends of his Harrow days were the friends of his manhood, but it seemed as though every circumstance conspired to pervert his nature and to make his life unfortunate. A lord when ten years old, he had none of the advantages of title and wealth. Mrs. Byron's fortune had been thrown away by her dissolute husband, and Newstead Abbey, the family seat, which was left to the boy almost in a state of ruin, had in after years to be sold to relieve Byron of his difficulties.

While still at Harrow he fell in love with Mary Chaworth, who seems to have amused herself with his affection. "She liked me as a younger brother," he writes, "and treated and laughed at me as a boy. . . . Had I married Miss Chaworth, perhaps the whole tenor of my life would have been different." Four years were spent at Harrow—"my own dear Harrow-on-the-Hill," he called it—and then Byron went up to Trinity College, Cambridge, where he wrote his earliest verse. The "Hours of Idleness" gave no indications of future greatness ; neither did the poet gain university honours, but by his own confession led a life of dissipation. In 1809 he came of age, took his seat in the House of Lords, and published his satire, "English Bards and Scotch Reviewers." It was a daring attack upon the critics and poets of the day ; full of injustice, as

satire so often is, but also not without sufficient
truth to make the poem a success. At this time
Lord Byron was living after his mad way with
racketing associates at Newstead, where he kept a
bear and a wolf, and drunk wine out of a skull-cup.

After this the story of his life is for some period
the record of his travels, which led him, by way of
Gibraltar and Malta, through Albania. On this
occasion he was nearly drowned in a Turkish man-
of-war, and showed what he never lacked—courage.
While the captain was crying, and expecting every
moment that the vessel would go down, Byron,
unable from his lameness to be of any use, wrapped
himself in his capote and fell asleep. When in the
Dardanelles he swam like Leander from Sestos to
Abydos, a feat of which he was proud. Swimming
and riding on horseback were his favourite forms
of exercise. His lameness did not interfere with
them, and they enabled him to conceal the defect
to which throughout life he was so strangely
sensitive.

On returning to England Byron published the
first and second cantos of "Childe Harold." They
were dedicated to his half-sister, Mrs. Leigh—that
dear sister of whom in the dark after-hours he wrote
so affectionately as the one joy of his life.

> " From the wreck of the past which hath perished
>   Thus much I at least may recall,
> It hath taught me that what I most cherished
>   Deserved to be dearest of all ;
> In the desert a fountain is springing,
>   In the wide waste there still is a tree,

> And a bird in the solitude singing,
> Which speaks to my spirit of thee."

The poem became instantly popular, and Byron leapt at a bound from obscurity to fame. The inspiration of success urged him on, and he published in swift succession the Eastern stories, which led Scott to feel he was beaten on his own ground, namely, that of a story-teller in verse. It may be doubted, however, if he was beaten. There are passages in the "Giaour," in the "Siege of Corinth," in "Mazeppa," above the mark of Scott as a poet, but there is a wholesome freshness in Sir Walter's verse, a manly simplicity and directness, and a truth to nature which we do not find in Byron's melodramatic tales. It is but fair to remember, however, that the poet did not reach in them the culminating point of his genius. Scott never produced anything in verse greater than "Marmion;" the fourth canto of "Childe Harold" is immeasurably superior to the tales which were so extravagantly praised at the time by Byron's critics.

For a while the poet became the hero of London society. The beauty of his features, his charm of manner when he chose to exercise it, his very haughtiness when he did not, his frankness on the one hand, his mystifications on the other, acted like a spell. He was the "observed of all observers." It was a period of wild excitement, but he was far from happy, and deeply in debt. His marriage to Miss Milbanke took place in 1815; about a year

later his daughter Augusta Ada was born, and five
weeks afterwards Lady Byron returned with the
infant to her father's house, never more to see her
husband. The separation from first to last is a
mystery not likely to be solved. Byron always
said he was ignorant of the cause, and always
expressed his wish that it should be made public ;
but Lady Byron made no sign. It may be said in
his favour that she knew by report at least what his
character was before accepting him as a husband,
and it may be said in her favour that a virtuous
and high-minded young woman who had seen
nothing of evil, may have been unable to realize
the unbridled depravity of a man like Byron. In
later years he said bitter things against his wife,
but two months after the final parting he wrote : " I
do not believe that there ever was a brighter, and
a kinder, or a more amiable or agreeable being
than Lady Byron." She has been absurdly called a
" Puritanic precisian " in her old age by a writer who
apparently did not know her ; but the testimony of
Robertson of Brighton may be set against this. A
devout Christian and a liberal-minded clergyman,
he knew her long and intimately. With a " Puritanic precisian " he would have had little in common,
but Robertson writes of Lady Byron's warm sympathy and manifold wisdom, and said of her that
she was one of the noblest and purest women he
had ever met.*

---

* It seems probable, however, that she was subject to halluci-
nations, and cherished opinions which had no foundation in truth.

Lord Byron had previously been hailed with acclamation; he was now treated with obloquy. Macaulay has described the change with his accustomed brilliancy and love of antithesis. You will read his essay. It is enough to say here that in 1816 "Childe Harold" left England for the last time. The troubles of his life had not sobered him. The year before leaving several executions had been served in his house, and two years later on he was forced to sell Newstead in order to pay his debts. But neither in Switzerland, where he lived for some time with the Shelleys, nor in Italy, which was his latest home, did he halt in his career of dissipation. At Venice he was again joined by Shelley, who modestly said he despaired of rivalling Byron as a poet; and there, too, Thomas Moore, who was destined to write the life of Byron, paid his friend a visit, which is turned to good account in the biography. Shelley could have felt nothing but disgust at Byron's reckless life. He was an infidel, but not a libertine; he held perverted views of morality, but he had no taint of vulgarity, and in all his instincts he was a gentleman. Byron liked to defy the laws of society as well as the higher laws of morality and religion, and he was only saved from falling still lower into the gulf of dissipation by his intercourse with the Countess Guiccioli. On this subject I am glad to quote the words of Mrs. Oliphant.

" It requires no great strain of charity, we think, to pardon Teresa Guiccioli. She was married at sixteen to an old man, according to family arrangement, as was usual; and had scarcely married when she met the fascinating English poet, about whom all Venice was raving, and who was young and noble and unfortunate—an object of romantic interest everywhere. It was according to the morals of her time and country to permit a lover, the tie between the old husband and the young wife in a *mariage de convenance* being so unnatural that permitted license has always been the consequence. This Italian girl had never been taught nor known better, and no hero of romance could have exercised a more powerful spell upon a young creature, full of romance and sentiment, yet shut out from all legitimate indulgence of the poetry of youth. . . . We will not be thought to approve an immoral connection in attempting to say a word of tenderness and pity for the sweet and tender Italian girl from whose lips there never falls an unwomanly word, and whose breast was pure of all interested and worldly motives." *

Byron was never a safe friend ; even in his lovemaking he had no sense of honour, and the girl who excited the strongest impression on his wayward nature is alluded to with coarse levity in the letters he sent to England. The only excuse which has ever been made for him is that he affected not to feel. He was never, however, so lost to the sense of right as not to acknowledge, " How awful goodness is ! virtue in itself how lovely ! " When at Pisa he received a letter from John Sheppard, a writer on religious subjects, and also a minor poet, describing the death of his young wife, and stating that among her private papers he had found a prayer offered on behalf of Lord Byron. The poet in his reply refers to the account he had received of Mrs.

* " The Literary History of the Nineteenth Century," vol. iii. p. 75.

Sheppard's last moments, and observes, "I do not know that in the course of reading the story of mankind, and still less in my observations upon the existing portion, I ever met with anything so unostentatiously beautiful ;" and he adds, " I can assure you that all the fame which ever cheated humanity into higher notions of its own importance would never weigh in my mind against the pure and pious interest which a virtuous being may be pleased to take in my welfare. In this point of view I would not exchange the prayer of the deceased in my behalf for the united glory of Homer, Cæsar, and Napoleon, could such be accumulated upon a living head."

This letter was written from Pisa at the close of 1821. In the summer of the following year Shelley and his friend Williams were drowned, and, in company with Leigh Hunt and Trelawney, Byron witnessed the burning of the bodies on the sea-shore— a terrible sight, which affected, as well it might, the sensitive nerves of the poet. His own death was not far distant, and in a skeleton biography such as this nothing is left to be recorded beyond the closing scene. Gleams of greatness and of nobility of character are visible as his short and tempestuous life drew to a close. Greece, about which he had written so much and so well, was struggling in a weak way for freedom, and Byron, whose name was a tower of strength to the insurgents, was led to engage in the enterprise. He seemed to have a strong presentiment of his approaching death, but this, instead of slacking his energy, served to stimulate it. He had sound sagacity and dauntless courage, but the people for whom he acted lacked unity, and seemed bent on ruining their own cause. It was too late to help, save by the memory of his self-sacrifice, the land he loved so well—too late to find, as he had wished to find, "a soldier's grave." From the time he reached Mesolonghi, where he occupied a most unhealthy position, he seems to have suffered constantly from ill health. One day he had a fit, and, after the ignorant fashion of the time, was bled till he fainted. On another day, when very hot and also wet through from a heavy shower, he returned home in a boat—an imprudence which brought on rheumatic fever. It proved rapidly fatal, and on the 19th of April, 1824, this great but unhappy genius died.

> " When Byron's eyes were shut in death,
>   We bowed our head and held our breath.
>   He taught us little ; but our soul
>   Had *felt* him like the thunder's roll.
>   With shivering heart the strife we saw
>   Of Passion with Eternal Law,
>   And yet with reverential awe
>   We watched the fount of fiery life
>   Which served for that Titanic strife."

Mr. Matthew Arnold, whose lines have been just quoted, himself a true poet, is also one of our ablest critics of poetry. Few thoughtful men will agree with all his arguments—to some of them, indeed, the opposition is likely to grow stronger the more they are considered ; but even when he fails to convince, his masterly style of criticism, bearing as it does the marks of consummate ability, will always claim and merit attention. In his selection from the poems of Byron Mr. Arnold agrees with Mr. Swinburne in praising the poet for his imperishable excellence of sincerity and strength. Strength, no doubt, he has in considerable measure, but sincerity, so far as I can judge, is by no means a powerful characteristic of his life or of his work. In his life he seemed constantly to be playing a part. He had a love of the theatrical, and liked to attract attention by dark hints of secrets he could not utter, of deeds he dared not acknowledge. Much of his poetry is weighted with the same defect, and to separate the false from the true is a business of no small difficulty. Mr. Arnold allows that there are two Byrons, and that readers who stop at the theatrical preludings do not know him. It may be so, and so far as he is a true poet it is evident his verses must be based on sincerity. He had strong feelings, and could utter them in vehement words; he had a genuine love of nature, as " Childe Harold " will testify ; * he had wit and powers of rhetoric and

---

* And yet Rogers, who travelled with Byron some time in Italy says, " If there was any scenery particularly worth seeing, he generally contrived that we should pass through it in the dark." Rogers, by the way, gives an amusing account of the poet's affectations. One night he dined with Rogers, to whom he gave the second place among contemporary poets, and met for the first time Moore and Campbell, whom he placed " both third." " When we sat down to dinner," says Rogers, " I asked Byron if he would take soup ? No ; he never took soup. Would he take some fish ?

satire which assuredly he did not play with. All this and more may be granted, and yet, if we study Byron's poetry, the impression grows that affectation rather than sincerity predominates. To see him at his best, and worst, a reader is generally told by the critics to look at " Don Juan "—a poem which, upon its appearance, amazed and disgusted every person of right feeling. Poetry, the divinest of the arts, should be the most elevating. Its object, indeed, as I have said more than once in the course of our "travel," is not to be distinctly moral and didactic, but it should stimulate the highest aspirations of the reader, instead of insulting them. It should give to virtue and vice their form and aspect, instead of sneering at what is good, or putting it on an equality with what is evil. The mind revolts at the travesty given by Byron, because it feels instinctively that if life were what he represents it to be, it were better to die than to live ; for then, indeed, would earth be

> " darkness at the core,
> And dust and ashes all that is."

No ; he never took fish. Presently I asked if he would eat some mutton? No ; he never ate mutton. I then asked if he would take a glass of wine? No ; he never tasted wine. It was now necessary to inquire what he did eat and drink ; and the answer was, ' Nothing but hard biscuits and soda-water.' Unfortunately neither were at hand, and he dined upon potatoes bruised down on his plate and drenched with vinegar. . . . Some days after, meeting Hobhouse, I said to him, ' How long will Lord Byron persevere in his present diet ?' He replied, ' Just as long as you continue to notice it.' I did not then know what I now know to be a fact— that Byron, after leaving my house, had gone to a club in St. James's Street and eaten a hearty meat-supper."

A coarse representation of vice may do no evil to the pure in heart, but a poem that sneers at whatsoever things are lovely, that treats what is essentially immoral as a matter of indifference, and, moreover, does all this with the wit and fancy and imagination that are at the command of genius, cannot but have an evil influence on the reader. The man Byron speaks out in the coarser features of his poetry, and also in its morbid egotism. Perhaps the fourth canto of " Childe Harold " presents his verse in its purest vein. He is a master of description, and can picture with a powerful hand a scene in nature or a work of art ; but the atmosphere even of this fine canto is not wholesome, for the diseased nature of the writer infects the beauty he describes. Only when forgetting himself, and exulting in the majesty or sweetness of nature, does he attain to the full height of his genius. He loved the mountains and the ocean, loved all objects of sublimity and even of terror ; but after rising with his theme and soaring higher and higher, he destroys our sense of congruity by a wilful plunge into the mire, as though he were mocking at the feelings he had himself excited.

Nothing can well be finer than Byron's description in " Don Juan " of a shipwreck, which rises to a climax in the following stanza, describing a ship going down head foremost :—

" Then rose from sea to sky the wild farewell,
    Then shrieked the timid and stood still the brave,—-

> Then some leaped overboard with dreadful yell,
>   As eager to anticipate their grave ;
> And the sea yawned around her like a hell,
>   And down she sucked with her the whirling wave,
> Like one who grapples with his enemy,
> And strives to strangle him before he die."

The slow and ghastly death of some of the men who escaped in the boats is pictured in part with great vividness and pathos, and in part with a humour which, under the dreadful circumstances, must be pronounced vulgar. A moment of hope dawns, for a rainbow appears. Here it is drawn by a poet, and wilfully blurred in the drawing :—

> " Now overhead a rainbow, bursting through
>   The scattering clouds, shone, spanning the dark sea,
> Resting its bright base on the quivering blue,
>   And all within its arch appeared to be
> Clearer than that without ; and its wide hue
>   Waxed broad, and waving like a banner free,
> Then changed like to a bow that's bent, and then
> Forsook the dim eyes of these shipwrecked men.
>
> " It changed, of course ; a heavenly cameleon,
>   The airy child of vapour and the sun,
> Brought forth in purple, cradled in vermilion,
>   Baptized in molten gold and swathed in dun,
> Glittering like crescent o'er a Turk's pavilion,
>   And blending every colour into one,
> Just like a black eye in a recent scuffle
> (For sometimes we must box without the muffle)."

Does not this sudden descent from beauty to buffoonery give a sense of pain rather than of pleasure ? And yet this is but one illustration, and a very moderate illustration, of the way in which Byron trifles with the feelings he creates.

There are always fashions in poetry as in dress, and Byron followed one of them in writing Eastern tales. They were read with amazing interest at the time, and no terms were too strong to express the admiration both of critics and of readers. Sixty or seventy years have greatly dimmed their lustre, just as it will tarnish the brightness of much of the poetical work that claims precedence in our day; but though weak as stories and artificial as poems, they have many noble passages, some rhetorical, some exquisitely poetical, which show the cunning hand of a master. Like so much that Byron published, they are hasty productions, written off, as it were, at a heat, though sometimes enlarged and improved afterwards. He seems rather proud of saying that "The Bride of Abydos" was the work of a week, while "The Corsair" occupied about a fortnight, and "The Prisoner of Chillon," quite one of his most beautiful poems, only two days. Passages from these poems, mummified in selections, have almost lost their charm by overmuch familiarity. The freshness of their colour has been brushed off, and we have lost, too, our interest in many of the subjects which in Lord Byron's day were deemed poetical. If this be true, and as far as it is true, Byron does not rank with the greatest poets of his country or of the world. The poetry of Homer and Dante, of Shakespeare and Milton, has lost nothing by time, nothing by changes of

taste, because its foundation rests on nature, the
source of all true inspiration ; much that Byron has
written has no such foundation, and must inevitably
decay. And another reason for believing this is the
carelessness of his style. His admiration of Pope
was undoubtedly genuine,* and Pope, though far
from being always correct, in the highest sense of
the word, was the most painstaking of poets. Byron,
on the other hand, is too often strangely indifferent
—not only wanting music, but even disregarding
grammar. "In order to enjoy Byron," said Lamb's
friend Cary, the translator of Dante, "the lover of
poetry must forget the harmonies of Spenser and
Milton and Dryden, and suffer him if possible to
enter the mind without passing through the medium
of the ear ; otherwise the effect is like that of good
music played on a jarring instrument by an unskilful
performer. . . . He must be read for the novelty
and vigour of the sentiments alone."

It is true that the ear that loves to listen to the
majestic harmony of Milton, or to the subtle music
of Coleridge, will not delight in hearing Byron's
poetry read, but on the untrained ear the swing and

* "Neither time," he wrote, "nor distance, nor grief, nor age
can ever diminish my veneration for him who is a great moral poet of
all times, of all climes, of all feelings, and of all stages of existence;"
and in another of Byron's letters he declares that all the poets of
his age were wrong except Rogers and Crabbe. "I took Moore's
poems and my own and some others and went over them 'side by
side with Pope's, and I was really astonished and mortified at the
ineffable distance in point of sense, learning, effect, even imagination, passion, and invention, between the little Queen Anne's man
and us of the Lower Empire."

energetic movement of his lines fall impressively;
and the familiar address to the ocean, " Roll on,
thou deep and dark blue ocean—roll!" the opening
lines of "The Corsair," the dying gladiator; the
noble imagery employed in "The Giaour" to represent the death-like state of Greece; the lines
on solitude in the second canto of "Childe Harold,"
which Rogers thought the best that Byron ever
wrote; "The Isles of Greece;" and, above all, the
splendid stanzas on Waterloo, in "Childe Harold,"
which describe how, amidst the sound of revelry by
night in Brussels, when "a thousand hearts beat
happily," and "all went merry as a marriage-bell,"
the opening roar of the cannon is heard,—take hold
of the mind, even when failing to satisfy the ear,
with a force not to be resisted.   It is when reading
passages like these that we feel Byron's greatness
as a poet.   There is, too, a buoyancy in his verse
especially attractive to the young.   Is there a girl
or youth under twenty who will not read the
following stanzas with pleasure?—

"Oh! talk not to me of a name great in story—
 The days of our youth are the days of our glory;
 And the myrtle and ivy of sweet two and twenty
 Are worth all your laurels, though ever so plenty.

"What are garlands and crowns to the brow that is wrinkled?
 'Tis but as a dead flower with May-dew besprinkled.
 Then away with all such from the head that is hoary;
 What care I for the wreaths, that can *only* give glory!

"O Fame! if I e'er took delight in thy praises,
 'Twas less for the sake of thy high-sounding phrases,

Than to see the bright eyes of the dear one discover,
She thought that I was not unworthy to love her.

"*There* chiefly I sought thee, *there* only I found thee;
Her glance was the best of the rays that surround thee;
When it sparkled o'er aught that was bright in my story,
I knew it was love and I felt it was glory."

The interest that attaches to Byron's poetry is
mainly personal. He had little dramatic art, and
the passion of the moment gives the brightest glow
to his verse. If he forgets himself it is chiefly when
inspired by the love of liberty and hatred of what
he deems oppression. I have already mentioned
"The Prisoner of Chillon." Read it, and learn it if
you will by heart, but take care also to read his
noble sonnet on the same subject. A poet is at
full liberty to write of himself when his muse
suggests no higher theme, and there are poems
written by Byron on this favourite topic which well
deserve attention. His stanzas to his sister Augusta
are as sincere as they are beautiful, and if one did
not know the hollowness of his address to Lady
Byron, beginning "Fare thee well, and if for ever,"
it would touch us with the same kind of sympathy
we feel for Burns's stanzas "To Mary in Heaven."
"The Dream," too, would make a similar claim
upon the reader were it not "an act of revenge,"
written six months after the separation from Lady
Byron. The fine verses suggested by his thirty-
seventh birthday create infinite pity for the man,
still comparatively young, who had lived out his life

so soon and found it vanity. It is for this reason, and in spite of himself, that Byron becomes, to those who have sense enough to learn from him, a great moral teacher.

"It is," writes George Brimley, "in his fearless attempt at solving the problem of life in his own way, his complete discomfiture, and his unshrinking exhibition of that discomfiture, that the absolute and permanent value of his social teaching consists. For he was endowed with such gifts of nature and of fortune, so highly placed, so made to attract and fascinate, adorned with such beauty and grace, with such splendour of talents, with such quick susceptibility to impressions, with such healthy activity of mind, with such rich flow of speech, with such vast capacity of enjoyment, that no one is likely to make the experiment he made from a higher vantage ground with more chances of success." *

Byron, in Mr. Swinburne's judgment, cannot be justly appreciated in a selection, since he rarely wrote anything faultless. Mr. Arnold thinks otherwise, and observes—

"Although the abundance and variety of his production is undoubtedly a proof of his power, yet I question whether by reading everything which he gives us we are so likely to acquire an admiring sense even of his variety and abundance as by reading what he gives us at his happier moments. . . . Receive him absolutely, without omission or compression, follow his whole outpouring, stanza by stanza and line by line, from the commencement to the very end, and he is capable of being tiresome."

This verdict of two poets upon a third is, it will be seen, in one important respect contradictory.

* Essays by the late George Brimley, p. 108 (Macmillan and Co.).

Whichever judgment be the true one, it is doubtful
whether any poetical student of our time has read
the entire works of Byron, and certain that he will
have gained little by so doing.   This poet's genius
lies upon the surface ; it speaks at once to the mind
of the reader, and makes the strongest impression
on a first perusal.   There are poets who, like
Chaucer, like Shakespeare, like Wordsworth, yield
more and more gold the oftener we dig for it ;
there are others who, like Goldsmith, Campbell, and
Moore, leave us nothing to discover on a second
perusal which we did not find upon the first; and
this is true also of Lord Byron.   You will observe
I am not placing these poets on a level.   To do so
would be ridiculous; for Byron is among the great
poets of his country, but he does not rank with the
greatest, partly because there are no depths to
sound in his work, partly because much which
he has done is slovenly and unartistic, and partly
because what was vulgar, empirical, and impure
in his life is reflected on the larger portion of his
poetry.

[Thomas Moore's " Life of Byron," in six volumes, is the foremost
biography of the poet, but the literature that has accumulated round
his name is considerable.   Lord Byron forms the subject of one of
Lord Macaulay's essays.   A selection from his works (now, I believe, out of print) has been made by Mr. Swinburne, and Mr.
Matthew Arnold in 1881 undertook the same labour.   There is a
life of Byron by Professor Nichol in the series of "English Men of
Letters " (Macmillan and Co.).   The latest contribution to Byronic
literature is a work, in two volumes, by Mr. Jeaffreson, entitled
" The Real Lord Byron."]

CHAPTER XVII.

POETS OF THE NINETEENTH CENTURY
(*Continued*).

JOHN KEATS—PERCY BYSSHE SHELLEY.

"I THINK I shall be among the English poets after my death," were the modest but proud words of Keats, and comparatively brief though the time has been since the death of "Adonais," we can say without rashness that his place among the immortals is secure. There is no poet of his century whose work is more intensely poetical, and if some of it bear the marks of immaturity, even that portion is rich in lovely imagery, pervaded by a sense of beauty, and totally free from prosaic elements. The faults of Keats are the faults of genius spurred on by a noble ambition, and wanting the restraints of experience. He was but a boy, be it remembered, when he published his "Endymion;" he was scarcely more than a

John Keats, 1795-1821.

boy when he died; but there is nothing more
remarkable in his brief career than the rapid intellectual growth which marked those few years.
"Endymion," published in 1818, is a poem of
promise—a garden of exquisite spring blossoms,
not an orchard of golden fruit; but the "Hyperion,"
the "Eve of St. Agnes," and the "Odes," published
a year or two later, show the vigour of imagination
and the consummate mastery of form which entitle us to speak of Keats as a great poet.

He was born in 1795, and received all the education he ever gained at school, from the father of
Charles Cowden Clarke, who had a seminary at
Enfield. There he studied in his own way with
great ardour, but his acquirements were limited,
and the poet who was influenced above all others
in our century by the romantic mythology of
Greece, never learnt Greek. At the age of fifteen
he was apprenticed for five years to a surgeon
at Edmonton, and long before they ended, the
boy, thanks partly to Chapman's Homer, and
more to the "Faerie Queene" of Spenser, had discovered the bent of his genius. Sympathetic and
gifted friends recognized it also, and on removing
to London to walk the hospitals he found an intimate associate in Leigh Hunt. The influence of
this friendship is evident, as it was natural it should
be, in Keats's earlier poems. Other men of genius
and talent welcomed the poet with open arms, and
life for a short time glowed with the "purple light"
of youth and hope. Medicine and poetry did not

agree together in the case of Keats, and to the
latter, poor though he was, he became wholly devoted. His brightest days were spent at Hamp-
stead, where, in the Vale of Health, then a spot of
rural beauty, Leigh Hunt had a cottage, and there,
too, occurred some of the saddest, for Love, alike
passionate and hopeless, seized the young poet
with iron grasp at the very time when Death, with
a hand still stronger, turned all his love to pain.
He knew his doom long before the end came, and
in resolving for a last chance of life to try the air
of Italy, he felt, as he said, "the sensation of
marching up against a battery." At Rome the
artist Severn watched over the dying poet with the
tenderness of a sister. The struggle for life was
terrible. Keats believed in immortality after the
fashion of a virtuous pagan, but he knew nothing
of the "good hope" which sustains a Christian,
and oftentimes does more than sustain him, when
passing through the dark valley. His mind, like
his body, was diseased. "His imagination and
memory presented every thought to him in horror."
When letters came to him from home he dared not
read them. One from the woman he loved, to
quote the emphatic language of Severn, "tore him
to pieces;" and he adds, "He did not read it—he
could not—but requested me to place it in his
coffin." The delirium of fever disappeared on the
near approach of death, much to the relief of the
friend who had been "beating about in the tempest
of his mind so long." "I feel," said the poet, "the

flowers growing over me ; " and he begged that this inscription should be placed on his tombstone : " Here lies one whose name was writ in water."

" Keats was buried in the Protestant cemetery at Rome, one of the most beautiful spots on which the eye and heart of man can rest." *

The sense of beauty pervades the poetry of Keats as with an atmosphere. His verse is full of the loveliness which we find in youth, full of the ardours and aspirations, the brightness and glory, that belong to the season of hope. The charm of his language cannot be described, but it is impossible to open the volume without being enchained by it. It carries the ear captive with its sweetness, and gladdens the mind's eye with its brilliancy of colour. The reader feels there is a spell upon him, and one from which he has no desire to escape. The faults of " Endymion " will be as obvious to the student as its beauties. The imagery is extravagant, the diction luxurious, the rhymes too frequently feminine. He " looked upon fine phrases like a lover," but he was too fond of fine phrases. " Oh for a life of sensations rather than of thoughts ! " he once exclaimed when writing " Endymion," and the poem is coloured by this desire.† To no one was the weakness of the poem more evident than to the poet himself, whose preface shows a sanity of judgment which is all the more remarkable since it is exercised on the first child of his genius. "Knowing within myself," he writes, "the manner in which this poem has been produced, it is not without a feeling of regret that I make it public. What manner I mean will be quite clear to the reader, who must soon perceive great inexperience, immaturity, and every error denoting a feverish attempt, rather than a deed accomplished. . . . The imagination of a boy is healthy, and the matùre imagination of a man is healthy ; but there is a space of life between, in which the soul is in a ferment, the character undecided, the way of life uncertain, the ambition thick-sighted ; thence proceeds mawkishness and all the thousand bitters which those men I speak of must necessarily taste in going over the following pages."

---

song," and Keats said that illness relieved his mind of a load of deceptive thoughts and images, and made him perceive things in a truer light. He did sympathize with what is pure and noble and of good report, and how heartily he despised the degradation of spirit which can use for purposes of buffoonery that which is in reality most terrible and solemn, is seen in his remarks upon a passage in Byron's "Don Juan." For thirty hours he had himself been in great danger in the Bay of Biscay. "After the tempest had subsided Keats was reading the description of the storm in 'Don Juan,' and cast the book on the floor in a transport of indignation. 'How horrible an example of human nature,' he cried, 'is this man, who has no pleasure left him but to gloat over and jeer at the most awful incidents of life ! Oh! this is a paltry originality which consists in making solemn things gay and gay things solemn, and yet it will fascinate thousands by the very diabolical outrage of their sympathies. Byron's perverted education makes him assume to feel, and try to impart to others those depraved sensations which the want of any education excites in many.'"

It would, of course, be open to a cruel critic to retort that the world does not ask from the poet "feverish attempts," but deeds accomplished, and that it is useless for a writer to express his regret at a publication which he was under no necessity to produce. This, however, would be purblind criticism. Keats knew, and the world soon found out, that his poem had in it the life of genius, and such life, however immature, is always precious.

Keats is the most sensuous of poets, and he is also one of the purest. Surely none but a poet pure to the heart's core could have conceived the lovely vision of Madeline, on the eve of St. Agnes, undressing in the light of the wintry moon, while her lover Porphyro gazes on her beauty unespied, hoping to win his bride by the kind help of the saint.

> "A casement high and triple-arched there was,
> All garlanded with carven imageries,
> Of fruits and flowers, and branches of knot-grass,
> And diamonded with panes of quaint device.

> "Full on this casement shone the wintry moon,
> And threw warm gules on Madeline's fair breast,
> As down she knelt for Heaven's grace and boon ;
> Rose-bloom fell on her hands, together prest,
> And on her silver cross soft amethyst,
> And on her hair a glory, like a saint !
> She seemed a splendid angel, newly drest,
> Save wings, for heaven :—Porphyro grew faint :
> She knelt so pure a thing, so free from mortal taint.

"Anon his heart revives : her vespers done,
  Of all her wreathèd pearls her hair she frees ;
Unclasps her warmèd jewels one by one ;
Loosens her fragrant bodice ; by degrees
Her rich attire creeps rustling to her knees.
Half-hidden, like a mermaid in seaweed,
Pensive awhile she dreams awake, and sees
In fancy fair St. Agnes in her bed,
But dares not look behind or all the charm is fled.

" Soon, trembling in her soft and chilly nest,
In sort of wakeful swoon, perplexed she lay,
Until the poppied warmth of sleep oppressed
Her soothèd limbs, and soul fatigued away ;
Flown, like a thought, until the morrow-day ;
Blissfully havened both from joy and pain ;
Clasped like a missal where swart Paynims pray ;
Blinded alike from sunshine and from rain,
As though a rose should shut and be a bud again."

More than this I must not quote, although the
poem grows in beauty to its close ; but I have
transcribed these stanzas because they are alike
characteristic of the poet's wealth of fancy and of
his delicacy in treating a difficult theme. "Isabella,
or the Pot of Basil," a poem which drew forth the
early genius of Mr. Millais, is divided chronologically from the "Eve of St. Agnes" by a very
slight interval. Yet it is more immature, and
although full of luxuriant imagery, contains no passage of supreme excellence. It proves at least that
Keats possessed the gift denied to many poets, of
telling a story poetically. He could do something
far higher than this. The "Hyperion," which
Byron called as sublime as Æschylus, shows how

noble Keats could be in effort when the full attainment of his ideal was denied him ; but the perfection of his art is to be seen chiefly in his " Odes." The " Ode to a Nightingale," with its two final stanzas, immortal in their loveliness ; the " Ode on a Grecian Urn," which is, perhaps, his most complete and perfect poem ; and the " Ode to Autumn," ripe with the glory of the season it describes—must ever have a place among the most precious gems of lyrical poetry.   Before poems such as these, the richest fruits of a fine genius, criticism is dumb, or must content itself with the expression of admiration.

As a sonnet-writer, too, Keats takes his place with the best in the language, his finest effort in this compressed and difficult form of poetical expression being inspired by Chapman's picturesque and fiery translation of Homer.

> " Much have I travelled in the realms of gold,
>   And many goodly states and kingdoms seen ;
>   Round many western islands have I been,
>   Which bards in fealty to Apollo. hold.
>   Oft of one wide expanse had I been told
>   That deep-browed Homer ruled as his demesne,
>   Yet did I never breathe its pure serene
>   Till I heard Chapman speak out loud and bold ;
>   Then felt I like some watcher of the skies
>   When a new planet swims into his ken ;
>   Or like stout Cortez when, with eagle eyes,
>   He stared at the Pacific—and all his men
>   Looked at each other with a wild surmise—
>   Silent—upon a peak in Darien."

" Beauty is truth, truth beauty," was the poetical

creed of Keats, and in his last illness he said, "I have loved the principle of beauty in all things." Who can doubt that with such a faith he would have risen, had his life been spared, to a region of spiritual thought in which the poet's voice has not only a lovely sound, but an utterance that is prophetic. He died with aims still uncertain, with hopes unaccomplished, at the age of twenty-six— the greatest English poet, whose genius has been confined within so narrow a limit.

> "Peace, peace! he is not dead, he doth not sleep!
> He hath awakened from the dream of life,
> 'Tis we who, lost in stormy visions, keep
> With phantoms an unprofitable strife."

These lines of farewell to Keats were written by his brother-poet, Shelley. Both were alike in their intense worship of **Percy Bysshe Shelley, 1792-1822.** the spirit of beauty, both lived a life of imagination. There was, however, a striking contrast between them. Keats was self-centred. His art was his world, his religion, his being's end and aim. His highest aspiration was to have a place with Chaucer and Spenser, with Milton and Shakespeare. He longed to "overwhelm" himself in poetry, and whatever there may have been of strength and backbone in his character is due to this absorbing passion for a single object.   ·   ·

Shelley had a passion, too, but it ranged over a far wider field. He was the poet of impulse

and aspiration, but his mind was always the most
strongly moved by objects outside himself. His
aims were often far from being wise; they were
sometimes fanatical and sometimes childish; but
his purposes were unselfish, and the high courage
with which he strove after the impossible, would
be worthy of respect had it been tempered by
humility. When a boy in years Shelley expressed
his contempt for all established authority. He
had no reverence for the "patrimony of experience," but entered the field as a reformer, "when
he had but begun to think, and before he had
begun to learn." "He was strong," it has been
well said by a living poet, "in zeal, but weak
through self-confidence; he rushed into the fight
without armour, though with boundless courage,
and, with the weapon of an idle and ignorant scorn,
he struck not only at abuses and corruptions, but
at truths older than either science or song, and
higher than his highest hopes of man." *

I shall not undertake to tell at any length the
sad story of his brief but most eventful life. To do
this impartially is a task of no common difficulty.
Shelley's admirers have not only exalted him as
a poet to a place beside Shakespeare and Milton,.
but they have lavished on him the most extravagant praise for the beauty and matchless purity
of his character. In their eyes he is a demi-god
or a prophet; not only the greatest of lyric poets,

---

* *Edinburgh Review*, October, 1849.

but one of the noblest of men. Some of the terms
applied to Shelley by his worshippers are, indeed,
ridiculous, some well-nigh profane, and those who
do not join in this worship are regarded as alike
ignorant of what goodness is, and incapable of
appreciating the higher mysteries of the poetic
art. A man can but utter what he feels, and give
the ground of his belief. I confess I hope to carry
the judgment of my young readers with me, but
I shall do my best to avoid prejudice, and in re-
lating the prominent incidents and characteristics
of this wonderful poet's life, will use as far as
possible the statements and admissions of his most
ardent admirers.

Percy Bysshe Shelley was born August 4, 1792,
at Field Place, near Horsham, in Sussex. The
family was ancient and wealthy, and had Percy
survived his father he would have been a baronet.
The earliest love of the future poet was centred
on his sisters. His father, narrow-minded, pig-
headed, and only conventionally moral, had no
sympathy with the youthful genius, and neither
heart nor intellect appear to have been much influenced by his mother. Good home-training must
have greatly moulded a nature so affectionate and
sympathetic, but as a boy Shelley's position was
well-nigh as unfortunate as that of Lord Byron.
Like Byron, he had the gift of physical beauty,*
and in the early years of boyhood there were in-

---

* The artist Mulready said in after years that he was too
beautiful to paint.

dications that in mind as well as body he was
richly endowed. At school he seemed to learn the
classic languages by intuition, and much of his
time was consumed in dreaming and in novel-
reading. He was a solitary boy, and at Eton exhibited the qualities that marked him through life
—fierce indignation at oppression, and the defiant
spirit that regarded all law as tyranny, and all
governors, whether of schools or kingdoms, as the
tyrants of the race. While at school he wrote two
or three novels—wild, incoherent rhapsodies, which
are intended to be tragic, but are in reality ridiculous. The marvel is that for one of these stories
Shelley not only found a publisher, but gained
£40. A brief love affair, and the publication of
more boyish novels and some verse, marked the
period between leaving Eton and matriculating
as a commoner of University College, Oxford.
Shelley's life there has been vividly described by
his friend Hogg. It ended characteristically. He
wrote a tiny pamphlet, called " The Necessity of
Atheism," and was expelled accordingly. Whether
at this crisis gentler treatment of a young man like
Shelley—such treatment, for instance, as he would
have received from a clergyman at once reverent
and sympathetic like Kingsley—might not have
changed the current of his life need not now be dis-
cussed. Shelley, whose father would not allow him
to return home, considered himself a martyr ; he
had no one to show him that he had acted like a
fool. Unlike the greatest poets of England, he had

genius without common sense, ardent enthusiasm without stability of purpose. These faults cleaved to him in a measure to the last, but there are signs towards the end of riper judgment and wiser aspirations—gifts which had to be gained through suffering.

At nineteen he eloped to Scotland with Harriet Westbrook, a " charming, sweet-tempered " school-girl of sixteen, and married her according to the rites of the Scottish Church. Shelley's restlessness prevented him from staying long in one place, and the boy and girl lovers were continually on the move. The rose of their love had a thorn even in the honeymoon, for Harriet was troubled with an elder sister, who undertook to rule, and did so with energy. In those days Shelley devoted himself to what he deemed the emancipation of the race, and Harriet was " the partner of his thoughts and feelings." Together they went to Dublin to distribute " An Address to the Irish People," which the boy-husband had written. " We throw them out of window," Harriet writes, " and give them to men that we pass in the streets. For myself, I am ready to die of laughter when it is done, and Percy looks so grave." The " Appeal " seems to have had little effect, and Shelley left for Holyhead. The police, he said, had warned him it would be well to leave. Strange to say, however, Shelley's statements about himself are not always to be trusted. He writes of fancies as if they were facts, of what he saw in his mind's eye as though it had been a visible object, and to this day his biographers cannot tell whether certain incidents in his career related by the poet with amplest details, were dreams or realities. Impulse without forethought, marked his conduct, and the story is told of a certain schoolmistress, unknown except by correspondence, whom Shelley and Harriet entreated to resign her school and live with them, never more to part. She came, was found disagreeable, and "had at last to be bought off or bribed to leave." Probably some of the poet's eccentricities were due to his diet, which consisted chiefly of pulse or bread, which he ate dry, with water. This, at least, is a better reason for his complete forgetfulness of sacred engagements than the reason advanced by Mr. Symonds, that he was "an alimental and primeval creature." Two years after the marriage Shelley's first child was born, and in the winter of the following year, the poet, having fallen in love with Mary Godwin, daughter of the philosopher, a girl "with an enthusiasm for ideas," discovered that Harriet, however attached and affectionate, was no fitting mate for him.* Having made the discovery, he acted

---

* Mr. W. M. Rossetti remarks: "When we have summed up all Harriet's attractions and merits—and they were neither few nor unsubstantial—we find that we have described at best a sweet young creature qualified to adorn any ordinary position in life ; we have not described a poet's ideal." But what poet, since the world began, ever married his ideal, or would have been happier if he had? Poets are but men, often very frail and helpless men, and would feel their helplessness all the more keenly were they to marry creatures

"too bright and good
For human nature's daily food."

upon it, and in the middle of June, 1814, suddenly abandoned his wife and child. Forty days after leaving Harriet, with whom a year before he was "the happiest of the happy," Shelley left London with Mary Godwin. In so doing he was acting up to the principles he professed ; but he forsook his young wife under circumstances which make the act all the more reprehensible, for soon after the separation she gave birth to her second child. Two years and a half later Harriet committed suicide, and the life "that once was dearest to him had ended in misery, desertion, want." Shelley, to his credit be it said, had married Harriet despite his contempt for marriage, and he now married Mary Godwin. There was sympathy between the two, but the tragic memories of the past pursued the poet through life. Nor was this all, for by a decree of the Court of Chancery he was not allowed to have the custody of his own and Harriet's children. If his faults were great, so also was the bitterness of his spirit, and no one who reads the whole of the sad story can fail to sympathize with the trials of this wayward genius. Pity the great poet as much as you will, but never let this pity for an intellectual giant lead you to think that because he was a giant he was less amenable to the sacred laws of morality than the lowliest of the race.

It does credit neither to Shelley's intellect nor to his heart to write, " Every one who knows me must know that the partner of my life should be one who can feel poetry and understand philosophy. Harriet is a noble animal, but she can do neither."

Only six more years of life were allotted to Shelley, and the greater part of them were spent in Italy. It was long enough to develop his supreme power as a poet and many noble qualities as a man. Unbeliever though he was, the spirit of the faith he rejected is seen in his charity, in his self-denial, in his readiness to feel for those in trouble. More than this of biographical incident I need not state here. You have all heard how this eventful life ended. Like "Lycidas," Shelley suffered "a sea-change." He was drowned in the Gulf of Spezzia with his friend Williams, and the tragic conclusion of a tragic career can be best read, perhaps, in the record of his friend Trelawney, who died but recently at Worthing. The poet's body was burnt on a funeral pyre in the presence of Leigh Hunt, Lord Byron, and Trelawney. The ashes were buried in the Protestant cemetery at Rome, not far from the grave of Keats, and the heart, preserved entire, is now at Boscombe, the seat of his son, the present baronet.*

---

* "The sea gave up its dead, and all of Shelley's body that was rescued from flood and fire lies now where the rise of the ground ends, in a dark nook of the Aurelian wall. So deep is that resting-place in shadow, that the violets blossom later there than on 'the slope of green access,' where, seen from Shelley's grave, the flowers grow over the dust of Adonais. We may be glad that both were buried in Italy rather than in England, for though no Italian could have written their poetry, yet it was—in all things else different— of that spirit which Italy awakens in Englishmen who love her, rather than of the purely English spirit. The Italian air, the sentiment of Italy, fled and dreamed through their poems, but most through those of Shelley. It was but fitting, then, that Shelley, whose fame was England's, should be buried in the city which is the heart of Italy" (Stopford A. Brooke).

Shelley, like Wordsworth, depends, I think, for the permanence of his fame upon his shorter poems. In the " Cenci," indeed, he has produced a masterpiece. It has been called, not wholly without justice, the greatest tragedy of the century, if not since the time of Shakespeare, but there are subjects too horrible to be used for purposes of poetic art, and the pleasure which the highest tragedy affords is denied to us in reading Shelley. While admiring the greatness of his work, we turn from it with revulsion. To most readers, then, he is known chiefly as a lyrist—as the greatest singer, although not the greatest poet, of the century. The " Ode to the West Wind," " Love's Philosophy," " The Cloud," " The Indian Serenade," " To the Skylark," the " Stanzas written in Dejection, near Naples," and that most lovely song addressed to the " Spirit of Delight," are so enchantingly beautiful that they alone would suffice to place him in the front rank among the lyric poets of his country. And in more elaborate poems such as " Alastor," " The Sensitive Plant," " Adonais," and above all in the " Prometheus Unbound," we see all the intensity and individuality of his genius. " When is man strong until he feels alone ? " asks a famous living poet ; and Shelley, the most lonely of poets, found his strength in solitude. He could not bear to see things as they are, nor could he grasp, as Wordsworth did, the poetry of common life. His vague but sincere philanthropy, his aspirations after a higher life, were the dreams of a poet whose

genius drifted him hither and thither with the irresistible might of a whirlwind, without directing
him to the firm anchorage for which his spirit
craved.   Truly does Mr. Hutton say that "the
sense of weakness, of a longing to lean somewhere,
without recognizing any strength on which to lean,
runs through his whole poems." *   His verse, therefore, while perfectly satisfying the ear, fails to
satisfy the intellect or the heart.   It has no secure
earthly resting-places like the poetry of Burns or
Wordsworth.   Well, indeed, is Shelley described by
Mr. Arnold as a "beautiful and ineffectual angel,
beating in the void his luminous wings in vain."

As a poet, Shelley is superior to Keats in scope
of imagination and in mastery of verse, but it
should be remembered that if Shelley had died, as
his brother-poet did, at twenty-six, his most ambitious works—"The Cenci" and "Prometheus Unbound," for instance—would not have been written ;
neither should we have had the loveliest of his lyrics,
or such characteristic poems as "Epipsychidion,"
"The Sensitive Plant," and "Adonais."   Not even
Shelley has surpassed Keats in the felicitous use
of words—in the rare power which transports the
reader, by what *legerdemain* he knows not, into a
new world.   What imagination is so dull as not to
feel conscious of "something rich and strange" in
the following stanza, which I take from Keats's
"Ode to a Nightingale"?—

---

* "Essays Theological and Literary," by Richard Holt Hutton,
M.A., vol. ii. p. 187 (Strahan and Co.).

"Thou wast not born for death, immortal Bird !
No hungry generations tread thee down ;
The voice I hear this passing night was heard
In ancient days by emperor and clown ;
Perhaps the selfsame song that found a path
Through the sad heart of Ruth, when sick for home,
She stood in tears amid the alien corn ;
　　　　The same that ofttimes hath
Charmed magic casements, opening on the foam
Of perilous seas in faery lands forlorn."

There is a wealth of colour in the works of Keats, and a capacity for bringing scenes vividly before the mind's eye, which makes him beloved by artists. Shelley's poetry is rarely susceptible of pictorial treatment. He is less of the painter than of the musician. His voice, like that of his own skylark, "showers a rain of melody," and so enchanting is the music that we are not always careful to ask whether we understand the meaning, or whether the poet meant us to understand it. Shelley loves the mists, and gains much of his poetical nutriment from the dews and rains. The dank moisture of caves oozes through his verse, and when he leaves the earth he sails through illimitable space. If he have a local habitation, it is in the clouds. His sense of beauty is exquisite, but master though he be of language, his expression is vague, and his intellect rarely leads him to a definite result. A man who likes to feel the earth firm beneath his tread finds Shelley unstable and insecure. There was no restfulness in his life, and there is none in his verse. The largest minds are

"true to the kindred points of heaven and home."
Shelley is too full of unsatisfied desires to enjoy
all the beauty of the green earth.   According to
Hazlitt he had the physique of a fanatic, and
writing to a friend he says himself, " As to real
flesh and blood, you know that I do not deal in
these articles ; and you might as well go to a gin-
shop for a leg of mutton as expect anything human
or earthly from me."   At the same time this poet
of the intangible and the vague was intent on
bettering the race by upsetting all that is stable and
venerable in society, and repelled readers in the
first place by his hysterical shrieks at Christianity
(it is well to remember they were youthful shrieks),
and then by a choice of subjects for poetry from
which a well-regulated mind instinctively turns
away.

I think he is best read in selections, and in small
portions at a time, and Mr. Stopford Brooke
deserves the heartiest thanks for the volume in
which he has garnered up this poet's choicest
words. You will read with pleasure, but perhaps
not always with assent, the elaborate preface prefixed to this selection.   It may be true that in
the strictly philosophic sense Shelley was neither
an atheist nor materialist, but if it be also true,
as it is undoubtedly, that "he had little or no
belief in a thinking or loving existence behind the
phenomenal universe," his belief or negation of
belief is practically atheistic.   It was this feeling
that led him to give utterance to the most awful

lines about the universe to be found in the whole
range of our poetical literature. It is Beatrice, the
heroine of the " Cenci," who speaks.

> "Sweet Heaven, forgive weak thoughts, if there should be
> No God, no Heaven, no Earth, in the void world—
> The wide, grey, lampless, deep, unpeopled world."

Knowing what we do of Shelley, it is impossible
to regard this as merely a dramatic utterance. If,
as I believe, this last line expresses Shelley's own
outlook into futurity, if he had no faith in a Divine
Ruler, Guide, and Comforter, then for him was this
world fatherless and forsaken, and we can understand the desolateness of feeling that rings through
his most beautiful lyrics. In one of them he says—

> "Alas ! I have nor hope nor health,
> Nor peace within, nor calm around."

And in his immortal lyric " To the Skylark," one of
the loveliest ever written by poet, there is a stanza
which might serve as a motto to Shelley's life and
poetry :—

> "We look before and after,
>   And pine for what is not :
> Our sincerest laughter
>   With some pain is fraught ;
> Our sweetest songs are those that tell of saddest thought."

" Shelley's intensest lyrics," says Professor Shairp,
" those which have started with the fullest swing of
rapture, die down before they close into a wail of
despair." This is a true saying, but there are exceptions to the rule even in his poetry, and in parting

2 C

with this singer of sad songs, I shall like to quote
one superb lyric already mentioned, in which the
soul of Shelley, despite some pining for what is
not, seems to be borne upon the wings of gladness.

> " Rarely, rarely comest thou,
>   Spirit of Delight !
> Wherefore hast thou left me now
>   Many a day and night ?
> Many a weary night and day
> 'Tis since thou art fled away.
>
> " How shall ever one like me
>   Win thee back again ?
> With the joyous and the free
>   Thou wilt scoff at pain.
> Spirit false ! thou hast forgot
> All but those who need thee not.
>
> " As a lizard with the shade
>   Of a trembling leaf,
> Thou with sorrow art dismayed ;
>   Even the sighs of grief
> Reproach thee, that thou art not near,
> And reproach thou wilt not hear.
>
> " Let me set my mournful ditty
>   To a merry measure ;
> Thou wilt never come for pity,
>   Thou wilt come for pleasure.
> Pity then will cut away
> Those cruel wings, and thou wilt stay.
>
> " I love all that thou lovest,
>   Spirit of Delight !
> The fresh earth in new leaves drest,
>   And the starry night ;
> Autumn evening and the morn
> When the golden mists are born.

" I love snow and all the forms
    Of the radiant frost ;
I love waves and winds and storms—
    Everything almost
Which is Nature's, and may be
Untainted by man's misery.

" I love tranquil solitude,
    And such society
As is quiet, wise, and good ;
    Between thee and me
What difference ? But thou dost possess
The things I seek, not love them less.

" I love Love—though he has wings,
    And like light can flee ;
But above all other things,
    Spirit, I love thee—
Thou art love and life ! O, come,
Make once more my heart thy home."

[The life, letters and remains of Keats, edited by R. M. Milnes (now Lord Houghton), appeared in 1848. He also prefixed a memoir (the best we have) to an edition of the poems published in 1868. Another edition of the poetry appeared in 1872, with a memoir by Mr. William Rossetti.

Of Shelley there are numerous editors and biographers. Ten or twelve years ago Mr. W. M. Rossetti published his poetical works in two volumes. Another and more elaborate edition, edited by Mr. H. B. Forman, appeared in 1876. The volume likely to attract young readers is " Poems from Shelley, Selected and Arranged by Stopford A. Brooke" (Macmillan and Co.) It contains the choicest work of the poet. His two volumes of essays and letters are likely, in Mr. Matthew Arnold's judgment, " to resist the wear and tear of time better, and finally to stand higher than his poetry."]

CHAPTER XVIII.

POETS OF THE NINETEENTH CENTURY
(*Continued*).

ELIZABETH BARRETT BROWNING—JOHN KEBLE.

THE biography of Mrs. Browning has not yet been
written, and perhaps never will be.
Much of it may be read in her poems
and in her correspondence, and it must
suffice to insert here the few dates and facts which
link together the different portions of her life.

Elizabeth Barrett was born in 1809, at Hope
End (near Ledbury), a house built by her father
in the Turkish style. Her childhood and youth
were spent in the most eager acquisition of knowledge, which extended to the poets and philosophers of Greece. Miss Mitford, who won her
friendship in 1836, describes her as "of a slight,
delicate figure, with a shower of dark curls falling
on either side of a most expressive face, large
tender eyes richly fringed by dark eyelashes, a

Elizabeth Barrett Browning, 1809-1861.

smile like a sunbeam, and such a look of youth-
fulness that I had some difficulty in persuading a
friend that the translator of the " Prometheus " of
Æschylus, the authoress of the " Essay on Mind,"
was old enough to be introduced into society—in
technical language, was *out*."

The next year Miss Barrett broke a blood-vessel
on the lungs, and after many months of ill health,
she was ordered to spend the winter at Torquay.
Her eldest brother—"a brother in heart and talent
worthy of such a sister"—accompanied her, and
there, at a later period, he was drowned within
sight of his sister's windows. " This tragedy nearly
killed Elizabeth Barrett ; she was utterly pros-
trated by the horror and the grief, and by a natural
but most unjust feeling that she had been in some
sort the cause of this great misery. It was not
until the following year that she could be removed
in an invalid carriage, and by journeys of twenty
miles a day, to her afflicted family and her London
home." Arriving there, she was confined to her
room, Miss Mitford adds, for many years, "reading
almost every book in every language, and giving
herself heart and soul to that poetry of which she
seemed born to be the priestess." In 1846 Miss
Barrett married Mr. Robert Browning, and began
a new and happy life in Italy. They settled at
Florence, and the one son was born (now well
known as an artist) whom his mother addresses
with such tenderness, in " Casa Guidi Windows,"
as her own young Florentine. Mrs. Browning died

in 1861, the year in which that Italy which she loved so well gained her freedom, and took her rightful place among the nations of Europe.

To say that Mrs. Barrett Browning is the greatest poetess of this country is to say little. There is no woman who stands near her on the poetic heights. If her power of execution were equal to the scope and buoyancy of her imagination, her place would be among the crowned kings of poetry. Unfortunately her splendid gifts were recklessly, or perhaps it would be more correct to say wilfully, trifled with. Her finest work is often marred by some defect in the execution, by perversity of taste, by eccentricities of language, or by jarring notes of rhythm which irritate the sensitive reader. And this flaw is the more remarkable, since from early years she had been familiar with the sanity and symmetry of Greek poetry.

"Aurora Leigh," a long, rambling poem, which might be almost called a novel in verse, was, in the writer's judgment, the most mature of her works, and expressed her highest convictions upon life and art. It has passages of almost unequalled beauty, but as a whole the poem is spasmodic, hysterical, unreal. The characters are lifeless, there is much in the descriptive passages of doubtful taste, and in the social judgments, of which there are not a few, one detects also an ignorance of human nature. Self-restraint and sustained energy are wanting, and these deficiencies compel the reader who would gain pleasure from "Aurora

Leigh" to search its pages for beauties. These are not difficult to find, and will always make the poem welcome. Not only are there lovely and accurate pictures of English scenery, but the work, rambling and diffuse though it be, contains also a number of tersely written and poetically suggestive sayings which are not to be found elsewhere in Mrs. Browning's poetry. Take a few examples :—

> " Better far
> Pursue a frivolous trade by serious means
> Than a sublime art frivolously."

> " Every wish
> Is like a prayer . . . with God."

> " I do distrust the poet who discerns
> No character or glory in his times,
> And trundles back his soul five hundred years."

> " My Father ! Thou hast knowledge, only Thou.
> How dreary 'tis for women to sit still,
> On winter nights by solitary fires,
> And hear the nations praising them far off!"

> " Death quite unfellows us,
> Sets dreadful odds betwixt the live and dead,
> And makes us part as those at Babel did,
> Through sudden ignorance of a common tongue.
> A living Cæsar would not dare to play
> At bowls, with such as my dead father is."

> " Good love, howe'er ill-placed,
> Is better for a man's soul in the end
> Than if he loved ill what deserves love well."

" There are nettles everywhere ;
But smooth green grasses are more common still :
The blue of heaven is larger than the cloud."

" Free men freely work ;
Whoever fears God, fears to sit at ease."

It would be uncritical to call "Aurora Leigh" a great poem, but it has many great thoughts, and some so full of life that we seem to be conscious of a new life in reading them. It was published at the close of 1856, within five years of Mrs. Browning's death. Some of her most ambitious poems, and also some of her best poems, which are, perhaps, among the least ambitious, had appeared twenty years before—about the time when Mr. Tennyson's "Poems, chiefly Lyrical," had given the world assurance of a poet. The young woman who had already translated Æschylus, and who (in 1844) was daring enough to compete with Milton in the high argument of "The Drama of Exile," was no mean rival in the poetic race. Whatever failure there is in her larger works, among which "The Seraphim," published in 1838, holds a noticeable place, is due to execution rather than to conception. The thoughts are often sublime, the expression staggering and uncertain, and the rhymes of the lyrics forced and grating.

The deep reverence and profound spiritual emotion that prompted "The Drama of Exile," in which it is attempted once more to produce a poetical conception of Adam and Eve, and of their arch-enemy Lucifer, is also seen in "The Seraphim," in which the crucifixion of our Lord is represented —a subject which I venture to think is beyond the grasp of poetry. And the poet seemed to feel this herself, when, at the close of the poem, addressing the " bright ministers of God and grace," she craves forgiveness and a pitying smile for her " hoarse music," and adds—

> " I, too, may haply smile another day,
> At the far recollection of this lay,
> When God may call me in your midst to dwell,
> To hear your most sweet music's miracle
> And see your wondrous faces.   May it be !
> For His remembered sake the Slain on rood,
> Who rolled His earthly garment red in blood
> (Treading the wine-press), that the weak, like me,
> Before His heavenly throne should walk in white."

It is not from " The Drama of Exile " and " The Seraphim " that the reader should be advised to judge of Mrs. Browning's power.   In each of them there is no doubt a large measure of genius, but it is genius untamed and ill regulated, and we are inevitably led to compare these fine and yet comparatively abortive efforts with Milton's majestic conception and incomparable execution.   True poet and true woman, it is nevertheless not given to her to rise to the height of great arguments like these.   On lower ground her step is more certain, and wherever she chooses to go she carries with her the light of a pure and fervent spirit.   By general consent, " The Rhyme of the Duchess May," and " Lady Geraldine's Courtship," rank among

her finest and most carefully completed poems.
The ballad describing the heroic duchess, with
its prophetic refrain, " Toll slowly," tells a noble
story in language unusually concise and simple.
" Lady Geraldine's Courtship" reminds the reader
too strongly of Mr. Tennyson's " Locksley Hall," a
more perfect, although not a more imaginative
poem.   That there is conscious imitation is not to
be supposed ; never was there poet more unlikely,
or who needed less, to wear borrowed plumes ; but
if the two poems are read successively, it will be
found that there is in some passages, as well as in
the metre selected, a likeness between both.   Ber-
tram, the hero of Mrs. Browning's poem, is a contemptible fellow enough ; and so, too, is Romney, in
" Aurora Leigh."   She could not draw a man ; but,
apart from this defect, the " Courtship " has many
enchanting qualities—a rush of winged words,
copious imagery, "thoughts that breathe," and the
indescribable charm of a poem that springs
" warm " from the author, who wrote it off, it is
said, within twelve hours.   It has defects of taste,
too, but the writer's energy prevents us from
noticing these until a second or third perusal.

Mrs. Browning's versatility is great, and her
lyrics are sung in a variety of metres.   She is most
successful when most simple, and some of her
shorter pieces owe their charm to the pathos, always
more beautiful than painful, which is allied to imaginative truth.   You will see my meaning if you
read " The Deserted Garden," " To Flush, my Dog,"

"Cowper's Grave," "The Pet Name," "A Child's Grave at Florence," "My Doves," and that poem of perfect beauty suggested by the wonderful Scripture words, "He giveth His beloved sleep." The poet lived in the present even more than in the past. Her sympathy with the Italians in their struggle for liberty was profound, and "Casa-Guidi Windows" is alike characteristic of the woman and of the age. The "Cry of the Children," like Thomas Hood's "Song of the Shirt," is a grand poetical protest against what may be called the tyranny of civilization. The passion of that vehement "Cry" takes the heart by storm. Happily the evil it denounced has been remedied.

The innermost heart of the poet is best seen, perhaps, in the so-called "Sonnets from the Portuguese." Love-poems so pure, so impassioned, so palpitating with life, were never before written in the form of sonnets, and the necessity for compression has been highly serviceable to the writer's style. She had been ill for years and had looked for death, but a "most gracious singer of high songs" took her by the hand, and she found life instead. How full that life was will be best seen in these richly worded series of poems, which stand alone in their intensity and in the "purple light of love" which encircles them.

Other sonnets, too, of great beauty were written by Mrs. Browning, all of which should be read. Although their inequality is striking, there is not one that does not hold as in a casket some beautiful jewel. Her finest poems of this class deserve to rank with the greatest we possess in the language. Note, too, in reading her poetry, the exquisite art with which Mrs. Browning pictures youthful life— the babe, the young child, the maiden—showing how large a fund of motherly tenderness she possessed. Children's ways and thoughts seem natural to her, and for the lower animals she has the tenderness of a Cowper or a Burns.

One of her poems is written in memory of Mrs. Hemans, a charming woman, with a nature singularly refined and spiritual. Many of her poems have been highly popular, and being set to music are popular

Felicia Dorothea Hemans, 1793-1835.

still. Sweetness and sensibility are their special characteristics. Her life was pathetic, and her verse is pitched throughout in a melancholy but by no means despairing strain. Loved and admired by every one who knew her, accomplished, beautiful, devout, and possessing more than the shadow of genius, hers might have been a happy course, had not an unfortunate marriage wrecked her life. She lost its joy, but was not without its blessedness, and her gift of song must have yielded many tranquil hours. Not one of her lyrics has been thought worthy of a place in Mr. Palgrave's "Golden Treasury," but many of them have found a home in the hearts of readers denied to much loftier verse. They have been sometimes estimated too highly, partly because they appeal to popular sentiment, and chiefly perhaps because their author,

who died in the prime of womanhood, is so worthy
of our love. It was Felicia Hemans's goodness and
her premature death which dictated the following
lines of Wordsworth. He will not mourn for Crabbe,
whose life had reached its full length—for why
should we heave a sigh over ripe fruit seasonably
gathered ?—but he adds—

> "Mourn rather for that holy spirit,
>   Sweet as the spring, as ocean deep ;
> For her who, ere her summer faded,
>   Has sunk into a breathless sleep."

[A selection from the poems of Mrs. Browning has been made by
her husband, whose great name, like that of Mr. Tennyson, ennobles
the latter half of our century, just as its earliest years were ennobled
by Wordsworth and by Coleridge. Dr. Peter Bayne has written
one of the fullest and most genial criticisms of Mrs. Browning's
poetry that has hitherto been published. I think he estimates some
of her work too highly, or rather thinks too slightly of the faults
by which it is marred ; but if this be an error, it is surely a generous
one, and will not lessen the pleasure of readers, young or old. See
"Two Great Englishwomen" (Clarke and Co.).]

No poet ever thought less of fame than John Keble,
and few, if any, writers of sacred verse
have received so large a share of it. **John Keble, 1792-1866.**
He lived to witness the publication of
ninety-five editions of the "Christian Year," and
we are told that at the close of the·year following
his death, the number had risen to a hundred and
nine. Keble was reluctant to publish the work at
all ; he never published it with his name, and his
biographer writes : "I am certain that he had not
the slightest idea at the time how important was
the gift he had made to the world, nor how decisive

a step he had taken in respect of his own character and reputation." Truly does Sir J. Coleridge call the " Christian Year " a wonderful book, and he is right in saying that it is not a library book or a book of the house, but " rather a book of each person and each room in the house." The good and great man who wrote what is now one of the most popular volumes in the language, lived for the most part the peaceful, happy life of a country clergyman.

He was born in 1792, at Fairford in Gloucestershire, and was the eldest son of the Rev. John Keble, the vicar of a neighbouring parish. The boy was never sent to any school, but so well was he grounded by his father that he was elected scholar of Corpus Christi, Oxford, before he had completed his fifteenth year. His college course was brilliant, and in 1810 he gained a first class both in classics and mathematics—a distinction which up to that time no one had earned but Sir Robert Peel. Other university honours followed in swift succession, and when one and twenty, being already Fellow of Oriel, he undertook the office of examining master. Then followed his ordination and appointment to a curacy, which, however, was not suffered to interfere with his Oxford engagements, to which before long was added the tutorship of Oriel. In 1823 he returned to his father's home at Fairford, and took charge of three small curacies, which yielded an income of little more than £100 a year. Two years later he accepted the curacy of

Hursley, but the death of a dear sister, whom he called his "sweetheart," led him to return to his father and only surviving sister at Fairford. "I do not think," says Sir John Coleridge, "that in the course of his life he sustained any loss which he felt more acutely." In the summer of 1827 the "Christian Year" was published, one of the most important events in the life of Keble and the most interesting to the public. Two years later Sir William Heathcote, his warm friend and former pupil, offered Keble the living of Hursley, but he thought it his duty to decline it, "because he would not quit the care of his father." Meanwhile he was engaged in editing the works of Hooker, a labour which was not completed for several years ; and the appointment to the professorship of poetry at Oxford forms another prominent incident of his studious and quiet life. It is unfortunate for the general reader that, according to the prevalent custom—which has since been broken by the happy innovation of Mr. Matthew Arnold—Keble's lectures were delivered in Latin. Other interests were greatly occupying his thoughts at this time. He was the friend and close associate of the most prominent Oxford men in that period of controversy, and Cardinal Newman states, in his "Apologia," that he has always regarded the publication of a sermon of Keble's as the starting-point of the religious movement of 1833. On the death of his father, in extreme old age, Keble was a free man, and we soon read, not only of his marriage, but of

his settlement at Hursley, in 1836, the vicar having
resigned that living on the ground of ill health.   In
this rural home, happy in his friends, in his work,
in his wife, honoured and useful and loved quite as
much as he was reverenced, Keble lived until 1866.
His wife had been in a dying state for some time,
and her one anxiety was for him ; but he was called
home first, after a week's illness.   Three or four
days before he died, being unable to stand, he was
wheeled out of her room, and "they who for so
many years had had but one heart and one mind,
parted for life, with one silent look at each other."
    To write of a book with the cold impartiality
of criticism, which, like the " Christian Year," lives
in the hearts of so many readers, is not possible,
nor, perhaps, is it to be desired.   Something must
be said, however, if only to account for its almost
unprecedented popularity.   This, it will be evident,
is not due to any meretricious qualities.   There
is a calmness, and at times almost a severity, in
Keble's style ; there is little of the strong emotional
expression which makes so much verse, which is
not poetry, dear to devout persons.   It is said that
Keble had not a keen or accurate ear for music,
and this deficiency may, I think, be detected in the
" Christian Year."   His rhythm does not generally
satisfy and soothe the reader, and we must look to
the *matter* of his poetry in order to explain the
success it has attained.   Sincerity and entire truthfulness mark it throughout.   The devout feeling
—nay, more than feeling, the firm belief—of the

writer is seen everywhere, and all that is pure
and earnest in the reader answers to the thought
expressed. It is a companion to the Prayer-book,
and as such is dear to all earnest Churchmen ; but
its influence extends more widely still, for it appeals
to every heart that is conscious of heavenward
aspirations. To say how this is done would be to
explain what we know only by its results—the
supreme art of the poet. But observe how much
is effected by the exact and loving observation of
nature. It was Sir John Coleridge who first made
Wordsworth known to Keble as a poet, and "the
admiration for his poetry which he conceived in
youth never wavered in after-life." A great master
among poets like Wordsworth, could not be loved
by Keble without also influencing him strongly,
but he did this probably by inciting his genius, and
assuredly not by lessening its originality. It is
interesting to remember that when Wordsworth
received his honorary degree at Oxford, Keble,
then Professor of Poetry, paid him a fitting eulogy,
delivered, according to custom, in Latin, as having
above all poets "exhibited the manners, the pursuits, and the feelings, religious and traditional, of
the poor—I will not say in a favourable light
merely, but in a light which glows with the rays of
heaven."

Some critics agree in thinking that if the
"Christian Year" be the volume which keeps the
name of Keble fragrant in all English-speaking
countries, his "Lyra Innocentium" is marked by

still higher poetical qualities. It may be so in a few instances, but there is nothing, perhaps, in that volume so beautiful as the poems in the " Christian Year " for the second, fifteenth, and twenty-fourth Sundays after Trinity; and it may be added that the " Lyra " is more dogmatic in tone than the earlier work—more distinctly Church poetry for Churchmen. I write only of degree, for this was surely Keble's aim throughout. He was not only a sacred poet, but he was a Church poet, and it is difficult to understand the late Dean of Westminster's assertion, that " Keble was not a sacred, but, in the best sense of the word, a secular poet." " Not George Herbert," he writes, " or Cowper, but Wordsworth, Scott, and perhaps more than all, Southey, are the English poets that kindled his flame and coloured his diction." In one sense this is true. Keble was no doubt greatly influenced by his contemporaries, for he had a sympathetic nature, and for Wordsworth and Scott, at least, his admiration was extreme. But of Scott he cannot write without regretting that he was not a poet of the Church, and that this was Keble's single purpose is evident from the whole tenor of his work. No doubt he gathered imagery from classical literature, and it may be true that "his descriptions of natural scenery display a depth of poetical intuition very rarely vouchsafed to any man." He had the wide culture of a scholar combined with the genius of a poet, and poet-like wisely gathered his materials from every source ; but his purpose throughout, as expressed in the "Advertisement" to the "Christian Year," is distinct and unwavering. It does not follow that it should appear with equal clearness in every poem he wrote. Not one, however, but has what may be called a religious note, and how happily this is expressed will be seen in "May Garlands," a poem quoted by Dean Stanley in illustration of his position that Keble was a secular poet. With these lines this brief notice of Keble must conclude, and with them also I must close a volume which, if it be the means of making poetry more dear to the reader, will serve also to make life more beautiful.

> " Come, ye little revellers gay,
> Learners in the school of May !
> Bring me here the richest crown
> Wreathed this morn on breezy down,
> Or in nook of copsewood green,
> Or by river's rushy screen,
> Or in sunny meadow wide,
> Gemmed with cowslips in their pride ;
> Or perchance, high-prized o'er all,
> From beneath the southern wall,
> From the choicest garden bed,
> 'Mid bright smiles of infants bred,
> Each a lily of his own
> Offering, or a rose half-blown.
>
> " Bring me now a crown as gay,
> Wreathed and woven yesterday.
> Where are now those forms so fair ?—
> Withered, drooping, wan, and bare,
> Feeling nought of earth or sky,
> Shower or dew, behold they lie,

Vernal airs no more to know :—
They are gone,—and ye must go,
Go where all that ever bloomed
In its hour must be entombed.—
They are gone ; their light is o'er :—
Ye must go ; but ye once more
Hope in joy to be new-born,
Lovelier than May's gleaming morn.

" Hearken, children of the May,
Now in your glad hour and gay,
Ye whom all good Angels greet
With their treasure blithe and sweet :—
None of all the wreaths ye prize
But was nursed by weeping skies.
Keen March winds, soft April showers,
Braced the roots, embalmed the flowers.
So if e'er that second spring
Her green robe o'er you shall fling,
Stern self-mastery, tearful prayer,
Must the way of bliss prepare.
How should else Earth's flowerets prove
Meet for those pure crowns above ? "

INDEX.

THE END.

PRINTED BY WILLIAM CLOWES AND SONS, LIMITED, LONDON AND BECCLES.

s. d.

Captain Jewell's Wife. By the Author of "Our Valley." With Three page Woodcuts. Crown 8vo. ...*Cloth boards* 2 0

Carl Forrest's Faith. By MARY LINSKILL. With Three full-page Woodcuts. Crown 8vo. ....*Cloth boards* 1 6

Cuthbert Conningsby : A Sequel to "Maud King-LAKE'S COLLECT." By EVELYN E. GREEN. With Three page Woodcuts. Crown 8vo. ....*Cloth boards* 1 6

Crab Court. By M. SEELEY. With Three page Woodcuts. Crown 8vo. ....*Cloth boards* 1 6

Dick Darlington, at Home and Abroad. By A. H. ENGELBACH, Author of "Juanita," &c. With Three full-page Illustrations on toned paper. Crown 8vo. ....*Cloth boards* 2 0

Dresden Romance (A). By LAURA M. LANE. With Four page Woodcuts. Crown 8vo. ....*Cloth boards* 2 6

Good Copy (A) and Other Stories. By F. B. HARRISON. With Three page Woodcuts. Crown 8vo. *Cloth bds* 1 6

Great Captain (The) : An Eventful Chapter in SPANISH HISTORY. By ULICK R. BURKE, M.A. With Two full-page Illustrations on toned paper. Crown 8vo. ...*Cloth boards* 2 0

Griffinhoof. By CRONA TEMPLE. With Four page Woodcuts. Crown 8vo. ....*Cloth boards* 3 6

Hide and Seek : A Story of the New Forest in 1647. By Mrs. FRANK COOPER. With Three full-page Illustrations on toned paper. Crown 8vo.................*Cloth boards* 2 0

His First Offence : A True Tale of City Life. By RUTH LAMB, Author of "The Carpenter's Family," &c. With Three full-page Woodcuts. Crown 8vo. ....*Cloth boards* 1 6

Home and School : A Sequel to "the Snowball SOCIETY." By M. BRAMSTON. With Three full-page Woodcuts. Crown 8vo. ....*Cloth boards* 2 6

In His Courts. By MARGARET E. HAYES. With Three page Woodcuts. Crown 8vo. ....*Cloth boards* 2 6

PUBLICATIONS OF THE SOCIETY.

s.

Isabeau's Hero: A Story of the Revolt of the CEVENNES. By ESMÈ STUART, Author of "Mimi," &c. With Four full-page Woodcuts. Crown 8vo. ....*Cloth boards* 3

Lapsed, not Lost: A Story of Roman Carthage. By the Author of "The Chronicles of the Schönberg-Cotta Family," &c. Crown 8vo. ....*Cloth boards* 2

Lettice. By Mrs. MOLESWORTH, Author of "Carrots." With Three page Woodcuts. Crown 8vo. ....*Cloth boards* 2

Magic Flute (The). By MARY LINSKILL. With Four page Woodcuts. Crown 8vo. ....*Cloth boards* 3

Miles Lambert's Three Chances. By MARY E. PALGRAVE. With Three page Woodcuts. Crown 8vo. *Cloth bds.* 1

Miscellanies of Animal Life. By ELIZABETH SPOONER. With Illustrations. Post 8vo. ....*Cloth boards* 2

Muriel's Two Crosses; or, The Cross she rejected AND THE CROSS SHE CHOSE. By ANNETTE LYSTER. With Four page Woodcuts. Crown 8vo. ....*Cloth boards* 3

Mutiny on the Albatross (The). By F. F. MOORE. With Four page Woodcuts. Crown 8vo....................*Cloth boards* 3

No Beauty. By H. L. CHILDE-PEMBERTON. With Three page Woodcuts. Crown 8vo. ....*Cloth boards* 2

Not in Vain. By MARY E. PALGRAVE. With Three page Woodcuts. Crown 8vo. ....*Cloth boards* 2

One Army (The). By S. M. SITWELL. With Three page Woodcuts. Crown 8vo.................................*Cloth boards* 2

Out of the Shadows. By CRONA TEMPLE, Author of "Her Father's Inheritance," &c. With Three full-page Woodcuts. Crown 8vo. ....*Cloth boards* 2

Paths in the Great Waters. A Tale wherein is comprised a record of Virginia's early troubles, together with the true history of the Bermudas or Somers Islands. By the Rev. E. N. HOARE. With Four full-page Woodcuts. Crown 8vo. *Cloth boards* 3

s. d.

Pirates' Creek (The). A Story of Treasure-quest.
By S. W. SADLER, R.N., Author of "Slavers and Cruisers," &c.
With Four full-page Woodcuts. Crown 8vo. ....*Cloth boards* 3 0

Pride of the Village (The). By A. EUBULE EVANS.
With Three page Woodcuts. Crown 8vo. ....*Cloth boards* 2 6

Prisoner's Daughter (The): A Story of 1758. By
ESMÈ STUART. With Four page Woodcuts. Crown 8vo.
Cloth boards 3 6

Shadow and Shine. By MARY DAVISON, Author of
"Lucile." With Three page Woodcuts. Crown 8vo. *Cloth bds.* 1 6

Sketches of Our Life at Sarawak. By HARRIETTE
McDOUGALL. With Map and Four full-page Woodcuts. Crown
8vo. ....*Cloth boards* 2 6

Three Sixteenth-Century Sketches. By SARAH
BROOK. With Three page Woodcuts. Crown 8vo. *Cloth boards* 2 6

Turbulent Town (A); Or, the Story of the Arteveldts.
By the Rev. E. N. HOARE. With Four page Woodcuts.
Crown 8vo. ....*Cloth boards* 3 0

Una Crichton. By the Author of "Our Valley," &c.
With Four full-page Woodcuts. Crown 8vo........... *Cloth boards* 3 6

Valley of Baca (The). By the Author of "Douglas
Deane," &c. With Three page Woodcuts. Crown 8vo. *Cloth bds* 1 6

Wild Goose Chase (A). By F. S. POTTER. With
Three page Woodcuts. Crown 8vo. ....*Cloth boards* 1 6

LONDON:
NORTHUMBERLAND AVENUE, CHARING CROSS, W.C.;
43, QUEEN VICTORIA STREET, E.C.; 26, ST. GEORGE'S PLACE, S.W.
BRIGHTON: 135, NORTH STREET.

www.ingramcontent.com/pod-product-compliance
Lightning Source LLC
Chambersburg PA
CBHW032310280326
41932CB00009B/767